ELIE HALÉVY: An Intellectual Biography

ELIE HALÉVY
An Intellectual Biography

MYRNA CHASE

New York
COLUMBIA UNIVERSITY PRESS
1980

The Earhart Foundation, through a special grant,
has assisted the Press in publishing this volume.

LIBRARY OF CONGRESS CATALOGING IN PUBLICATION DATA

CHASE, MYRNA, 1935–
ELIE HALÉVY, AN INTELLECTUAL BIOGRAPHY.

BIBLIOGRAPHY: P.
INCLUDES INDEX.
1. HALÉVY, ELIE, 1870–1973.   2. HISTORIANS—FRANCE—
BIOGRAPHY.   3. GREAT BRITAIN—HISTORIOGRAPHY.   I. TITLE.
DA3.H28C47   941'.007'2024 [B]   79-24314
ISBN 0-231-04856-4

For Gail
and for Steve
with many thoughts of
golden days . . .

Contents

Acknowledgments

I HAVE BEEN fortunate indeed to include among my friends and mentors several scholars and writers who, over the years, have shared with me or clashed with me to my benefit. Those who have helped me know that they have, but because they might not ever stop to think of their importance to this book, I would like to thank them here. My special thanks to Nina Kressner Cobb, Daniel Gordon, Donald Harvey, Eric Kent, Merle Kling, Irving Kristol, Melvin Richter, and William Shanahan.

My debt to Gertrude Himmelfarb is immeasurable. I have felt it from my first days as a graduate student when I was excited by the rigor of her approach to the study of the history of ideas and I was aware of it again during the research and writing of the dissertation which was the center of this work. Her criticism and her suggestions for this manuscript and indeed, the challenge of her difficult questions, have contributed mightily to my understanding and to my rethinking of many of my most fundamental assumptions.

I would like to express my gratitude and respect for Dr. Henriette Noufflard Guy-Loé, Halévy's niece and literary executor. She shared his papers, his home, and her memories with me. Continuing the family's traditional hospitality to visiting scholars, she opened the world of the Halévys and their friends to an American whose only connection was an ever-deepening respect for Halévy's work. In her courage, her character, and her convictions I saw his living heir.

Two dear friends, Gail Benick and Stephen Levine, have left their mark on this book and its author. Without being responsible for its confusions or its author's judgments, they shared this manuscript and the passions and enthusiasms of graduate school at the City University of New York in the late sixties and the early seventies. This study of Elie Halévy, a historian of integrity and vision, is dedicated to these dear friends and fellow historians. For Miles Wortman, who did not share with me the joys of this work but who did share the final burdens and pains of publication, I hope some day to write another.

The manuscript of this study improved through the process of critical reviewing for publication and I want to thank those reviewers who are known to me for their criticism and encouragement—Robert Nisbet, Bernard Semmel, Stephen Tonsor, and R. K. Webb. My appreciation of my editor, Bernard Gronert, and the staff at Columbia University Press can best be expressed here in the book they helped to make possible. A grant from the Earhart Foundation made it possible for this work to be published. I deeply appreciate their commitment to the free exchange of ideas.

Finally, there are individuals and institutions who have helped to make this piece of scholarship possible. I want to thank Pierre Petitmengin, the chief librarian of the Ecole Normale Supérieure, and his able assistant, Mme Marie-Claire Boulez, as well as the staff of that remarkable academic institution. Mlles Humbert and Py made the Xavier Léon papers at the Bibliothèque Victor Cousin available for me when the library was closed. I am indeed grateful for their courtesy. Throughout my research the New York Public Library was a treasury. Baruch College and the Graduate Center of the City University of New York have assisted this work. I would like to express my appreciation to my schools and to my colleagues who have often unknowingly furthered the completion of this work.

ACKNOWLEDGMENTS

Introduction

ELIE HALÉVY was one of the most distinguished historians of this century. More than half a century after its publication his six-volume *History of the English People in the Nineteenth Century* remains a classic, its theses still sparking some of the most heated controversies in British historiography. His *The Growth of Philosophic Radicalism* is the definitive work on a critical subject of the British intellectual and political tradition.

But Halévy was more than a historian, or rather he was a historian in the grand tradition of his master Thucydides, the *philosophe manqué*. The speculative nature of his inquiry into British civilization transcends historical narrative and places him in the philosophical tradition of the great French observers of England's "miracle" of liberty, civic morality, and stable representative government, the tradition of Voltaire, Montesquieu, Guizot, Tocqueville, and Taine. Like his predecessors, he found in England alternatives to revolution and tyranny. His *History* is, as it was intended to be, a history of individual liberty and of progress in a modern society. While England is his text, his theme encompasses universal problems of the governed and the governing. In his study of the eighteenth and nineteenth centuries the implicit comparison of England and France is a great unwritten history hidden, so to speak, between the lines; his preoccupation with questions of revolution and stability and liberty is almost palpable.

There is in Halévy's work an incomplete history as well as an unwritten one. In addition to the monumental English history Halévy's oeuvre includes seven other books, among them one unfinished history and another not prepared by him for publication. These works supplement the English experience of freedom and underline his universal political and philosophical theses. These two fragmentary histories, the *Era of Tyrannies* and the *Histoire du socialisme européen*, were relatively unknown in the English-speaking world until a decade ago. The first is a book of essays which over the course of his career dealt with problems of contemporary history—war, socialism, militarism, and the concentration of authority in modern states. The second is a posthumous collection of lectures at the Ecole Libre des Sciences Politiques on various aspects of socialism, fragments that reveal the scope of the labor of half of his lifetime. Socialism was the polemical target of much of Halévy's life. Like his great contemporary Émile Durkheim, Halévy tended to pose the problem of contemporary society as one of a conflict between the forces contributing to individualism and those leading to socialism, a conflict in which he emphasized the role of ideas, values, and beliefs, rejecting a determinist and materialist interpretation of history as well as a materialist philosophy.

To this day, his work remains at the center of several major historiographical controversies because his insights into the complicated problems of European socialism, modern warfare, and nationalism were important, even prophetic. His creativity as a historical commentator on contemporary events is astonishing. The facts of publication—a solid body of work on nineteenth-century England, a fragmentary history of European socialism, and many essays on contemporary history—have bifurcated his reputation and it is the intention of this book to set forth his work as a single body of thought devoted to the major concerns of contemporary history, rather than divided into two separate projects.

Yet the sweep of these disparate fields of historical investigation influence our assessment of the historian. One can think of other historians whose accomplishments within a single field might be seen to match his, or of those who have established or confirmed and extended a new historical tradition such as that of the Annales, but it is difficult to think of another whose mastery of two disparate fields could match Halévy's. But for Halévy the grand *History*, the small volume entitled *Era of Tyrannies*, and the *Histoire du socialisme européen* reveal not disparity but the full range of his thought and the underlying unity of his life and work. He was first a philosopher concerned with the problems of the individual and the community, liberty and authority, democracy and tyranny. There was no shift in the themes of his work, only in the content. At first he tested his conception of liberty and of progressive society with the French experience of revolution, instability, militarism, and caesarism on a grand scale. He was a master in a great tradition of nineteenth-century historiography. But around the First World War the reality of contemporary experience—the social unrest on the eve of the war, the war, and then socialism and tyranny—as he saw it, became the measure of freedom and progress. It was then that he took his place as historian of our century.

Once understood this unity makes it possible for us to comprehend the larger philosophical design and intent of his historical writings. His greatness as a historian rests on more than his skills, on more than the sweep of his subject; it stands on the moral and philosophical profundity of his conceptualization of contemporary history as well.

The present study is the biography of a mind. Halévy's life was his work. His biography is singularly uneventful, although he was "cursed with living in interesting times" as the Chinese proverb goes, and he responded to and influenced those times as might a scholar in a society in which the intellectual elite mattered. His mind grappled with his times vigorously and honestly, just as it did with timeless problems and values. It is the mind of this historian who was trained for philosophy and practiced the art and science of writing history that is exciting, stimulating, important, and often profoundly contemporary. For Halévy, ideas, beliefs, and values were the moving forces of the world and as a historian he wrote the history of ideas as well as history in which ideas and ideologies played a creative and dynamic role. His work merits study for the ideas themselves, which is what he would have understood as the task of a scholar. His life and work also deserve examination in terms of the complex of liberal, secular, and republican principles which infused his history and his political and intellectual commitments. They evoke an intellectual culture that we cannot find in this world today.

Often the drama of a life of the mind unfolds in painful *crises de conscience*. There were causes enough in Halévy's life—the Dreyfus affair, the First World War, the depression, and the Popular Front—but they provoked no *crise de conscience*. Throughout his career there is a timeless, unchanging quality, a firm core of skepticism in all his observations of human behavior, in his understanding of liberalism, in his pessimism, in his morality.

By 1901, when he began to publish *The Growth of Philosophic Radicalism*, he had, during a fertile and enormously active decade, already made the major decisions of his life: to write history rather than philosophy or sociology, to reject the easy alternative of teaching at the Sorbonne in order to undertake a political as well as a pedagogic mission at the Ecole Libre des Sciences Politiques, to found and edit the *Revue de Métaphysique et de Morale* and to organize the Société Française de Philosophie. Thus, at the age of thirty-one, he had arranged the tasks of his lifetime. It was then too that he ardently defended Dreyfus and became one of the first men of letters to wear proudly the abusive name "intellectual." He threw himself wholeheartedly into l'Affaire, participating in politics more completely and actively than he ever would again, although he remained throughout his life steadfastly republican and morally and politically liberal.

Constancy and consistency characterized Halévy's values, friendships, and actions. Although a professor in the "republic of professors," he never became the office-holding, party-member professor-bureaucrat that is our image of the Third Republic's professoriate. He maintained a critical detachment from the university at the "sciences po." Similarly, he remained loyal to the *Revue*, its men, and its purposes until he died. Even the friends he chose in youth—Xavier Léon, Léon Brunschvicg, Emile Chartier (Alain), and Celestin Bouglé—remained the friends of his old age. They might differ in their interpretation of the role of intellectuals as critics, as prophets, as rational men, as philosophers, as "clercs," but they held in common a sense that it was an intellectual's duty to perform such a special role.

How did his historical work—his choice of problems and his principal theses—express his political values and his active concern for contemporary French and European problems? It is, after all, the historian of England who is a giant. The *History of the English People* and the *The Growth of Philosophic Radicalism* are works that stand as masterpieces of the art of history. But this giant of historical writing is, even when seemingly immersed in the past or in recording the events of another country and another culture, always a Frenchman of the Third Republic. His nationality and his political commitments in his native land too often are not given due weight in the consideration of his work.

By virtue of his place between two worlds he gained valuable distance and objectivity. His studies of England, socialism, and contemporary European history gain an added dimension through his love of France. While he loved England deeply and became a symbol of the *entente cordiale* insofar as one may say it still existed after the First World War, he was no more a simple Anglophile than he was merely a laissez-faire liberal, and in fact he did not consider English culture and intellect to be equal to French. But he thought the English had created the miracle of a responsible politics representing both the masses and the special interests without succumbing to demagoguery or failing to develop an adequate national policy. He believed that France could be taught a lesson by the English experience, one which he felt they had to learn if democracy was not to lead to caesarism, an authoritarianism exercised ostensibly in the name of the masses.

His political impulses were not as simple as the terms—republican and secular—that describe them. Not a party man, yet committed to uniting his thought and his action according to a standard of "perfect sincerity," his position on various issues was neither predictable nor easily categorized. His English friend H. A. L. Fisher called him "a man of left-wing sympathies"; his niece, who knew him well in the 1930s, insists that he was a "man of the left." A *Times Literary Supplement* reviewer faulted Halévy for seeing "the face of the socialist bogey in every non-conservative dictatorial regime" and accused him of liberal prejudices.[1] On the other hand, Halévy's countryman, Hubert Bourgin, a man whose political evolution from left to right resembled that of Halévy's brother Daniel, characterized Elie as one of the leading Jewish, socialist secularists whose commitment to democratic parliamentarism, English radicalism, and German-Jewish Marxism subverted France under the Third Republic.[2] Julien Benda respected and remembered Halévy for his Olympian impartiality before all the doctrines, before all the pleas of party.

It is the signal achievement of Elie Halévy, a great questioner and a disciple of Socrates and Plato, that in an age of accelerating political complexity he posed basic questions in a luminous and provocative manner. While his allegiance to truth and "sincerity" enabled him to reassert in all its freshness the human passion for reason and autonomy, he also learned—and taught—how to evaluate the lure of the many opposed dogmas. That Halévy has been cited in support of thoroughly embattled views is the mark not of his lack of clarity but of the cogency of his questions. His questions about democracy, republicanism, and socialism continue to be an acid test for both conservative and revolutionary political systems. It is no accident, then, that current attempts to reconstruct the history of nineteenth-century England in terms of rigid class divisions and class conflicts face in Halévy's masterly history an Olympian obstacle.

It is clear that Halévy's political values cannot easily be located in a simple schematization of French political life divided into two rival camps: republican and royalist, anticlerical and catholic, progressive and traditional, revolutionary and counter-revolutionary. Nor do Halévy's politics fit any more conveniently into David Thomson's responses in the tradition of a republican and a socialist left and a right divided into liberals or Orleanists, Bonapartists and liberal Catholics.[3] Neither are Halévy's political values easily subsumed under Albert Thibaudet's groupings of Traditionalists, Liberals, Social Christians, Socialists, and Jacobins of two varieties—Radicals of Bonapartist tendencies and Radicals of the ilk of Alain's men of the provinces.[4] Finally, Halévy cannot be dismissed as merely an Anglophile whose French politics have a foreign cast.

Halévy's politics have a principled cast at the same time that they are responses to particular political issues. The wisest course is to pursue his political values wherever they lead, particularly in moments of crisis, and to hope thus to capture their nature. Precisely because Halévy was a man of such moral and intellectual stature that in his thinking and his writing of history he is *sui generis*, he can illuminate for us many aspects of liberal republicanism by his political actions, opinions, and exchanges.

Different audiences have understood and appropriated different parts of Halévy. Among the English-speaking peoples his reputation rests on his writings about English thought and institutions. But French students of various political hues esteem his work on socialism, compiled from scattered articles and lecture notes, as the basic guide to this complex subject. In France, his *History of the English People* was out of print until recently, while his *Histoire du socialisme européen* has always been readily available in an inexpensive edition and widely read and quoted.

This partial appreciation of his work is illustrated by the

response to his death in 1937 as well. In England historians regretted that he had left unfinished volume four of the *History of the English People*, the volume concerning the Victorian period, the high point of the British liberal century. They thought this era would have been the most congenial to him. He had, after all, described it as the great epoch during which the British people cherished the "splendid illusion that they discovered in a moderate liberty, and not for themselves alone but for every nation that would have the wisdom to follow their example, the secret of moral and of political stability." He had first studied England because he had shared a large part of that splendid illusion.

Yet the volume that he did write, instead of completing volume four, represented in a political sense, if not in a chronological one, a necessary continuation of his discussion of English liberty. He was a man eminently capable of abiding by the priorities and schedules he set for himself, of ordering his days and weeks and months around his work, but the postwar period raised questions for the historian that the philosopher in him felt called upon to answer at once. He broke his chronology and wrote England's history in the years 1895–1914, examining the various forces he had witnessed which he thought had undermined the English achievement. He thought he saw the English people lose confidence in their ability to secure peace and prosperity by liberal and stable government. He postponed his *History* to investigate the origins of the war and to examine a variety of social and political aspects of socialism, all seemingly peripheral matters to those who would have had him write his history of Victorian England. Had he decided that the ideal of moderate liberty as a guarantee of political and moral stability was merely a splendid illusion?

In France, however, the brilliant teacher of the Sciences Politiques was mourned otherwise, with many expressing regret that he had left uncompleted his work, not on England, but on European socialism. And yet, had not the nature of that work, which had developed almost dialectically with the

History of the English People, drastically altered since the outbreak of the Great War? Feeling called upon to say something about the nature of socialism and its relationship to bolshevism and fascism and to war, Halévy had made radical new departures in *Era of Tyrannies.*

Immediately afterward he expressed his desire to return to his Victorian volume. Was this a return to the solace of the splendid illusion, to the values of another generation, to the moral and political aspirations of his youth? Or was it, rather, the renewal of his youthful pledge to those values of liberalism and to the science of history to which he had thought he could make a contribution? Was it in fact not a return at all since there had been no departure? His work, whether on England or France, whether on socialism or liberalism, whether on past or present, was, as is to be demonstrated, a continuous design, sometimes modified as to schedule of execution but consistent in its conceptions and aims.

CHAPTER ONE

The Making of A Historian

ELIE HALÉVY was born in the year of the defeat of France and of the Paris Commune. He was born at Etretat in Normandy to a Parisian *haute bourgeoise* family of Jewish and Protestant descent. His family was both talented and wealthy, bringing together Academicians, diplomats, artists, statesmen, and men of business and commerce. Orleanists in politics and social circle his family and many of their friends rallied to support the Third Republic, a republic by default, during its precarious first years, the years of Halévy's youth.

Elie was known to joke that he suffered no pangs of guilt about the origins of his father's wealth. Delighted theater audiences had given Ludovic Halévy his fortune. In that era of enormously successful operettas he was the prolific librettist for Georges Bizet, Henri Meilhac, and Jacques Offenbach. His popular novels earned his considerable fortune and ultimately one of them, *Abbé Constantin*, was so popular that he was elected to the Academy. His wife, Louise Bréguet, was a serious, cultivated, and intelligent woman and family legend has it that she was the strongest moral influence on her eldest son. She came of a family of Calvinist watchmakers who had returned to France from Switzerland in the revolutionary era. Having founded their wealth on clocks and watches, the Bréguets contributed to the development of telegraphy and aeronautics in the nineteenth and twentieth centuries. Elie was also known to tease his parents with his habits of hard work and self discipline, which he said he had acquired from the bourgeois Bréguets.

The Halévy family had been distinguished and well-established in France for several generations. Elie's paternal great-grandfather, Elie Halphen Lévy, after whom he was named, established the family in France during the rule of Napoleon. During the Restoration he founded a paper, *L'Israëlite français*. Grandfather Léon was a poet and one of the talented young disciples of Saint-Simon. He succeeded Comte as the prophet's secretary and edited *Le Producteur* until religious mysticism split the movement. Estranged from the "mystics" of the "new Christianity," Léon published his recollections of the master, hoping to preserve the rationalist elements of Saint-Simon's critique and vision of modern society. In the Halévy family respect for that rationalism, perhaps even aspects of the social goals, survived, and in the immediate circle of friends and relatives there were several men whose first friendship had grown in the movement. Daniel Halévy traced his first feelings for socialism to his father's explication of Saint-Simon's teachings.

Halévy's great uncle, the composer of *La Juive*, Jacques Fromental Halévy, was responsible for the development of the new French opera form. He was the first Jew to be elected to the Academy of the Beaux Arts. He married into the Rodriques family of bankers, a family which had also been Saint-Simonian. Fromental's daughter, Geneviève, married his most talented student, Georges Bizet. Bizet and Ludovic Halévy collaborated on the creation of *Carmen*, the artistic, if not the financial triumph, of the third generation of the Halévy family. Later, Geneviève's salon was to be the headquarters of the Dreyfusards during the Affair, a center for the various intellectuals who defended the Jewish captain.

Elie's uncle, Marcellin Berthelot, was one of France's most internationally respected scientists in the era of Louis Pasteur. A noted research chemist and physicist, the pioneer of chemical synthesis, he was also the Minister of Education in the 1890s and the champion of university reform, particularly the reorganization of scientific studies. He too was an amazingly prolific writer—thirty books and more than a thousand articles. His popular articles offered the promise that with the development of science and technology man might eliminate material want, humanize his environment, perhaps even realize "the dreams of socialism." Berthelot was in politics a Radical, briefly serving as foreign minister (his heirs would shape and carry out French foreign policy between the wars). There was an Orleanist cast to his moral thought, however, when he worried about the social effect of the plenty and leisure which it seemed the technological revolution might bring about.

Several Halévy's, Bréguets, and Berthelots were elected to the different branches of the Academy, but one of the most notable of the family was Lucien Anatole Prévost-Paradol. Prévost-Paradol was Ludovic's illegitimate brother, Elie's uncle, though Ludovic and the rest of the family were ignorant of that fact.[1] When Napoleon III seized power, Prévost-Paradol's circle of "normaliens," academicians, and intellectuals became the Orleanist liberal opposition to Bonapartist despotism in the grand tradition of Constant and Madame de Staël. Their salons became the center of their political campaign; the *Journal des Debats* became their organ for public controversy and the Academy their meeting place. At the very heart of the opposition Prévost-Paradol became one of the outstanding political thinkers of the Second Empire. His thought is said to have influenced the men who framed the complicated safeguards of the Third Republic constitution. It certainly influenced the values, attitudes, and politics of his family.

Long before Napoleon III's reign relaxed into the "liberal empire," allowing representation and public criticism, his government permitted its critics among its officials. Several of the opposition, including Prévost-Paradol and Ludovic Halévy, actually held diplomatic, administrative, and legislative positions in the Empire. Halévy held a number of posts, finally as secretary to the Corps Legislatif and to the Duc de Morny, the illegitimate brother of the Emperor and one of his most important advisors.[2] Ludovic resigned his post, disillusioned with politics and eager to make his way in literature and the theater. In 1870 Prévost-Paradol was posted to Washington, D.C., as French ambassador. There he took his own life. Ludovic's *Carnets* are a moving tribute to his brother, whom he knew only as his dearest and most admired friend. The Orleanist sympathies and liberal political opinions that they shared, amply documented in these memoires, were the milieu of Elie's youth. Ludovic and Lucien shared a profound respect for England as the model of liberal, constitutional, parliamentary principles and institutions—a respect which was a mainstay of Orleanist politics.[3] On questions of religious belief Prévost-Paradol and Ludovic Halévy were genially tolerant, easily accommodating Protestants, secularists, Jews, and liberal Catholics among their close friends and family. Because it was the Halévy custom to raise their children in the religion of their mother there were a variety of religious beliefs within the family itself. Ludovic's sons were reared as Protestants, while Prévost-Paradol's daughter became a nun. From generation to generation the Halévys were flexible in their religious opinions.

It was not his indifference to public life but his practical experience of politics, especially in the Corps Legislatif, that profoundly disillusioned Ludovic Halévy with French politics and with the professional class of French party politicians and administrators. When he resigned his post with the Corps Legislatif, Ludovic wrote: "From the seven years that I spent in the company of the representatives of my country I was overcome by the profoundest political indifference. So many ambitious people had acted around my modest person. As for convictions . . . they were absent, completely absent, as much on the right as on the left, merely men who weren't much and who wanted to become something."[4]

In fact, however, the man who resigned from government service to write musical comedies and novels was not indifferent to political questions, or even to French politics, only to narrow concerns of elections and offices. His influence upon his sons, Elie and Daniel, was such that they shared his disdain for the ambitions of French politicians. Sharing their father's informed interest in foreign and domestic affairs and his deep concern for social problems, neither son contemplated a career in administration or in politics.[5] His father's distaste for political life is a strain running through Elie Halévy's more private thoughts recorded in his youthful journals and his letters to family and close friends. But there is no trace of indifference to public affairs, only a keen sense of the limits of a moral man's involvement in politics.

If politics were beyond the pale of legitimate aspiration for the young Halévy, the world of literature, music, and the arts and sciences was within easy reach. Some of the most gifted personalities of the era, including Renan, Taine, and Degas, met in the Halévy home. Taine was one of Ludovic Halévy's close friends. The great painter Degas was a regular visitor and Daniel has left a testimonial to the powerful influence the old man exerted on his life before they were irrevocably alienated during the Dreyfus Affair. When questions of tolerance and religion became national political issues, rather than personal prejudices, the painter's anti-Semitism separated him from his friends. Statesmen and politicians, French and foreign, mingled with intellectuals in the rue de Douai, which Célestin Bouglé remembered as a "sort of kaleidoscope" revealing all the colors, combinations, and variety of French intellectual, artistic, and political life.

The precocious child of a wealthy, prominent, and cosmopolitan family, Elie was free to choose any profession, any style of life he could reconcile with his conscience. His conscience was not easily reconciled, however. He longed for an active life; he chose as his own philosophy one of action, of duty, and yet he ruled out politics as immoral as a matter of course. He cross-examined his own aspirations, suspicious of any desire for advancement or fame or even for a life of peace and quiet;[6] he strove for perfect sincerity. His wealth and his self-discipline gave him the freedom to do and think as he chose, independent even of the necessity of earning a living that his father had faced and that his own friends had to contend with. He chose a life of scholarship and trained and disciplined himself in the study of philosophy. Yet even this choice was not free from pitfalls; the prospect of teaching as a salaried functionary of a government displeased him. So also did the thought that he might become one of a scholarly coterie, subjecting himself to a doctrine or even to a friendship that might jeopardize perfect independence of thought.

At first glance, Elie Halévy, a young man of austere conscience and deep commitment to scholarship, seems to share relatively little with either his father or his brother. He had little patience with the kind of writing his father and brother both did—memories, reflections, and musings, and history as belles lettres. He thought his brother was often guilty of intellectual affectation. Certainly his political views, values, and intellectual circles differed considerably from Daniel's. There is a family photo of Ludovic and his two sons in formal attire at the funeral procession of Emile Zola in 1902, a grand manifestation of Dreyfusard sympathies by the Halévys and thousands of others. Politically, however, by that date the brothers shared only a general Dreyfusism, republicanism, and concern for social questions as they had already begun to move apart in their opinions.

Elie's Orleanist tolerance and skepticism, which he imbibed with his family, did not affect his behavior in the same way that it did that of his father and brother, who showed a certain ease in joining together beliefs from the entire range of the French political spectrum and an ability to appreciate the actions of men whose politics were opportunistic. There is a rigor to Elie's political judgments missing in his brother and even his father. There were few traces of the dilettante about Elie Halévy, which the family tradition ascribed to his mother's influence. Without the letters of a dutiful and loving eldest son written to his parents from many travels, the sparkling sense of humor, the elegant literary taste, the keen eye for the detail in person and place of a born and indefatigable traveler would be lost. His public humor tended to the wit of debate. His love of the arts, literature, and the theater, his close ties to his artistic family and to that of his wife, Florence Noufflard, would be obscured by the shadow cast by the scientific historian and serious scholar that he was. His home was less a kaleidoscope world than his father's, but his was also always open to scholars and to students. His commitment to "perfect sincerity" was the legacy of Prévost-Paradol and of his mother to which he was the faithful heir.

Elie and Daniel attended the Lycée Condorcet, one of the best right bank schools of the period, known for the quality of its faculty, which included Mallarmé as English master and Alphonse Darlu, the idealist philosopher. The school attracted some of the brightest, most creative, and wealthiest of young Parisians, including Elie's life-long friends Léon Brunschvicg and Xavier Léon, both of whom became philosophers, and Daniel's classmates Marcel Proust, Robert Dreyfus, and Fernand Gregh, the poet, and Jacques Bizet, the Halévy's cousin. At Condorcet Mallarmé and Darlu symbolized the two dominant cultural interests of the day, symbolist literature and idealist philosophy. In a sense each attracted one Halévy brother. The moral authority and intellectual power of Darlu impressed both boys and both studied English with Mallarmé, but their ways parted slightly at school as Elie and his friends followed Darlu, while literature and poetry became the passionate bond of Daniel's group. Proust, Dreyfus, Daniel Halévy, and friends titled their first literary magazine *Le Banquet* to honor both Mallarmé and Darlu; the first published work of Proust, Barbusse, and Léon Blum appeared there. In *Jean Santeuil* Proust left us a portrait of Darlu in the schoolmaster and turned the life and atmosphere of the school and the boys into literature.[7]

In Darlu's class Elie, Brunschvicg, and Léon first dreamed their dreams of effecting the moral regeneration of France through the teaching and writing of philosophy. While still in their early teens, they planned a philosophical journal which would be the forum for critical, secular, rationalist, and idealist thought. With their journal they hoped to batter down the walls within which evolutionist and positivist throught had confined French philosophy. Darlu remained their intellectual mentor as they formed the *Revue*, wrote their books, and shaped their careers. For Elie the founding of the *Revue de Métaphysique et de Morale* was only one respect paid to his teacher; he also dedicated his *Growth of Philosophic Radicalism* to Darlu. And Darlu was more and more included within the Halévy family circle, especially around the Affair when he replaced Degas.[8]

Elie was a brilliant and confident student. He placed first in the *concours général de philosophie* the year that he left Condorcet for the Ecole Normale Supérieure. His career at the Ecole Normale was as bright as his years at Condorcet had been; he was second in his graduating class. He loved the Ecole for its monastic life of intellectual rigor and for the vibrant intellectual exchange with the true friends he found there, Emile Chartier (Alain) who was first, and Celestin Bouglé. Halévy studied philosophy—Spinoza, Pascal, and Plato—and he conceived his study of the philosophic radicals there.

Despite his profound affection for the Ecole and the life that he led there, those years do not seem to have been truly formative years in any intellectual, moral, or political sense. He had already been formed at Condorcet and, earlier, in his family. None of his professors became his mentor as Darlu had, despite the fact that among them were Georges Lyon, the author of *Idealisme en Angleterre au XVIIIᵉ siècle*, Henri Michel, the author of *L'Idée d'état*, and Léon Ollé-Laprune, the Catholic philosopher whose dismissal by Jules Ferry was a cause célèbre at the rue d'Ulm. There are, in fact, no recognizable references to Lyon or to Ollé-Laprune in his letters and only critical comments about Michel, whose essay in French political and social theory since the revolution touched on problems and individuals that interested Halévy but in a way that was clearly not satisfying to the student.

French political life during his *normalien* years also failed to exercise a formative influence on him. As he remarked later, he had become a *normalien* shortly after the fiasco of Boulanger's abortive coup d'état and in the midst of the Panama scandal he left the Ecole to begin his research in London. He thought these events accounted for the apolitical attitudes that he shared with his classmates in those years. He commented, by way of explaining his political beliefs, that in the years 1889 to his *agrégation* in 1892 there had been no socialists at the Ecole.[9] There were, however, those among his acquaintances who would become socialists, although most would be radicals. During these years idealistic men were more likely to turn away from politics. Léon Blum, for example, spent his time at rue d'Ulm writing poetry and criticism and acting in amateur theatricals. Jaurès had already achieved his *agrégation* before Halévy reached the Ecole and the great librarian, Lucien Herr, did not exert the powerful influence for socialism that he would in the years of the Dreyfus Affair, five years after Elie left the school. It was Daniel Halévy's friends, Albert Mathiez, Charles Péguy, and Albert Thomas, four or five years younger than Elie Halévy, whom he came to regard as the socialist generation of *normaliens*. The Affair politicized the generation.

But political choices are not merely a matter of timing and chance. Elie Halévy was modestly dismissing his commitments as a function of time and environment and his statement does not account for the fact that he and his brother Daniel took such different turns after the Dreyfus Affair. Daniel moved further left after the Affair, throwing himself into socialist causes, helping to found *L'Humanité* and in *Pages Libres* and *Cahiers de la Quinzaine* contributing to the study and propagation of a uniquely French socialism that drew upon Bergson, Proudhon, Sorel, and Péguy for its inspiration and the Bourses du Travail for its example. After the First World War and prior to the second debâcle Daniel's elitist polemics against democracy and the politics of the Third Republic earned him some notoriety as an apologist for fascism, a reputation that did not do justice to the complexity of his political thought, to the logic inherent in it, but the accusation indicates the distance he had travelled from his brother and his youth. Elie Halévy was never a socialist, never ceased to be a democrat, and was the outspoken opponent of both fascism and communism. By his own description his political principles were "liberal," "liberal" in an anticlerical, democratic, and republican sense. (It is interesting to note that in a French political context he felt it necessary to enclose the word "liberal" in quotation marks.) His response to everyday politics, as well as to great causes such as that of Dreyfus, was individualistic, moral, and intellectual to the core.

What did it mean to be "liberal" in the political milieu of Halévy's youth? What was the nature of his anticlericalism, his republican and democratic principles? How did a young man who refused to think of public office and political activity propose to join thought with action in order to realize the moral reform of France? How did an idealistic individualist with a limited ability to join movements and express himself in political slogans hope to further the principles that he espoused?

When Halévy and his friends established the *Revue de Métaphysique et de Morale* they aimed at nothing short of the moral reformation of France. Pushed to action by the sordid republican politics of the 1890s the step they took was the founding of a philosophical journal. They added the word "morale" to their title to make explicit their intention to improve public life and to contribute to the secularization of French society by providing a rationalist alternative to both positivism and to religiosity. As they expressed it in 1893 their ambition was to join thought and action, to realize the abstract idea of duty as a concrete end in society and to reunite the several elements of their social and political life through ethical laws.[10] To the men of the *Revue* there was a vital connection between the moral thought of the elite and of every individual on the one hand and the institutions and the material ends of society on the other. For them, and particularly for the young Halévy, shallow beliefs had undermined respect for moral ideals or spiritual objectives. The progress of irrationalism or of naive scientism could be reversed by the revival of a proper regard for the element of moral commitment involved in scientific knowledge.

They thought that the conscientious efforts of even a few men could elevate life and intellect, revitalize a demoralized elite, rejuvenate a dying public life and a stagnant science and culture. They took Charles Renouvier and the neo-Kantians as the model of the power for good of an ethical ideal held fast by an intellectual elite. Renouvier and the neo-criticists (so-called for the Kantian position they took in the name and content of their journal *La Critique Philosophique*, 1872–89) had called for a science of morals independent of religion, that is based on reason, which could lead men progressively toward perfection. In more specific proposals Renouvier had advocated a conversion of France to Protestantism as the faith best capable of instilling in man the knowledge of his limitations and the desire for self-perfection through self-discipline. The appeal that this image of Protestantism had for that generation, including Taine, Ferdinand Buisson, Renan, and others, was such that this school of somewhat eccentric Kantians became one of the prime resources of the republican spirit. With the followers of Renouvier as one of their models and within four years of the demise of *La Critique Philosophique* Halévy, Brunschvicg, Léon, and others of the *Revue* made their program the improvement of public life and the secularization of French society by providing a rationalist alternative to both positivism and Catholicism.

They insisted on the free exchange of ideas. Through the journal and through the Société Française de Philosophie, which they founded, they were hosts to the greatest French, European, and American scholars of all philosophical opinions. They created a congenial climate for philosophic dialogue. Ultimately, they exerted a powerful intellectual influence in France, exactly as they had hoped to do. Whether or not they had worked the moral reform of republican France was another question and one which a skeptic such as Halévy would probably have answered in the negative. Perhaps theirs was more a holding action than a victorious campaign over forty years of the life of the Third Republic, from the 1890s to the 1930s.

In Halévy's mind the success of such a campaign depended upon the moral authority of the intellectual elite, both the worldly, committed intellectuals and the men whose labors were purely speculative pursuits of the ideal of truth. Though the intellectual elite as a whole must struggle against ignorance, superstition, and injustice the actual battle was fought daily by individuals. It was the only combat in which he willingly engaged. There were other intellectuals who shared his belief that the national welfare depended upon the public ethic and who also wanted to reinforce the conscience of individuals, but they tried to achieve this end through public office or power in the university. There were those among Halévy's fellow Dreyfusards, including some of his close friends, who thought national reformation could be realized through command of the school curriculum, of the journals, the bureaucracy, and the legislature. Unlike Alain or Bouglé and Durkheim, Halévy did not accept the image of the intellectual as professor *engagé*. Neither could he agree with those, including his brother and the *normaliens* who became the followers of Jaurès, Herr, Péguy, and Sorel, who thought a moral reformation impossible in capitalist and liberal republican France. The conflict of ideas, the spread of learning of an ethical nature through journals, societies, and schools, the education of an elite for individual action—these, and not the drastic reordering of institutions by group or by class action, were Halévy's way to raise the level of public life.

It has been suggested that the generation of the 1890s felt themselves to be mere *epigoni* to some race of intellectual giants that had preceeded them.[11] Halévy's circle, at any rate, did not seem to share this feeling. On the contrary, the legacy

THE MAKING OF A HISTORIAN

of Comte, Darwin, Marx, Renan, and Taine represented very real evils of positivism, scientism, and determinism, which this handful of young scholars attacked with great zeal, firmly convinced that there was much for them to do. The era seems to have had more than its share of talent that paid no homage to intellectual ancestors in literature, music, and the arts. Philosophy appears to have attracted the interests of the generation, especially idealist philosophy, in the last two decades of the nineteenth century. Greater numbers of the best students chose the Ecole Normale over the Ecole Polytechnique and the public lectures of Renan and Taine, and the general popularity of the two thinkers indicates a revival of interest. Nonetheless, there were only two philosophical journals in France at the time—the flurry of important reviews of philosophy, science, and sociology at the turn of the century followed the founding of the *Revue de Métaphysique* in 1893. This paucity of philosophical publications both encouraged and discouraged Halévy and his friends—discouraged them because it indicated the low state of philosophy in France, but encouraged them because there was so much for them to do and they were so confident it was worth doing. When they founded their journal, it was Léon who suggested the title, playing on the almost pejorative common usage of "métaphysique" and deliberately calling attention to the fact that they intended to combat religious excess and narrow-minded positivism by examination of general theories of thought and action, knowledge and existence.[12] They intended their *Revue* to be the focal point of French philosophy, capable of meriting its subsequent description as the "most profound organ" of contemporary thought in France.[13]

As early as 1891, when Halévy was still at the Ecole Normale, he and Léon had agreed on the basic format of the magazine and on the division of labor. Léon would be the editor and would be financially responsible. But the mundane aspects of establishing a journal seemed to appeal to some practical, active side of Halévy's nature because he too threw himself into the work. He prodded Léon, not always tactfully, about business matters. He collected opinions from his father's friends about the comparative advantages of various publishing firms; he explored family connections that could be used to launch the magazine. He recruited Bouglé, Louis Couturat, and Chartier, the latter in his opinion the best mind among his classmates. Dominique Parodi and Halévy's cousin, René Berthelot, also joined the circle. He visited professors and other eminent scholars, explaining the journal, reassuring the secularists that "métaphysique" should not be understood in any religious sense, and winning promises of contributions from men of considerable reputation.[14] He wrote to philosophers, societies, and journals throughout Europe, including Russia, and the United States. While in England in 1892 and 1893 working on the philosophic radicals, he made contacts for the *Revue.*

Halévy and Léon proposed the principles by which the journal would stand. Halévy promised to write articles and book reviews, insisting that all reviews be anonymous as in the best English periodicals. He constantly generated topics for articles and discussions. He suggested special features, for example *Questions pratiques,* which would deal with social or political problems in their broadest sense, and the *Supplément,* which would review important journals, books, and articles from all major countries, summarize the arguments of young philosophers when they defended their dissertations, comment upon the meetings of philosophical societies, and even describe the courses relating to philosophy offered each year at all French universities. The diligence with which he pursued any particular project through the years varied greatly, but he never lessened his involvement and he maintained the *Supplément* as an abiding concern. By editing it he kept abreast of current developments in philosophy long after his own research had shifted to subjects that could be considered more purely historical or political science.

Before the first issue Halévy wrote to Léon: "It is necessary to act against the miserable positivism, which we are departing from and the irritating religiosity which we risk getting stuck in, to build a philosophy of action and reflection, to be rationalist with a passion."[15] An uncompromising rationalist, Halévy was never very comfortable with the rebirth of irrationalism and mysticism at the turn of the century. An inveterate opponent of Bergsonian thought, he was the foe of positivism as well, though his anti-positivism grew from other roots than those of the thought of Bergson, Péguy, Huysmanns, or the neo-Catholics. Insofar as the positivists and the sociologists were rationalists and believed in and aspired to a science of man he was much more at one with them than with their enemies. As he once confided to Bouglé, the only time he was tempted to belief was when he passed the positivist church in the Latin Quarter. The positivists' vision attracted him and their belief in the possibility of a science of man and society was part of his ideal, after all. "I ask myself sometimes with some anxiety if the only thing that keeps me from being a Comtist isn't a vague aristocratic feeling, worldly, or a little intellectual, à la Daniel Halévy."[16]

Léon was as much a rationalist as Halévy, but his manifesto introducing the *Revue* was cautious: the *Revue* would be devoted to pure philosophy, not to science or to the history of philosophy or to religion as the dogma of any particular church. Careful not to offend religious sentiments Léon, the Jewish secularist, promised the journal would not be irreligious, saying "philosophy is the science of eternal things."[17] The *Revue's* rationalism, polemically expressed in Halévy's letter, would not be scoffing nor would it be insensitive to questions of the ideal or of the spirit. Still, for the lifetime of its founders, it remained secular and anticlerical.

The *Revue* hoped to compel philosophical thought in France to develop publicly, freely, and vigorously by examining first principles. Their teachers, men like Darlu, Jules Lagneau, and Emile Boutroux, had reawakened youth to Plato and Kant, thereby launching a revival of metaphysical idealism in France. The men of the *Revue* took Charles Renouvier and the neo-criticists as their example, admiring them for altering the conscience of a nation in the generation after the

Franco-Prussian War. They thought that a mere handful of men with a journal had "strengthened and fortified the public mind" by their respect for the "dignity of person and inviolability of the law." [18] The *Revue* hoped to exercise the same moral influence in their generation.

The editors and contributors of the *Revue* held Comte and Cousin responsible for the decay of metaphysics in French philosophy. Comte's disciples believed that he had closed the era of systems of philosophy and that all that remained for science to do was to ascertain the facts. Following Victor Cousin, the eclectics thought that all systems might be synthesized by drawing the best elements from opposing philosophies. As a result, philosophy had become on the one hand the history of philosophy and on the other, the sterile mechanical pursuit of special studies in the name of science. To Halévy it seemed that philosophy was weak and under constant attack, caught between a positivism that did not reach beyond the elementary facts and a revival of mysticism that only furthered superstition. To him "mysticism" meant Bergsonianism and other currents of irrationalism which he felt would drown rational inquiry. Privately he expressed his fear that the times were with the mystics, that unfortunately only Chartier of the *Revue* group had the genius to combat them. [19]

In the first issue of the *Revue* Halévy and Brunschvicg discussed the vicious cycle begun by the decay of genuine philosophy. The decay affected the institutions that were responsible for the creation of a nation's elite and for the recognition of scholarship, perpetuating the mediocrity of the national intellectual life. They criticized the Collège de France where scientism dominated to the point that only the history of philosophy and experimental psychology were taught there. [20] Perhaps the professors of the broad generalization, like Michelet, no longer taught at the Collège, but in the process of ridding the school of that style of philosophy the ethical concerns of men like Michelet had also been discouraged. Special interests dominated the Collège, partly as a result of positivist attitudes and partly because professorships were created to suit a co-opting elite.

This attack on the Collège de France was part of a broad campaign for educational reform in France in the 1890s, a campaign that involved the *Revue* circle for a period of twenty years. The structure and curriculum of secondary and university education were under constant attack in France as they had been since the Franco-Prussian War. Critics claimed that French education was dominated by literary and philosophical studies to the detriment of scientific inquiry and that this dominance caused the relatively slow rate of industrial growth. Marcellin Berthelot, the Minister of Public Education and Halévy's uncle, combatted this view of science as essentially a technical study with all the weight of his enormous scientific reputation. Halévy and the other young men of the *Revue* came to the defense of philosophy, especially metaphysics and ethics, as the necessary core of the French educational system. Broadly defined, the *Revue*'s educational reform campaign was a defense of humanistic learning, particularly of philosophic inquiry, as the core of republican morality that France most needed to fortify. One tactic of the campaign was to attack the control of the nation's youth by the positivists or by the religionists. Another was the advancement of idealist philosophy and the defense of humanistic and secular learning. Through the years, and especially in the aftermath of the Dreyfus Affair, Halévy and the *Revue* maintained this position.

An aspect of the reform movement in the educational system can be seen in an article in the first issue by Halevy and Brunschvicg on the Collège de France in which the youthful philosophers accused the Collège of blindly succumbing to German philosophical currents. France had been enriched when Michelet, Quinet, de Staël, and Cousin introduced Herder, Fichte, and Schlegel, but the worship of German thought became an affront when Renan's disciples used their control of the Collège to teach Bopp, Miller, and Strauss.[21] The previous generation had already felt the first stirrings of French philosophical rejection of German domination—*la crise allemande*. For the generation of the nineties the *Revue* expressed a more developed, self-conscious desire to throw off this intellectual hegemony or, at the very least, to judge German thought on its own merits. Several members of the *Revue* circle were very much influenced by German thought, among them Charles Andler, Lévy-Bruhl, Léon, whose major interest lay in Fichte, and the sociologists. There was a certain fashion of Nietzsche among the French intellectuals. There was, however, a general revival of interest in metaphysical and scientific questions, a flourish of classical revival, and a strong current of English political and psychological concerns, which combined in the *Revue* to encourage an independent and critical stance.

The *Revue* resisted the Prussianization (for that was how they viewed it) of the French educational system as well. In the spring semester of 1895 Halévy went to Germany on a grant to observe the seminar method in the teaching of philosophy. He observed classes on all levels, including the institutes that were established outside the university for the study of psychology. He published an article expressing his severely critical opinions of the total environment of philosophic inquiry and instruction in Germany.[22] He urged the French to resist imitating the German system, his criticism coinciding with the opinions of the Berthelot ministry and following the general observations made by Charles Seignobos in the previous decade. He was particularly critical of the practical, materialistic atmosphere in German universities.[23]

It was true, Halévy wrote, that Germany excelled in all the material requisites for industrialization, which was one of the arguments that critics of the French system made. But innumerable circumstances contributed to and resulted from this excellence, including the domination of German universities and intellectual life by material concerns and practical learning. In Germany the true concerns of youth and professors alike were social or economic questions. What Frenchmen did not understand was that this concern could hold the interests and activities of German youth indefinitely without any corresponding development of liberal or democratic government. Frenchmen tended to identify social reform with radical movements, with an urge to emancipate mankind, but in the German Empire dramatic social measures, which were revolutionary by French standards, were merely an aspect of the power of the state. Halévy doubted that the concern for social problems there could ever go beyond attention to material needs.

There are so many aspects of the mature Halévy's thought in this 1896 article, especially in his interpretation of the impulses to social reform in Germany, that one is tempted beyond the central theme. However, that theme is fundamental to Halévy's approach and to the idealism of the *Revue*. He and the others around the *Revue* believed that the moral idea of a people could be seen in their basic institutions and his perception of the German idea was a materialist, bureaucratic, and autocratic one. To preserve their republican insti tutions Frenchmen must hold to their own ethical ideal. The transplanting of German institutions to French soil would disturb the life of the French republican ideal either by adding to the materialistic, autocratic, and bureaucratic strain or by failing to take root at all. He added that some Germans, albeit a minority, but the best minds, shared his opinion and desired the reintegration of philosophy into the secondary curriculum for the spiritual enrichment of German youth. This demand was being expressed in Germany at the very moment that "unauthorized voices [in France], unfortunately too much heard, demand the total suppression of the teaching of philosophy in our schools . . ."[24]

Halévy's commitment to the *Revue*, from its founding in 1893 when he was preparing for his examinations to his death in 1937, was profound and unstinting. His friendship with Léon and his relationship to the journal were such that he was never able to ease out of the burdens of editorship, particularly toward the end of Léon's life when Halévy accepted the tasks of full editorship, without the title, always hoping to find someone to take over the responsibilities. His letters often were concerned with the time-consuming task of editing, including the meticulous reading of proof, even in the 1930s when he was burdened with the fourth volume of the *History of the English People* and his history of socialism. Frequently, he was the editor who signalled new developments and young philosophers, especially those from without France, but his contribution to pure philosophy, as opposed to practical questions of the social sciences, ended by the time he published *The Growth of Philosophic Radicalism.* For more than thirty years, however, he continued to fulfill the obligations to the *Revue* and to the Société that he had undertaken as a young man because his principles remained very much the same.

Sometime before 1896, when he published his thesis on Plato's theory of science or knowledge, Halévy decided that he did not want to be a professional philosopher. He wrote to Bouglé in 1896: "The true way to be a philosopher would be to live; to do philosophy in a professional sense of the word is a totally inadequate way of being a philosopher. I would give a fortune to have been a lieutenant of the artillery like Descartes . . ."[25] To the first sentiment, against a career in philosophy, he remained true; the second needs some explanation. He wanted action and public responsibility, not for the excitement, but for the realism that public experience could bring to his thinking.[26]

He was not stimulated by contacts with men of political power; if anything he was repelled by French political men. He accepted completely the Platonic suspicion of the actual world as a distraction from one's true objective of gaining wisdom. And the world of political action in France seemed so blatantly corrupt to him that it could never distract him as it did some of his friends. He also accepted the Socratic ideal that public life should not be contrary to the "progress of reason, of wisdom, and of speculative thought . . ."[27] For him then, realizing his thought in his actions, leading an active public life would be teaching at the Sciences Politiques, writing and refusing to shirk difficult issues, not active political engagement.

The rigor of his training would affect his writing of history, but, more than that, Platonic thought made a formidable impact on the moral cast of his mind and his perception of the problems facing liberal republicanism in France. He believed the rational morality of the Greek tradition from Socrates to the Stoics valid and vital enough to provide a secular ethic for his contemporaries and for himself. He usually referred to his own beliefs as stoic. It does seem the best description of them.

Of course, understanding the precise way each generation of Frenchmen defined the Greek rational tradition would constitute an intellectual history of the nation; it is nonetheless valuable to see the way Halévy and his colleagues meant to follow this ideal. First, they understood a rational, secular ethic as anticlerical. They felt it essential to the well-being of the republic to break the hold over the minds of Frenchmen of the Catholic Church, traditionalism, and anti-republicanism. Even before the Dreyfus Affair made the question a pressing one, most of Halévy's friends participated in organizations that furthered a modern, secular, republican ethic.[28] Halévy was not drawn to these activities even though he lacked some action more congenial to his principles. He might attend a session of the Société Française de Philosophie on the problem of formulating a secular catechism, but his skepticism led him to see the residues of religion and the inherent futility even in causes he held dear. Certainly, he accepted the obligation to contribute to the secular morale as much as Bouglé, Durkheim, Léon, Brunschvicg, Andler, or Chartier did, but he took the position that in an age of sectarianism and nationalism these secular humanist groups could offer little more than messages of hope, fortitude, courage, and charity.

Halévy did not feel compelled to search for a naturalistic

and secular ethic in the same way that Durkheim and his disciples did—as a rational substitute for traditional religion. He thought that the teachings of the classics provided a secular civic ideal. His contribution to the realization of a secular ethic for modern France might be made by writing a history of Platonism or perhaps a life of Socrates. These were works in which he believed and that he was able to do without straining to reconcile his thought and his actions. He said that he hoped his life of Socrates might be the book for secularists that Renan's *Life of Jesus* was for worldly neo-Catholics.[29] Halévy shared this ambition to draw some civic lesson from Plato and from Socrates with all his friends, especially with Alain who was writing and drawing similar messages from the classics at the Lycée Henri IV. He saw no need to reach the popular mind directly, trusting somehow to the dissemination of this ethic by those who were educated. The truth would filter down. In the aftermath of the Dreyfus Affair, the problem of reaching the masses became a more vital concern.

But Halévy did not write a history of Platonism or a biography of Socrates. Between 1896 and 1905 he decided that history was his science, rather than philosophy or sociology. He made the decision in stages. In 1896 when Bouglé teasingly warned him not to write another history of England, he responded, "If I must not write a history of England, I will write a philosophy of history, or a critical examination of fundamental social notions, or quite another thing in that order of ideas."[30] Every choice still seemed open to him. He was attracted to problems that were philosophical in the Greek sense, in which history was the subject of philosophic meditation on the passions and actions of men and groups. Hadn't Hume too ultimately turned to history as the foundation of a science of ethics? When Halévy embarked upon the writing of *England in 1815*, having definitely resisted sociology and having rejected professional philosophy, he explained. "Another history? Yes, it is unfortunately my only way to do science. It would be better to do physics or astronomy but I can't and I seek where I can for explicative relationships."[31]

This motif of science runs through Halévy's writing for the first decade of his career. He said that he was drawn to a science of politics, and he was, for all his skepticism, deeply influenced by the hope of applying the methods and principles of science to man and society. He did not mean by this the establishment of any grand scheme of general laws such as Durkheim aspired to; he meant merely the application of the tools of reason to political and social problems. He believed that a political science was feasible, if there was a rigorous and thorough examination of first assumptions. He was convinced that it would be difficult, if not impossible, for moral law to shape social and political life without rational inquiry into the nature of politics and without the acceptance of the obligation to act according to the implications of that rational inquiry.[32] The Platonic cast of this conviction molded his whole life. As a young man it was the frame in which he placed his thesis on Plato, the subject of some book reviews, and one of the themes of his work on the philosophic radicals. The theme remained secondary to other considerations in the latter work but may very well have been the original motivation behind the work—the investigation of the assumptions and premises of a group who believed they had developed a science of governing men according to a few simple principles.

Halévy shared with others around the *Revue de Métaphysique* his concern for political science as the instrument with which moral law might shape social and political life. They were strengthened in their will to invigorate critical philosophy by their fear of the practical effects of the permanent separation of philosophy and social science, which they thought would continue unless they combatted the trend toward the isolation of philosophic from other concerns. In their long critique of the Collège de France Halévy and Brunschvicg called for the reordering of priorities in order to break down the barriers between philosophy and social science and thereby encourage the rigorous philosophical examination of the metaphysical implications and the critical tools of social science. They thought that positivistic social science was characterized by inaction or resignation to slow and fatal evolution. Furthermore, without a social science there was no adequate intellectual challenge to utopians of all varieties, including socialists who claimed to base their political actions on the "scientific nature" of their theory. It was one of the persistent themes of Halévy's earliest studies of socialist writings to question the validity of their economic science. To Halévy and to Brunschvicg the alternatives facing a society devoid of some sound principles of political science—if only the exercise of sustained criticism of the philosophical assumptions of political scientists—was inaction or foolhardy action.[33]

In Plato's dialogues Halévy found a kindred spirit searching for a science of politics through which morality might be infused into society. He stressed this theme in 1896 in *La Théorie platonicienne des sciences*, the work that he presented for his *agrégation*. Unlike most of his contemporaries and teachers Halévy thought there was a unity in the Dialogues:[34] Plato's desire, that is, to resolve the contradictions between purely critical philosophy and merely empirical politics and to reconcile the philosophical and the political life for the true welfare of the polis. Plato's task was to found the state, to realize social happiness, and to organize society, all impossible undertakings unless an ideal existed by which a moral and rational individual could judge and act to build, to justify, and to condemn. The task was, of course, the same one that Halévy and the men of the *Revue* saw before them; it was the duty of moral men from time immemorial.

The key chapter of Halévy's volume on the Platonic theory of science was one on practical and political science in which he argued that a science of politics was absolutely essential for the reconciliation of the ideal of justice and the reality of politics. He argued that according to Plato man left to his common sense would be merely utilitarian about justice in society, willing to accept repression in order to destroy vice. If the highest aim of the state was the realization of virtue, not merely the repression of vice, then ignorance must be overcome through education. To realize virtue and to discern any other goals that might exist for the state presupposed a science of politics.

Plato did not, of course, consider all men equally able to practice the science of politics. The philosopher alone was capable of establishing the general principles of government and society; an aristocracy or an elite was able to understand and apply the rules of governance; but the masses were rarely able to perceive general rules or purposes. The dialectic was the fundamental tool of the political scientist. The ability to recognize the vital relation between the critical dialectic and the positive dialectic distinguished the philosophic mind. The critical dialectic discovered truths and discarded untruths by examining fundamental propositions, such as body and soul, the state and the individual, theoretical and practical science, common moral education and philosophical education, and the problems of participation in civic life. The positive dialectic joined true propositions together in an attempt to discern scientific laws. In an effort to seek explicative relationships Halévy borrowed this critical dialectic as the essential tool for the philosopher's true work—"to found, to justify, and to condemn." [35]

Charles Gillispie's brief analysis of the method of this work first pointed out the similarity between Halévy's dialectic and the one that Halévy described as Platonic. Halévy characteristically resolved contradictions into systematic dichotomies—"an analysis that unfolds a subject through layer after layer of conceptions until it comes to a core of basic attitudes and assumptions. . . ." [36] Once he discovered the core assumptions, usually two opposing aspects of a subject, he then organized his own exposition and criticism. This negative dialectic was certainly fundamental to his treatment of all questions of ideology and even historical narration. In making what purported to be a summary Halévy indicated inherent contradictions, thereby confronting each doctrine or political action with a variety of alternative interpretations as he apparently summarized them. Even his historical narrative is written from the center of events describing in effect the dialogue between contemporaries on any major problem.

The impact of Platonic thought left its traces on Halévy's method, as well as on the moral cast of his mind, but it was as a historian and a teacher, not as a philosopher, that he would practice his science. Following his trip to Germany and the publication of *La Théorie platonicienne des sciences*, he chose his career, a decision which he described, in characteristic fashion, as a matter of chance.[37] He might just as easily have been part of the university, he thought, because he had asked Liard, the rector of the Ecole Normale, to find a teaching position for him while he prepared his thesis. When nothing developed from Liard's many connections at the Ministry of Higher Education, he took Léon's advice and sought out Emile Boutmy, the director of the Ecole Libre des Sciences Politiques and one of the foremost interpreters of English civilization in France.[38] Boutmy, the close friend of Hippolyte Taine, was a Protestant, an Anglophile, and an economic liberal. At the very moment that Halévy sought him out Boutmy was in the middle of reorganizing the teaching of political economy at the Sciences Politiques. He offered the young scholar the position in English political economy and institutions.

Halévy hesitated to accept the offer only momentarily, fearing he would have to hurry his study of Benthamism. He began teaching. He expressed no doubts about the Sciences Politiques as an institution or about teaching the children of the *haute bourgeoisie* whose reasons for resisting the university were various but often included some feeling of detachment from the ardent republicanism of its professors. Halévy was himself deeply and profoundly committed to the Republic. Later, in the general soul-searching and assessing of responsibility for the fall of France in 1940, it was maintained that the Sciences Politiques was a bastion of reaction which trained the government's servants to undermine the Third Republic,[39] a charge that cannot be taken for truth out of its political context. Halévy saw teaching as an active life in which he could serve usefully. He had no fear that he would endanger the perfect independence of his thought by teaching in an institution that trained a class of government officials and was policy oriented in general. Halévy intended his criticism of France and French politics to contribute to practical, realizable reforms, and perhaps that is why he preferred teaching administrators and diplomats. To him an anti-establishment stance made little sense in a republic that was under severe attack from its birth, was threatened from the Right when he began teaching, and held on under fire from Right and Left throughout the years of his academic career.

When, later, he was offered a post at the Sorbonne, he rejected it. He was offended by the practice of filling professorships by co-optation and made ironic comments about the impossibility of maintaining one's independence at the university. He seemed to think it almost as difficult as preserving one's independence in politics. He expressed jokingly a desire to continue the family tradition of distance from the Sorbonne. He refused an appointment in philosophy there at least twice, once in 1905 when Henri Michel's position at the Ecole Normale was free[40] and again in 1911 when he was considered for another chair in philosophy. But he admitted that he might have been seduced by the vacancy in contemporary history, which was out of the question until he completed his *History of the English People,* and so he remained at the Sciences Politiques all of his professional life.

The Sciences Politiques stood in opposition to the Sorbonne, if not to the Republic. The institution was a challenge to the university from its founding by Boutmy and Taine shortly after the Franco-Prussian War. They hoped to reshape the French government after the debâcle by the thorough training of an elite administration and foreign service. It was greatly admired in England by the Fabians and others around the London School of Economics for the high quality of its students, its curriculum, and its faculty. The Sciences Politiques took a policy-oriented approach. Instruction there was much less specialized than in the law faculties of the university. Heavy emphasis was placed upon modern subjects such as history, international relations, administration, economics, and public law. Modern languages, travel, and even sports were stressed. The patrons of the school and its founders were biased toward the social sciences, and in the early years of Halévy's tenure Manchester economics dominated the school through the influence of some of the most important patrons, such as Adolphe d'Eichthal. Among the social scientists there was a definite bias toward individualist methodology as well and more than a trace of hostility toward the campaign of Durkheim's followers to dominate the university and the social sciences in France.

The school's approach was popular. By the 1890s three to four hundred students were enrolled, at least ten per cent of them foreign students. The success of the school was so great that between 1907 and 1927 153 of the 192 men appointed to diplomatic or consular vacancies held diplomas from the Sciences Politiques. Many of them studied with Elie Halévy. The school's influence upon the public administration of France was comparable to its preponderance in the foreign service.

Halévy's choice of the Sciences Politiques indicates the breadth of his concerns in the 1890s—political science, sociology, and economics as well as philosophy and history. He was moving away from the purely philosophical concerns of his friends of the Ecole Normale and the *Revue* circle though the bonds of friendship did not slacken. He had already begun his study of British history as the testing ground for principles of liberalism and democracy, a commitment which predated his teaching. As a matter of fact, if any of the major problems to which he devoted his life developed at the Sciences Politiques, it was his interest in socialism. During the first years of teaching he discovered and then wrote a small volume on Thomas Hodgskin, the English working-class radical. He also began his essays on the birth of Methodism and decided the length of his history of England and its basic outline. All these inquiries were part of his attempt "to decipher the most indecipherable people, the most moral, the least familial, the most mobile, the most adaptable, the frankest and the most hypocritical,"[41] but the aspect of Hodgskin the socialist and the study of socialism in general developed and strengthened at the Sciences Politiques.

Halévy's position was not important in defining the intellectual choices that he made, but it did allow him the kind of political and intellectual freedom he sought. He taught European socialism and British institutions and ideas, two subjects within the limits of which he could happily work out the major problems that interested him.

The grand test of the Third Republic reinforced Halévy's individualist and moral politics and his emphasis on the obligation of the elite to elevate republican public opinion. In a sense, however, the Dreyfus Affair which tested France can hardly be said to have been a test for Halévy. It was not a turning point, not a crisis of conscience. His commitment to the cause was deep and sincere and made long before the sides were drawn and the case had become the Affair, a crisis of conscience for a generation, for a nation, and for the republican regime. Halévy was a Dreyfusard from the first hour, one of the first young men to be convinced of the innocence of the captain and to act to redress the injustice. The Herculean task of reversing Dreyfus' conviction, the many setbacks during the years of agitation reinforced Halévy's ethical and individualist manner of perceiving political causes. It helped to set the limits of his political activism and in the process strengthened his fundamental belief that moral ends were best achieved through the morally regenerative forces of education. The Affair cannot be said to have altered his basic attitudes about the nature of his involvement in the real world; when it was over one could say that it had served only to reinforce his ordering of priorities toward teaching, writing, and research as his way of joining thought and action.

There was remarkable public unity in the reaction to the Dreyfus case in its first months. The union behind the government of Moderates and Catholics which had convicted Dreyfus was all the more remarkable in view of the fact that it drew disparate political forces together which only months previously had threatened to dissolve the fragile political mechanism. The Third Republic's parliamentary leadership had just brazened out a flurry of charges, counter-charges, and indictments for the corruption and improper influence that accompanied the Panama scandals.

During that enthusiastic moment of unity when Dreyfus' guilt was generally accepted and the papers called for a full hearing only in order to root out any accomplices of the convicted spy, the Halévy brothers first heard gossip to the effect that the captain might be innocent. Their informed sources were regular visitors to their home and that of their aunt, Geneviève Bizet Straus. At Trouville, Madame Straus's summer home, in August 1897 Joseph Reinach, the nephew of the notorious Baron de Reinach of the Panama scandals, demonstrated that Esterhazy had written the *bordereau* and was the guilty man in the espionage case.[42] But Halévy was not won over by rumor and inside information. In the middle of November he became firmly convinced of Dreyfus' innocence simply on the basis of evidence printed in the daily newspapers.[43] He and Daniel immediately began to recruit *normaliens* and professors, as well as famous intellectuals, to sign a protest manifesto, the first of a long series of demands for a review of the case and a reversal of the verdict.

From the beginning Elie Halévy's position was fundamentally a liberal one: it was a matter of redressing a wrong done to an individual who had been deprived of his liberty and position by a miscarriage of justice. Halévy did not, as so many republicans did, move beyond the issues involved in the Affair to an ideological definition of himself. He did not first become aware that he was a citizen of the Third Republic in reaction to the Affair; he and his family had accepted the Republic from its beginnings. Father and sons, mother and aunts had always been as one in their republicanism. Now they were also Dreyfusards. But if the Affair worked no fundamental change in Elie Halévy, it did engage him completely and uncharacteristically in furious political activism. To save Dreyfus was to save republican justice.

There is a way, of course, in which some assimilated Jews defended the universalism of French republican justice with special fervor. Many explain the commitment of Dreyfusards by the fact that they bore Jewish names and were of Jewish descent, but if one can trust his own estimation of his motives Halévy entered the fray as a republican, not as a Jew, or rather as a Protestant-born secularist of Jewish descent. Alain Silvera, the biographer of Daniel Halévy, found Daniel's choice "dictated by a certain racial origin hitherto ignored."[44] Daniel's relationship to Jewishness seems to have been more difficult than Elie's and it remained problematic for him; the loss of the friendship of Degas was a great blow to him personally. But there appears to be no "racial consciousness" in Elie Halévy's commitment. There is only a single comment in his correspondence, the first letter on the question, asking Bouglé, a French Christian, if he would tell Halévy if his conviction of Dreyfus' innocence was an "illusion of caste" because he bore a Jewish name and was a Protestant.[45] His assimilation certainly seems to be complete, his passionate involvement in the cause testified to his desire that France be vindicated as the home of religious and political liberty, a common enough hope of French radicals and liberals.

Liberal and republican principles, rather than identification with the Jewish captain, dictated Elie Halévy's choice, or so it would seem. He found Picquart more admirable than Dreyfus when he voluntarily faced indignities and imprisonment for the sake of justice and in spite of his personal prejudice against Jews. All the same, the issue of anti-Semitism in France engaged Halévy's passions. He urged Léon to organize his co-religionists to fight for Dreyfus and to struggle openly against anti-Semitism. When Bouglé wanted to write a work on anti-Semitism, Halévy offered his father's papers and passed on his father's reminiscences of the place of Jews in the Second Empire and in republican scandals.[46] He shared Bouglé's generally depressed mood, confiding that the phenomenon of anti-Semitism in modern times oppressed him unbearably. He feared the anti-Semitic coalition, which joined "powerful religious passions" with "socialist passions" by allying the old aristocrats and the old bourgeoisie, the traditionalists and the Catholics with sections of the masses through a shared hatred of "financial feudalism" and the *nouveaux riches*.[47] Halévy refused to believe that the socialists, who at first took a plague-on-both-your houses stance, would remain anti-Semitic for long, even as a tactic. He predicted pessimistically, however, that "the day that one must choose between socialism and anti-Semitism," the hatred of Jews in France would be very strong.[48] This conjunction of tribal passions with class hatreds was totally repugnant to him. He indicated this in a propaganda theme that he sketched for Bouglé as "Orient and Occident." He characterized anti-Semitism as part of that tendency of the East to form regimes of castes, with religious and racial communities isolated from one another. It was, of course, the antithesis of the individualist West which measured men by their work and their personal value. The wave of anti-Semitism in Russian Poland, Austria, Germany, and now Algeria too was, for Halévy, the progress of the oriental mind. The Dreyfusards must redouble their efforts for France to remain an island in Europe of the western mind.[49]

Halévy's liberal commitment in the Dreyfus Affair remained just that—a liberal commitment—with respect to a number of issues other than anti-Semitism. He shared the conviction of the "intellectual party" that militarism, clericalism, and anti-Semitism were inseparable and he agreed that unless they acted immediately the "twentieth century would be a sad disavowal of the nineteenth,"[50] a prediction he would have thought fulfilled in the decade before he died. He did not share the political stance of many Dreyfusards, however. He never adopted the antimilitarist position that many espoused in reaction to the role of the military in the Affair. Neither did he join the socialists in fundamental antipathy to the establishment that willingly perpetrated, for a time, this crime of state. Nor did he take up the leftist idealization of the masses who, it was asserted, would never have allowed this injustice to take place, if they had had political power.

Halévy would not leap from a liberal position defending a soldier unjustly convicted in a military trial to a condemnation of the military as a whole. "One must desire with all one's strength that, for the honor of France and the army, all will be righted."[51] He thought the intellectuals' antimilitarism was a luxury that France could ill afford so long as her neighbors, England and Germany, were armed to the teeth. His hatred of war was as deep as that of his dear friends Alain and Bouglé, but unlike them he could not believe that he promoted peace by campaigning against his country's army. Peace might be advanced by rational understanding of international politics and genuine love and respect for the culture and civilization of other nations but not by undermining the military position of France, which he regarded as a state on the defensive in European politics. He held this position throughout the affair and long after when, prior to the Great War, he refused to accept any part of Jaurès's or Hervé's opposition to the three-year military service bill. For one thing, he saw the revolutionary implications of Hervéism long before Leninism imitated its antimilitarist tactics. The international political situation, as he saw it from an England embroiled in the Boer War, taught him a sobering lesson that reinforced his political realism.

THE MAKING OF A HISTORIAN

And what will become of our work of republican defense, what will be your attitude on the day more or less near when England will be in war with one or more continental powers, and when the universal brawl without precedent in the history of the world begins? They will massacre each other in Africa, in Oceania, in China, in America and in Europe. We are not yet familiar with these ideas, having preoccupied ourselves from birth with the last European war but we will become habituated to everything and in short order. Some wars, more or less European, like the Cuban war or the South African war will suffice to achieve our adaptation.[52]

As he said in the beginning of the Dreyfus crusade in a period of relative optimism: "We are dealing with a crime by 'virtuous' men. The crime will be repaired. . . . I only ask the reparation of this particular injustice and after that silence."[53]

Halévy did not join the socialists during or in the aftermath of the Dreyfus Affair. In this he broke with his brother and with all that generation of *normaliens* who followed Herr and Jaurès from a liberal struggle to the socialist cause. Daniel Halévy began his pilgrim's progress in French ideologies at this time, becoming involved with Georges Sorel and with Péguy in the *Cahiers de la Quinzaine*, where he first published his re-examination of the Dreyfusard commitment.[54] There were among Elie's classmates those who, like Bouglé, envied the socialists their faith and their goals, but Elie never contemplated the jump from Dreyfus to Marx or even to Jean Jaurès.

It seems to me that I am no more or less socialist now than eighteen months ago. I work to calm the exalted ones who declare themselves socialist because Dreyfus is innocent. What is the relation between the return of Dreyfus from Devil's Island and the taking by the state of private property? Better if they called themselves anarchist![55]

In the period following the socialists' move from neutrality to activism in questions of justice among the bourgeoisie, the Dreyfus Affair made strange bedfellows. Jewish bankers and anarchist miners, Protestant pastors and naturalist writers joined together to demand appeal and Halévy joined them because he saw clearly that Dreyfus was innocent. "But beyond that point I cease to see clearly. I continue therefore to examine my ideas every day, waiting until they arrange themselves."[56]

As he waited, his ideas did not change, not about socialism, not about democracy. He was a self-proclaimed democrat and a republican, but his language and point of view seemed Orleanist, reflecting a Burkean belief that complex institutions are the genuinely liberal safeguards. Halévy found repugnant the entire aristocratic affectation that passed for a critique of democracy. "I could become authoritarian. I would be indeed astonished if I were to become anti-democratic. The most tenacious prejudice of my nature is a lively antipathy for the aristocratic religious and provincial sentimentality. . . ."[57] He was a republican with serious reservations about civic education in France, especially among the masses. However, he had little of the enthusiasm of those republicans who saw the masses as the repository of republican virtue incapable of committing or perpetuating a crime comparable to the imprisonment of Dreyfus. A democratic republican, he was perfectly aware of the problems of democracy. The danger of universal suffrage was that it might, by periodic elections, ratify the crimes of the state against the fundamental tenets of the republic. To Bouglé he would admit that corruption might be an inherent vice of a democratic regime. That did not mean that it was any the less necessary to be republican. As he wrote, quoting Renan, "It is still Caliban who defends Prospero against the Cagots."[58] "It is necessary to work, whatever the costs, to make the French republic last, though it lasts only by a *miracle*, as one knows from the last five years."[59]

Faced with the apathy of the public to Dreyfus' plight, Halévy saw it as part of the same general degradation of public opinion and public morality that had prompted the founding of the *Revue de Métaphysique et de Morale*. The press, the League of the Rights of Man, every person, and every available institution had to be activated and had to testify in Dreyfus' behalf. "Ultimately, those who are the ruling classes, those who must be liberal by profession, the lawyers, professors, keep silent because they haven't any organ with which to speak. The press belongs to a special class of adventurers whom no one respects but everyone listens to."[60] New tactics had to be devised to compensate for the level of the press and of the populace. He wrote long letters of Dreyfusard tactics to everyone: Bouglé must organize the League of the Rights of Man in Brittany to combat the Montpellier anti-Semitic league; Havet's lecture on freedom of association must be published; friends and acquaintances must sign official letters of protest. They gathered 3,000 names for the January 16th protest in *L'Aurore*, timed to coincide with Zola's *J'accuse*. Halévy also participated in the great student demonstrations.[61]

Halévy said that his commitment to political action ended on the January day that Dreyfus solicited and accepted a pardon (that is, when he allowed others to assume the implication of guilt rather than continue his struggle for exoneration). Halévy wanted now to "ignore politics." "A man disposed to fulfill his civic duties, but resolved to keep intact the greatest part of his time for the accomplishment of tasks properly intellectual, must rigorously limit the practical part of his existence. I ignore the Dreyfus Affair, I ignore politics; . . ."[62]

The issues of public opinion had widened in the Affair, however, steadily bringing into question the depth of republican roots in France. So although he had decided to ignore the Affair he took up missionary activity in the school. He and his brother threw themselves into the *universités populaires* movement, which was an attempt on the part of students to reach the lower classes.[63] He argued that in a republic the school is fundamental, not secondary, and "must therefore be honored as befits an instrument of the truth. . . . I would like to demonstrate to the people the vanity of enthusiasm and the usefulness of institutions."[64]

Political combat ended. Halévy returned to alternative

republican duty, propagating the ideal of the school and the laic ideal, responding thus in the same fashion as most of the elite of the republic of professors. His friends, all convinced secularists and anticlericals, continued their efforts as well in the League of the Rights of Man and in anticlerical organizations. They all supported the laic laws and the anticlerical policy of the Radicals. But Halévy's correspondence indicates that he held to the logic of the laic ideal by a more consistent, and perhaps less liberal, anticlericalism than that of his friends. When Combès crushed the orders and suppressed religious schools, even Halévy's close friends expressed qualms over the morality of discriminatory laws against the orders. Bouglé, whose support of the Radicals in this period was almost as consistent as that of Alain, the party's 'official philosopher,' and Léon whose anticlericalism dominated his republicanism, both had their doubts. Elie's position was much more hardheaded. He chided Léon that he wanted to be rid of the influence of the church without the use of pressure or power. But that was not possible.

No less aware than his friends of the morally ambiguous position of liberal republicans who advocated freedom of speech and inquiry and at the same time urged repressive measures against the religious, he nevertheless believed that in France individual liberty could be won and preserved only by a struggle against the preponderance of special groups and societies, especially the Church.[65] Its control over the minds of youth was so great that rationalism could not take root there until its hold was broken, he reasoned. The laic laws were obviously not laws of liberty, not even after the fashion of Rousseau, whereby the law replaced caprice even at the risk of imposing the despotism of the group over the individual. His argument was very much like that of his fellow Dreyfusard, Emile Durkheim, who also saw the state as one of the liberating institutions that free the individual from the bonds of such elementary groups as the family, patriarchy, the commune, and the church. As he explained to Bouglé, liberalism admitted the necessity of the state but was fully aware that

that state could become tyrannical. Therefore, the state must be constituted to remain useful, although deprived of the opportunity to become tyrannical. The state might actually be the weapon by which the capacity of men to be free was strengthened. On the question of anticlericalism, which touched so closely the issue of free minds and a liberal public opinion, Halévy thought that the French state might have to pursue a policy of persecution of the orders so that France might ultimately be liberal. "There is a sense of the words *liberty* and *liberalism* in which these words are synonymous with state anticlericalism," he wrote.[66]

Some men of a left-Dreyfusard persuasion, men like Daniel Halévy and Charles Péguy, were disgusted by the laic laws and with the bourgeois political game, even as played by their Dreyfusard allies. They argued that the state had turned from the persecution of the Jewish captain to the harassment of priests and nuns and that there was something immoral in the ends and means of the bourgeois state. The abuse of power by the Radical coalition that enacted the laic laws prompted Péguy to his famous epigram, "Tout commence en mystique et tout finit en politique." The bourgeois state, even when it included their ally Jean Jaurès in the inner circles of government, appeared incapable of realizing their ideals. The experience deepened their feeling for socialism. For Elie Halévy, whose expectations of states were much more limited, the politics of anticlericalism won his allegiance more than any other policy carried out by the government from the time of the Affair to the outbreak of the war.

Halévy's liberalism was not merely Radical politics, however. In practice he tended to vote Délégation des Gauches, either Radical, or Moderate, but that tells a small part of the story. In Radical doctrine, at least as it was expounded by Alain for the provincial voter, the role of the state was a negative one—to prevent disorder, to prevent the usurpation of authority and the corrupting influence of power, to prevent the growth of government or of overmighty interests. The essential problem of political organization was to maintain order without which there could be no liberty; the government's duty was the preservation of both order and liberty without falling into tyranny or anarchy. Liberty was both personal and public, the distinction corresponding to the realm of freedom of the private individual with which the state ought not to interfere and the sphere of public life in which opinion, expression, and beliefs were exercised openly and freely under the states' protection.

There was little in these Radical tenets that Halévy did not espouse and yet commentators have tended to regard his liberalism as nearer to the English variety than to the French strain. There is something to be said for this view. At its worst, Radicalism expressed a mean, suspicious, negative view of civic responsibility, of political leadership and representation. In this political framework Halévy's ideals did seem more English than French. Radicalism was individualist, as was Halévy, but Radical individualism intended only to narrow the scope of public action that the society or the state could demand of the citizen. But Halévy's individualism aimed not only at preserving the citizens' privacy and his right to free inquiry but also at guaranteeing him the possibility of participating in public life. Radical individualism was, in effect, a right to inaction; Halévy's individualism, a right to take action. Radical parliamentarianism too differed from Halévy's view, as a advocate of parliamentary democracy, that the parliament must elevate the public ethic and seek to preserve peace. The Radical representative understood parliamentarianism only as a means of serving his constituency and faithfully voting for its material interests, without necessarily concerning himself with the social good.

Halévy assigned a positive role to the state and to political leadership—a duty to educate, to affirm an ideal of political and social justice, to express the public will without partisan spirit and without representing special interests or constituencies. Although he was fully aware of the dangers of caesarism, he had a most un-Radical appreciation of the importance of leadership and institutions, as well as the condition of the public ethic, to the good governance of the republic. The problem of French democratic republicanism was that there were no institutions that could wield power in any other way than to check it. A watchdog mentality permeated the Chamber, the administration, local government, and party politics. The result was an executive handcuffed in emergencies and nearly immobile in even the best of times. Halévy understood the value of state power in achieving social goals and the necessity of active leadership whether it was exercised by great men, such as Peel or Lloyd George, or by an elite, as in the case of the English reformed aristocracy. In France, representatives were primarily delegates of constituencies, rather than of the society, who blocked any concentration of authority, individual or institutional. There was an appearance of enormous activity but little movement. This state of affairs might have been acceptable in a society troubled by few differences or divisions. Even before the war, however, there were signs of great social strain, particularly among the working classes. Halévy argued for social reforms and a progressive income tax, which was then thought to be the confiscation of property, and it was one of his bitterest disappointments that policies resembling the new liberalism of Lloyd George and Winston Churchill made so little headway in his country. He was not, as some critics would have it, a laissez-faire liberal. He argued that artificial obstacles to the development of the individual must be removed in a democratic state. His was a liberal social philosophy that justified state intervention in the economy to alleviate distress, to open opportunities, and to secure justice. At the same time he was a hard-headed critic of economic schemes (such as imperial tariffs in England), which purported to lessen the burden on the workers but which could not fulfill their promise; they were demagoguery and nothing more.

There is a tension in Halévy's political thought which as a young man he refused to resolve by posing oppositions of liberty and authority, individual and society and democracy and leadership. His forte was critical intelligence, pointing out problems and drawing on vast historical and political knowledge for analysis and for solutions. In his view the intellectual's role was a critical one and the critical function was integral to the fundamental idealist morale. Absolutely basic to his personal idealism, his Platonism so to speak, was a belief that society's purpose was to enable men to be moral. The precondition of morality for him was the free individual acting according to ethical principles freely chosen. But the other side of that coin of liberating and reforming man and society was the acceptance of a stringent self-discipline by the free agent and the society as a whole. Stability in society and self-discipline of the individual were necessary conditions for a free society. He found it paradoxical that in general liberalism was founded on hedonist and materialist principles. He thought in fact that freedom rested on the recognition of the absolute sacredness and dignity of the individual, the acceptance of his privacy, his autonomy, and his right to self-development and personal independence. These rights were the ones he chose for himself and he chose for others. This paradox ran through his *History of the English People.* He thought the future was democratic and that democracy was morally valid because it seemed best suited to the cultivation of the individual, but he, like Tocqueville, found at the origins of democracy a contradiction between liberty and equality, between the individual and society. He found in his time the contradictions expressed most clearly in his concept of socialism and this theme ran throughout his observations on the subject. These problems and these principles would infuse his entire life of scholarship and citizenship.

CHAPTER TWO

The Growth of
Philosophic Radicalism

HALÉVY DEFINED his intellectual problems for the next thirty years in the decade following his *agrégation.* Generally speaking, by 1904 when he published the third volume of the work which began as his dissertation— *The Growth of Philosophic Radicalism*—he had established the concerns of his scholarship. He widened his scope and changed his priorities after the First World War, but basically he was himself following the two courses that he taught at the Ecole Libre des Sciences Politiques—the history of British institutions and thought and the history of European socialism.

He indicated the internal logic of his major problems in a letter to Bouglé in 1896. Drawing three concentric circles on the page, he wrote that he would next undertake "a theory of society, a theory of modern democracy, or a history of England, or something else entirely in that line of thing."[1] Then, mocking his own seriousness as was his habit, he commented that destiny would let him know in which of these three circles he would enclose himself. It would be an error to believe that he ever confined himself within the perimeter of a single one of these circles, that by choosing to write a history of England he put aside a theory of society or of modern

The political influence of this seemingly simple idea interested Halévy who proposed in his dissertation:

> to write the history of certain ideas, of certain individuals and of a particular milieu. But I wanted to place on the first step the history of ideas; I wanted the individuals to remain on the second step and only to appear as the vehicles of the ideas. James Mill is only a doctrine made man. I would almost say as much of Bentham.[8]

He wrote a history of Benthamite doctrine, not merely the ideas of Bentham himself. He saw his study of the utilitarians as "a problem in the philosophy of history: what is the historical importance of a doctrine?" He was bothered by this question when he thought of Hodgskin, Pecqueur, and Marx and again when he speculated about the impact of the Wesleyans. He returned to this question again and again in that first decade following his *agrégation*.

Halévy's method was the chronological and topical treatment of the thought of the utilitarians organized around the events of Bentham's life. The men in the work were the vehicles of ideas, especially those ideologues who came under Bentham's influence or who influenced him, such as James Mill, David Ricardo, and Francis Place.[9] The three volumes of *The Growth of Philosophic Radicalism* cover the youth of Bentham, the evolution of the doctrine, and the formation of philosophic radicalism. Within each volume Halévy discussed the currents of political and economic opinion that influenced Benthamism either to contribute to or to challenge its principles. In doing so, he was able to reconstruct much of the intellectual and political life of England around these English doctrinaires, first for the period from Bentham's birth to the French Revolution and then to the Reform Bill of 1832.

Halévy's central theme supplied the organization and the critique of *Philosophic Radicalism*. He held that there were two strands of utilitarian thought and that they were inherently incompatible. One, under the influence of Helvétius and of Bentham's own predisposition to administrative and legal reform, justified the artificial identification of interest between the subject and the state. By structuring government and law and ultimately society itself to reward preferred behavior and to punish undesired conduct, the legislator or administrator artificially created a harmony between the interests of the individual and the greater good of society. The other strand, which was incorporated by the Benthamites into their thought from classical economics, assumed the natural harmony of interests, the impossibility, that is, of conflict in the long run between the desires of the individual and the greater good of society.

As Halévy pointed out, the central problem of the social order, first raised by Hobbes and then by Locke, remained the issue for the utilitarians, who never squarely faced, if they grasped, the problem. Hobbes had posited that the conflict of interests between the individual and the state must be resolved by the sovereign for the sake of peace. But in the English tradition the Hobbesian solution had not prevailed; rather, the Lockean natural harmony of interests of the individual and society was assumed.

The utilitarians never directly confronted the conflict in the assumptions of Locke and Hobbes. They used both theories. Though it could be said in general that Benthamite legal and administrative thought resorted to the artificial identification of interest as in Hobbes and that utilitarian economic policies tended to assume natural harmony, there were times when even this rule did not hold.

Many apparently divergent political economists expressed their positions in the language of utility and Halévy's unravelling of the strands was a *tour de force*. His discussion placed utilitarian causes into one or another category throughout the period. He indicated that what appears to be an irreconcilable conflict between the artificial reconciliation of interests and the natural harmony of interests was, in practice, often completely obscured by the particular issues. The New Poor Law, by which the agency of the state incarcerated subjects in an attempt to discourage public dependency, was an example of artificially created harmony. The argument for the repeal of the Corn Laws, on the other hand, rested on the principle of the natural harmony in that the state was not to be allowed to protect the special interests of the agriculturalists. Thus, at one time the utilitarians might promote the growth of the power of the state and at another pursue commercial and industrial laissez-faire policies and at no time recognize any theoretical contradiction.

Halévy broke utilitarian doctrine into three components, which roughly corresponded to three different periods in Bentham's life—juridical concerns, matters of political economy, and political reform. Within each volume he described the theoretical considerations and the currents of opinion that contributed to the finished dogma of Benthamism. The first book included the theories of penal reform and legislation of Beccaria and Helvétius that shaped Bentham's formulation of a philosophy of law as well as the economic thought of Adam Smith. He summarized the development of Benthamism by 1789, noting that in every particular Bentham's juridical theory was complete and ahead of its time. He thought utilitarianism reflected the spirit of the age in economics where its premises and teachings were drawn from Adam Smith. But in politics, at the moment of the Revolution, the utilitarians were skeptics and authoritarians and were far from the Radical program they were to develop over the next generation. The doctrine of utility was so universal a philosophy in England, however, that all reformers in the era of the revolution "were forced to speak the language of utility if they wanted to make their opinions accepted or even understood by the public to which they were addressed." [10] Halévy pointed out that Bentham and Burke both assumed the principle of utility to be hostile to the principles of republicanism and democracy. Burke based his traditional philosophy on a utilitarian argument and Bentham refuted the Declaration of the Rights of Man point by point on utilitarian grounds. In 1789 Bentham, the future leader of the philosophic radicals, was far from a democrat, but in spite of him the rhetoric of utility came to be identified with the principles of democracy and republicanism.

If Bentham's ideological development stood still during the upheavals in France, that of the Jacobin sympathizers did not. Halévy noted that Paine's doctrines reflected the assumptions of natural rights and utility. In effect, Paine attempted to apply Smith's ideas to political problems, positing the natural harmony of interests. Others, Halévy noted, particularly Godwin and Hodgskin, applied the natural identity of interests even more faithfully and more consistently than Paine did. They ultimately denied the need for government at all. Thus, Halévy reasoned that if the language and principle of utility coupled with the assumption of the natural identity of interests implied radicalism, including even radical anarchism to some, then the character of Benthamite ideology depended upon other theorems than these two. From Bentham's disciples a mechanism of the egoistic passions determined whether they were naturally or artificially reconciled for the well-being of society. Therefore, although Godwin expressed his thought in utilitarian language, at the heart of all his philosophy was a belief in the individual personality and a hope for the intellectual emancipation of the individual. Halévy thought that by its nature this hope separated Godwin from the utilitarian tradition. Similarly, Godwin expressed his economic views in utilitarian terms, but ultimately he aspired to a society in which individual property would cease to exist and would be replaced by the egalitarian sharing of abundance.

A doctrine of scarcity, not abundance, dominated Benthamite economic utilitarianism. For the philosophic radicals the Malthusian prospect of insufficient products for human consumption overwhelmed and overshadowed Godwin's fear of the harmful effects of a maldistribution of goods. The philosophic radicals incorporated Malthusianism without any explicit recognition that there might be a conflict between Smith's optimism and the pessimism of Malthus. The ease with which they joined philosophically incompatible beliefs could be explained only by historical conditions. Halévy's reason for approaching his subject historically was masterfully demonstrated in his explication of the conditions in which the philosophic radicals came to favor education, a direct result of their Malthusianism.[11] Their espousal of laissez-faire ought to have led them to oppose compulsory education, but the spirit of Malthus so overwhelmed their thought that they hoped education would tame the sexual instincts.

The Benthamites' political activity leading to the Reform Bill of 1832 was the center of the last volume of the book. Halévy described a school of propagandists around Bentham, established by James Mill, the most capable and ardent propagandist of the groups' principles.[12] Halévy argued that Mill converted Bentham to democracy. A series of rejections at the hands of men whom he saw as the agents of corporate privilege running the complex machinery of aristocratic government in such a way as to foil true reform convinced Bentham of democracy. If he could not make reform at the top, then perhaps he could win support for it among the people at the bottom.

After 1815 the Benthamites mounted a strenuous propaganda attack on the common opinions held by Englishmen. Utilitarian economists campaigned against protection, which they argued favored corporate or "sinister" interests over the general interest. They defined the general interest as the aggregate of the interest of consumers, which avoided the theoretical problems that conflicts of interest between producers posed for any idea of natural harmony of interests. They assumed that as consumers, individuals have similar interests. Government was chief among the "sinister" corporations because the aristocratic elements of society controlled it, using it to further their individual and class interests. Utilitarians, therefore, adopted the tactic of reducing or ending state intervention in behalf of any particular group or class. Ultimately, the Ricardians argued for the world-wide free exchange of products among individual consumers without regard for group, class, or national boundaries.

In utilitarian political theory after 1815 the democratic or egalitarian argument supplied the rationale for the call to reduce corporate privilege. The Radicals advocated democracy for its greater equality, but, more important for them, for its dispatch in enacting reforms and realizing progress that would ordinarily be delayed by the complex machinery of aristocratic government.[13] Bentham's moment of truth had come from the frustration he experienced as a would-be reformer batting his head against the wall of official indifference and, so he believed, corporate resistance. In truth, Bentham had only slightly more ideological commitment to democracy than he had to liberal institutions. The method by which he attained his goals was incidental to the goals themselves. Instead of making the facile identification of Benthamism with radicalism, which was common in France, Halévy drew a parallel to the ideal benevolent despots of the philosophes. For want of a despot, Bentham accepted universal suffrage.

Utilitarians believed the chief political fallacy they had to combat was the widespread assumption in England that complex and liberal government were one and the same thing. To them complex government protected corporate privilege; it was the refuge of special interests and class government, not the bulwark of popular liberties. And so the Radicals attacked the restraining devices of the English system whether they held back the state or the masses. Similarly, they attacked the philosophers of complex government, Montesquieu, Blackstone, and de Lolme. Halévy saw this tactic as a reflection of contradiction inherent in the very origins of liberal ideology.

Halévy thought, in fact, that liberalism might spring from many sources, including this Whig "fallacy" that complex government was liberal, which Benthamites attacked. A liberal society might also build on the mores of a people of strong Christian habits, historical traditions, and even on the necessities of the industrializing economy. But in the eighteenth century liberalism came to be justified by two arguments—utility and the rights of man. Halévy chose as his subject the emergence of the argument of utility to preeminence among the English Radicals rather than the doctrine of the rights of man, which had appealed to the French. The utilitarian position, however, no less than the doctrine of the rights of man, was shot through with contradictions. First, there was the grand contradiction, which permeated the doctrine, between natural and artificial identification of interests, between the legacy of Bentham and that of Smith. If individual interests had to be artificially reconciled with the public welfare, might not there be a threat to individual liberty in that reconciliation? Secondly, the spring of classical economics fed diverging streams of social thought; the socialism of Godwin, Owen, Holcroft, and Hodgskin as well as the Manchesterism of MacCulloch, Cobden, and Bright could be found at this source.

With regard to the first contradiction, which was the theme that bound his book together, Halévy was the first scholar to call attention to the fundamental ambivalence toward liberty in the Benthamite tradition, in its origins and in its influence. He alone of historians in England and France insisted that this ambivalent strain ran through the utilitarian philosophy. Neither Leslie Stephen nor A. V. Dicey saw the difficulties that he raised. The former noted with approval the Benthamite contributions to the development of state machinery. Rejecting the rise of collectivism, Dicey used the concepts Benthamism and Individualism interchangeably.[14]

Halévy, the French liberal, held liberty to be the highest good. He believed that one of the best safeguards of liberty was a complex constitution,[15] but even this might prove inadequate if public opinion did not respect the sacred nature of the individual with an almost superstitious awe. England possessed a complex constitution and the elaborate mechanism of an honored legal system. Furthermore, evangelical pietism had imbued English liberalism with a respect for the incomprehensible, the irrational, and the spark of divinity in every human being. With these and other moral controls England had resisted the authoritarianism inherent in Benthamism. France did not possess these mechanisms or these moral controls and there both caesarism and anarchy were a constant threat to liberty. Halévy feared caesarism as much as, if not more than, anarchy. The omnipresent threats to liberty in France deepened his sensitivity to the indifference to personal liberty in the thought of the English philosophes, a trait they shared with their French counterparts.

In *Philosophic Radicalism* Halévy returned consistently to the theme of the Benthamites' indifference to liberty. His comment on Bentham's Panopticon scheme pointed it out: "Liberty is not, according to Bentham, an end of human activity; the doctrine of utility is not, in origin and in essence, a philosophy of liberty." [16] Commenting on Bentham's simplifying mania, which could advocate a single remedy for penitentiary, factory, madhouse, hospital, and even school, he concluded: "He hoped to make the principles of the doctrine of Helvétius, which were despotic, philanthropic and utilitarian, but not in the least liberal, triumph in his own country. . . ." [17] This utter lack of regard for questions of liberty was not merely a personal quirk of Bentham, but one shared with several others, such as Owen or Godwin, who were also under the influence of Helvétius.

In his discussion of Bentham's *Rationale of Judicial Evidence* Halévy contrasted the accepted English procedures with Bentham's recommendations. He concluded: "On Bentham's doctrine, the judge is free to put what restrictions he likes, for reasons of nonpertinence or of superfluity, on the production of evidence, without any rules of exclusion, with a view of arriving at a knowledge of the truth. . . ." [18] He repeated: "Utilitarianism is not a synonym for liberalism; in the doctrine of utility, liberty is not a good in itself." [19] Halévy pointed out that Bentham only once, and then under the influence of James Mill, defended the institution of the jury. Summarizing Bentham's proposals for juridical reform he wrote:

> In short, the judge, as conceived by Bentham's doctrine, is a kind of monarch isolated in his tribunal, delivering his sentences without legal forms, and without any really efficacious control to prevent eventual abuses of power, other than the purely moral control exercised on him by public opinion. But such a doctrine bears almost no relation to the so-called liberal doctrine: it was almost in the same terms as those that the Caesarists of the nineteenth century were to demand the establishment of a government which should be personal, and responsible just insofar as it was personal.[20]

Halévy suspected the Benthamite zeal for strong government by experts precisely because it was coupled with this insensitivity to threats of liberty. He distrusted this passion in the political tradition of France, among his contemporaries as well as historical figures, and he frequently remarked it in his English friends the Webbs. He thought that the Webbs, who saw themselves as the intellectual descendants of Bentham, might have prejudiced his sense of socialism because they defined it as a strong centralized government controlling the peoples' welfare and efficiency. There are those, of course, who see Bentham as the father of English socialism in that he ardently advocated using public authority for social reform and social engineering. This view is particularly strong among those who are favorably impressed by the Fabians, but Halévy, whose definition of socialism centered on precisely this willingness to use state authority for intervention in economic matters, did not see Bentham as father to English socialism. For Halévy, whose dread of Hegelian statism was as great as his rejection of Marxian class warfare or economic determinism, the greatest influence on the English statists at the turn of the twentieth century was neo-Hegelianism translated into English, the influence of German administration and bureaucracy on British reformers. In Halévy's final estimation, the Benthamite "greatest good for the greatest number" remained individualist and democratic in practice and in thought. To his mind it differed substantially from Saint-Simon who aimed at "the amelioration of the most numerous and poorest class" as a class, not as simple individuals.

Halévy's judgment of the Benthamite passion for centralization and government by experts was that, fundamentally, the conception was detrimental to liberty. "The State, as conceived by Bentham, is a machine so well constructed that every individual, taken individually, cannot for one instant escape from the control of all the individuals taken collectively." [21] "Pure democracy" meant to Bentham a government as free as possible from every constitutional complication and from every juridical fiction. [22] Bentham's willingness to create anew ancient tyranny in more rational forms was not lost on Halévy, any more than it was on Bentham's contemporaries at the *Edinburgh Review* or on Thomas Hodgskin, but it had been lost on Bentham's heirs.

The other flaw that Halévy found in philosophical radical theory was the fact that one could defend both laissez-faire capitalism and socialism on the basis of the assumption of either natural harmony of interests or the labor theory of value. He found an interesting parallel of the contradictions of philosophic radicalism in two different phases of its history, which he thought underlined his theme and justified the use of historical rather than philosophic methodology. Godwin had founded his economic and political system on Smith's natural harmony of interests. On that foundation he had advocated the end of private property and of government because coercion was inherently evil. Halévy pointed out that later, in the era of the Reform Bill, William Thompson and Thomas Hodgskin had turned Ricardo's labor theory of value against his political and economic conclusions. Both argued that the divergent interests of labor and capital followed inevitably from the realities described by the labor theory. Ricardo stressed the conflict of interests between the landlords and other classes of society, but not the struggle of capitalist and laborer. But that struggle was based on a natural divergence of interests of the class of capitalists and the class of wage earners encompassed in Ricardo's theory. Ricardo was accused of preaching economic optimism and quietism in its most complete form because the theory accepted the momentary or dynamic changes of the economic system as merely short-run problems that would be resolved in the long-run of the economy.[23]

Halévy was attracted to the democratic, individualistic radicalism that viewed all men, rich or poor, as belonging to a single class. Yet, even there, in the origins of liberal thought he found an inherently contradictory doctrine with regard to the utilization of state power and in "left Ricardianism" the germs of a class analysis that was incompatible with liberal individualism. Certainly, as he pointed out years later in the *Era of Tyrannies* discussion, radicalism changed once it admitted that there were classes in society arising from the natural evolution of the economy which were constituted in such a way that in one class all individuals were hereditarily favored by fortune and in the other hereditarily denied advantage.[24]

Such problems occurred to few of Bentham's contemporaries. In spite of the contradictions in philosophic radicalism, the doctrine was capable of fully satisfying a young and talented intelligence like that of John Stuart Mill around 1825. Halévy himself, however, was acutely aware of Benthamite failure to reconcile theoretical difficulties. The relative harmony between liberal and radical at the time of the Reform Bill could best be explained by the social ethic and the political programs of the period, not by the logic of arguments. Intellectually, the values of a man like Hodgskin diverged noticeably from the philosophic radicals, but in practical program they differed very little. Halévy thought the doctrine of natural harmony had so totally captured the imagination of some of Bentham's contemporaries that in practical terms the distance between libertarian socialist or anarchist and laissez-faire Ricardian was very small. Furthermore, Ricardo's explanation of the fact that workers and masters joined together against the landed interests seemed to describe the political reality of the particular moment, a moment in which Peel's economic reforms of 1846 were realized.[25]

Once he moved from theoretical difficulties to the social and economic realities of the 1830s, Halévy came very close to a class explanation of the popularity of the ideology. In his volume on Thomas Hodgskin, which was written as he worked on *Philosophic Radicalism,* he had made the point that this precursor of Marx was utterly unwilling to rely on the state or to interfere with the natural harmony of the economy. There were no differences in the program of Hodgskin's Mechanics' Institute and that of the advocates of laissez-faire once they secured the abolition of special privileges. As a result, the aristocracy of labor concentrated on the virtues of natural harmony and progress—self-reliance, self improvement, and prudence.[26]

But it was not working-class acceptance of the ethos of industrial and commercial laissez-faire that played the decisive role in the ascendance of that ideology. The working class mattered relatively little. Neither did Halévy believe that the government policy of free trade derived from the conversion of the elite to Ricardian principles alone.[27] Rather, these principles fit the spirit of the age, he said, and in fact, he indicated that they fit the needs of a class; that is, "merchants needed the thesis of the identity of interests to be true, in order to secure the most extended market for their products." "Manufacturers needed to believe in the theory of indefinite progress . . . , consequently it mattered little that certain economic laws brought serious restrictions to bear on the harmony of interests, or set a limit to the progress of the human race. . . ." "The industrial revolution, like the political revolution in France thirty years earlier, was demanding its principles."[28] The youthful Halévy in the rhetoric of the history of ideas offered as explanations facile connections of class and ideology, explanations he would test in the *History of the English People.*

THE GROWTH OF PHILOSOPHIC RADICALISM

The Growth of Philosophic Radicalism should be seen in the context of the political and scholarly issues that stirred Halévy, and indeed the French intellectual community, in the years 1894 to 1904. An extremely complex book, *Philosophic Radicalism* must be seen as an attempt to examine critically the fundamental propositions of much of liberal thought and as a reasoned defense of much of the liberal, radical, and democratic tradition against a French intellectual current which hoped to drown that legacy. It is a masterpiece of descriptive analysis of the English utilitarians' theory and practice as it evolved in response to specific political, social, and economic problems and theories. It has not been replaced as a work of scholarship in more than seventy years. In this work of scholarship Halévy sought political wisdom about the problems of modern society, especially those relating to change, order, security, and liberty. The relentless logic with which Halévy organized the argument of the utilitarians and the dialogue with their critics took a position as well as it described one. Finally, *Philosophic Radicalism* deserves our treatment as one part of a developing Halévy thesis about the nature of English society in the nineteenth century.

Liberal political economy was the object of attack from many directions in France, as well as in England, at the turn of the century. There were, as there had always been, political attacks in France, but there were cracks in economic theory as well, reflecting the influence of Marshall, Pareto, and the German Historicists. Marshall and others refused to accept the view of economics as merely the science of the satisfaction of human wants. Pareto was groping toward a view that even on the basis of an individualistic and capitalistic theory society could and ought to structure its needs on terms other than individualist utilitarian ones. Another utilitarian assumption, that of equal desires of equal intensity among equal individuals that were amenable to measurement, was a problematic one; the Benthamites had not solved the simple difficulty of measuring the intensity of wants of any given individual or group of individuals merely by declaring *a priori* that the wants were equal. There were, in short, serious questions as to the meaning of individualism for economics, society, and even for psychology.

Halévy was, as we have shown, committed to the rational investigation of politics and society. His skepticism was joined with a belief in progress through rational inquiry and protracted personal effort. He was a liberal, an individualist, an idealist, and a rationalist; all positions that were steadily confronted in intellectual debate and political positions from the 1890s on. This book was a systematic investigation of utilitarianism, Anglo-Saxon political economy, and associationalist psychology to determine how much had stood the attack of a century as well as an exercise in intellectual history. Thus, not merely utilitarianism as a political-economic school and democratic radicalism as practical politics but as a psychology were being examined to see if an individualist position were defensible.

Of course, Halévy wanted to examine the utilitarians for what they were and how their ideas developed, much as Lucien Lévy-Bruhl had studied Comte and the Comteans, integral positivism so to speak, revealing the dominant ideas of the movement and holding them up for a close look. Lévy-Bruhl had laid bare the passion for classification of science, the establishment of sociology, the narrow definition of politics, and the Comteans' aim to establish intellectual and social harmony often at the cost of descriptive honesty. His work had sharpened the debate among sociologists and other social theorists as to the nature, legacy, and methods of their enterprise. It had also revealed Comte's passion for authority and order and the relation of these values to his classifications, his sociology, and his educational attitudes. The assumptions of English political economy seemed both an alternative to sociology and integrally related to English liberty and good government to Halévy. Therefore, he intended a study of the philosophic radicals, of their doctrine and the actual evolution of their thought, which was comparable to Lévy-Bruhl's and which he hoped would continue the dialogue between opposing political philosophies. Critical examination of the intellectual origins of a doctrine was a way to make a contribution to social thought.

The philosophic radicals, the utilitarians, had a poor reputation in France. Since the Revolution French social thinkers had been thoroughly critical of utilitarian assumptions: first, on the grounds of their ahistorical nature, and then on the basis of the primitive conception of human psychology and of society. The Saint-Simonians, for example, argued with the utilitarians that human societies were not created to fulfill men's desires, either individually or collectively, and that societies had their own laws of development, which were neither made by or very often understood by the members of the society. According to Saint-Simon, societies develop in history, and the method of the social sciences must therefore be historical in order to determine the function of any given institution within the society at a given stage.[29] Furthermore, in the eyes of the Saint-Simonians the utilitarians' indifference to religion and unwillingness to acknowledge the political importance of class were grievous faults.

Comte had criticized the utilitarians for their failure to include a concept of progress in their social theory (a criticism which Halévy disputed), and for their crude egoist psychology. The positivists complained that the Benthamites thought their rationalism was scientific when, in reality, it was deductive and sentimental. The positivists argued that the only true social science must be based on empirical observation of social facts and upon true quantification, not on an abstract felicific calculus.[30] In part, Halévy's study was a reaction to this positivist reduction of social science to mere statistical methods as if compilations did not make value assumptions.

Halévy sought to right common French misconceptions of the Benthamite utilitarians and to assert the positive role that these men had played in shaping reform in England. He wanted to prove that Bentham was a "reformer" not an "empiricist," that rather than "sensationalists" or "empiricists," as they were categorized, the Benthamites were rationalists and their methodology was deductive.[31] He pointed out how much they tended to assume the natural harmony of interests, how much more stoic than hedonist they all were in behavior, and how much their view of human nature posited man avoiding pain rather than seeking pleasure. He observed that the "habit of happiness" had never been engrained in Stuart Mill and Herbert Spencer, those great descendants of the utilitarians.[32] Self-restraint and abstinence motivated these "hedonists" rather than self-interest or the pursuit of happiness; they were certainly not libertines. The hedonist ideas of these utilitarians, whose actual behavior pointed to an ingrained stoicism, had misled serious-minded Frenchmen for a couple of generations. Halévy suspected that the true secret of English liberal society lay in that habitual stoicism, in all the varieties of experience which reinforced the very habit that he thought his countrymen lacked.

Concluding his book, Halévy defended the utilitarians against their critics, past and present. Perfectly aware of their colossal naiveté, their aberrations and short-sightedness, their shallow view of man and society, he nevertheless shared their hope of applying to man and society the methods and principles of science. It was for their efforts and goals, for their will to enact practical reforms, their power for good that Halévy made his defense of the Benthamites. He defended the part that Ricardo had played in the organization of the science of economics, though his political economy had been refuted for a century.[33] He traced the Benthamites' individualist positions, particularly in the theory of the origins of law, the principles of political economy and psychology. He examined their assumptions and areas of confusion and their terrible penchant for simplification, which was the appearance rather than the reality of an exact science—as it was with the Comtists. It was true that Bentham postulated his rationalism more than he justified it, but if he had not been the maniac of logic, calculation, and language that he was, "he would not so thoroughly have infected public opinion with these truths . . . that 'all pain is evil' and that the 'happiness of the worst man in the species is as much an integrant part of the whole mass of human happiness as is that of the best man.' "[34] Furthermore, the second postulate of Bentham's system, the individualistic, egalitarian propositions led step by step to an egalitarian perception of society, in spite of Bentham's lack of concern for equality. And Halévy believed equality was a worthy end to have contributed to. By implication, further, the French counterparts of this English philosophe had advanced the same view of society and of man. If the outcome was not the same, the fault did not lie in the value.

Halévy's concluding defense carried on the dialogue with the Durkheimian sociologists with whom his relations were complicated. A critique of Benthamite inadequacies ought not to create the illusion that individualism was merely a "philosophical eccentricity" or that the need for a social science based on the individual was a popular fallacy of a past period and no more. The methodology of the philosophic radicals might be simplistic, but this fact ought not to lead others to believe that a social science of collective representations, passions, and institutions was an easily realizable alternative. And further, for Halévy, collective representations implied moral and ethical assumptions to which he was philosophically hostile. He was sure that the practitioners of the new sociology were often dimly aware, if they were aware at all, of these assumptions. If social science purported to be explicative, he thought it had to be based on the individual who was the indivisible atom of all collective representations. And if one ceased to explain social facts and merely attached them to their predecessors in time, as many positivists did, then social science ceasing to be explanatory would become merely narrative, neither history nor social science, handicapped by the inherent limitations of its mechanistic assumptions.[35]

In the French context, the debate over secular morality fed many currents of thought, Halévy's as well as the sociologists'. Durkheim, with whom Halévy shared a concern for social order, objected to the naive assumptions upon which the utilitarians built their economics and politics, that human happiness could be achieved, and increased, through greater divisions of labor to satisfy material needs or that human happiness could be isolated into individual units. Actually, Durkheim expected modern society to increase human diversity and freedom rather than conformity, which Tocqueville and Mill feared, but one of the sociologist's major concerns was the relation of the individual to the group, a relationship which took on great significance because he thought that values and ideas had lost much of their power in modern society to be replaced by institutions and groups, or the social context. Morality was a problem of social discipline and it was a problem of society to make an environment for man which was both disciplined and personally intimate. Both the *Division of Labor* and *Suicide*, written and published between 1893 and 1897, challenged any simple view of the effect on the individual and on society of rationalized economic practices.

The concern for social discipline, joined with individual liberty, was common territory for Halévy and Durkheim, but the approach to the individual and to moral values was quite different. Halévy, like many idealists, was critical of sociology's claim to perform traditional tasks of moral philosophy. He thought sociologists often confused the "origin" of morality with the "standard" of morality—even sociologists who were sensitive to the taint of biological evolutionism in their thought—and this confusion diminished the importance of man's moral nature. Halévy did not accept Durkheim's assumption that it was within the province of sociology to ascertain ethics by descriptive methodology. The idea that society was a collective major work in which the individual has a part implied to Halévy an ethical decision and involved the mixing of problems with which he was unsympathetic. He was hostile to "collective consciousness" or "collective representations" or the social basis of morality or the assumptions about primitive peoples that were common to some investigations of religion by some of Durkheim's disciples.

Halévy's history was, nevertheless, in a grand sense, sociological. His manner of formulating *The Growth of Philosophic Radicalism* owes much to a French historical convention which ascribed the Revolution to the ideas of the philosophes. It was the same tradition which had at its heart a concern for the possibility of a society based on a secular morality which had fostered the development of French sociology. Halévy's problem in the history of ideas, as he explained it, was one which we may see as a sociological inquiry. The effect of comparable ideas in two nations could be quite different, calling for an explanation in other terms than the ideas themselves or human nature. Halévy did not think he needed to take sides in the debate between sociologists and historians. He thought it possible to formulate general theory as a historian. As he wrote to Bouglé, "Thucydides is more of a philosopher than Gumplovicz."[36] He was, like Seignobos who carried on the debate with the sociologists, unwilling to allow history to be absorbed by sociology or even to be thought of as adjunct to the new discipline. He wanted to write the history of social institutions rather than continue the everlasting emphasis on diplomacy and like Seignobos he aspired to works of synthesis of contemporary history, in the most philosophical sense.

Halévy responded to Bouglé's constant advice not to write history—it was a standing joke between them—by rephrasing his historical problems *à la sociologique*.[37] These conceptualizations are very interesting because they indicate his consciousness of the sociological implications of his themes. The themes that motivated his work—stability, the social significance of institutionalized religion, the basis of socialist movements in the working class and party structures, the nature of bureaucracy—are characteristically sociological concerns. His conceptualizations from his first period of writing and research from 1895 to the First World War, indicate clearly the close connection between *The Growth of Philosophic Radicalism*, his Methodist essays, and the history of England; the role of ideology in social reform; the part played by a religious impulse in the creation and influence of a social ethic; a theory of progress in modern society in terms of the relation of economic, political, and social factors to stability and to change: a theory of modern democracy and a theory of modern socialism. His concern for the problem of a social stability which allowed for change and for the resolution of conflict in pacific and progressive ways was, in a sense, sociological in inspiration. It was most certainly liberal in values. His examination of England in the crucial period of free trade and electoral and social reform suggested to him a general thesis of progress and liberty without violence and revolution. France was his model in the sense that it provided an implied basis of comparison with England.

In spite of genuine and deeply felt areas of disagreement, Halévy was at one with diverse sociologists, philosophers, and historians who shared his rationalism. It was *Revue de Métaphysique* and *Revue Philosophique* which gave the Durkheimians their precedence as sociologists, perhaps because they were preferable to the more conservative followers of LePlay or because of common interests in religion, morals, and metaphysics or perhaps on the basis of personal connections around the Ecole Normale Superieure. Halévy might agree with Gabriel Tarde or René Worms on specific issues but all could join in an antipathy to the irrationalism of intellectual culture at the turn of the century and in a desire to make social science possible. Men like François Simiand, Bouglé, Henri Berr, Charles Seignobos, Halévy, Charles Gide and the philosophers of the *Revue* were friends, shared common political attitudes, especially as they rallied around Dreyfus and the Third Republic. Halévy's disagreements with many positivists and sociologists were quarrels among friends in the milieu of *fin de siècle* Paris. The staking of territory by disciples who thought themselves at a new frontier was much less important to Halévy than common values and common opponents.

The period of intense political activity around the Dreyfus Affair and his involvement with "schools" such as the sociologists or his own around the *Revue* actually contributed to Halévy's appreciation of the power for social good of individuals acting in unison.[38] Perhaps this explains Halévy's sudden and somewhat uncharacteristic rhetoric in the conclusion of *Philosophic Radicalism:* "There is no doubt that the young Benthamites had their faults and made themselves hated because of these faults. But were not their very faults respectable, if their exclusiveness and their pedantry can be explained by their fidelity to an idea which was the object of their considered allegiance?"[39] Further, he admitted that the idea to which they were faithful was narrow, did not account for all they assumed it explained, and that they systematically disregarded many aspects of human nature. After this devastating critique Halévy continued, almost as if to excuse it,

> If, in active life, it is the definition of courage to defend to the last extremity, in spite of all its risks, a position which was at first freely accepted, is it not likewise a sort of speculative equivalent of courage to dare to take an idea as the principle of all one's opinions and of all one's acts, and then to accept without flinching all the consequences which this original idea involves?[40]

For such an unHalévyan sentiment one must seek the explanation in the passions of the moment.

The philosophical discussion waged around the Dreyfus Affair allowed the issues of individualism and anarchy versus order, hierarchy, and authority to come to the surface once again in French politics. On these issues there was no easy division of Dreyfusards and anti-Dreyfusards, rationalists and irrationalists, and many of the most ardent critics of liberal individualism were in the camp of Captain Dreyfus. In the French context, in either camp, individualism was thought to have the effect of encouraging merely private morality, isolating citizens and undermining the public interest. For a century naive critics had been charging laissez-faire policy with contributing to anarchy, atomization, egoism, anomie, to social dissolution, in short. It was part of Halévy's genuine contribution to this discussion among historians that he did not take classical economists or philosophic radicals as they were purported to be but returned to them to stress the degree to which their freedom made order and stability a necessity. Readers of his work or of the masters who impressed him so much—Smith, Ricardo, and Bentham—ought not to think it necessary for him to point that fact out, but to his contemporaries and to historians who succeeded him it has been important to repeat this theme, as the work of Lionel Robbins testifies.

The French intellectual tradition which dominated Halévy's time discredited the legacy of the philosophes, blaming the failures of the French Revolution on the naiveté of the liberal and individualist vision of society. Some of the most esteemed men of letters—Saint-Simon, Comte, Taine, and such lesser figures as Paul Bourget, Ferdinand Brunetière, Jules Lemaitre, and Emile Faguet—held to this tradition. But in the 1890s there were faint murmurs rejecting this interpretation and defending the Enlightenment tradition in one aspect or another. Halévy first decided to investigate the English philosophes, the work of Gustave Lanson, Daniel Mornet, Louis Liard, and a few others constituted the beginning of a revisionist view of the origins of modern France. Halévy's professor at the Ecole Normale, Henri Michel, whose careful study *L'Idée d'état* tried to rehabilitate "individualism" from its negative French connotation, nevertheless thought the Enlightenment heritage essentially destructive. This point of view was well within the mainstream of French social criticism.

Halévy did not, of course, see individualism or liberty through these French glasses alone. His work has its place among the fine pieces of scholarship which took this revisionist view. His formulation of one of the problems of the history of England, a formulation that he was making as he worked on *Philosophic Radicalism*, brought the question of stability and social dissolution to the fore. English critics have regarded as unwarranted and peripheral to the discussion of the utilitarians Halévy's emphasis on the continental aspects, particularly the French influences, of Benthamite thought. Stephen's and Dicey's volumes, which were contemporaneous, saw fit to mention French influences very little, if at all. But Halévy's work was written from a different context, written as a test and a defense of individualism, liberty, of the philosophes' contribution to human freedom.

Bernard Semmel has suggested that the powerfully conservative influence of Hippolyte Taine on Halévy's evaluation of English society was decisive.[41] There were few men among the generation preceeding Halévy's who were not influenced by Taine. His studies of English literature and of the origins of the French Revolution were accepted as classics virtually at publication, and his lectures were outstanding in a long tradition of great professorial orators. The power and popularity of his view of the Enlightenment was fairly widespread. Halévy's interest in Taine's thesis was two-fold: one, as a democrat and a liberal republican he wanted to test the impact of the philosophes; two, he was drawn to Taine's hypothesis that popular religion in England led to deference and stability in contrast to the disorder and social impudence of the French "mob." Halévy's scholarship rigorously measured generalizations that were merely impressionistic in Taine's work. He rejected his thesis with regard to the philosophes and he refused to accept Taine's mode of explanation, which was determinist and heavily emphasized racial or national characteristics. His refinements and conclusions of Taine's view of popular religion made of it a genuine historical problem rather than a national prejudice.

Halévy challenged Taine's interpretation by arguing that the English philosophes had not moved English society to revolution. And England needed reform every bit as much as France did, especially in law and the judiciary and in its anomalous electoral system. Halévy was perfectly aware that a simplistic grouping of the philosophes did not do justice to disagreements among them—they had not posed their principles as absolutely or as systematically as Bentham had—but his revision of Taine did not make this case. He accepted the parallel and then denied their ideas had had the effect that Taine had described.

Halévy treated philosophic radicalism sympathetically. He thought utilitarianism was a philosophy of emancipation, very different in its inspiration and principles, but akin in many of its applications, to the sentimental philosophy of Rousseau. He paralleled the English and French centuries of liberalism: "to the century of the French Revolution corresponded, on the other side of the Channel, the century of the Industrial Revolution: to the juristic and spiritualistic philosophy of the Rights of Man corresponded the Utilitarian philosophy of the identity of interests."[42]

Cousins though the two philosophies of emancipation were, their progeny differed astoundingly. "The philosophy of the Rights of Man eventually led, on the Continent, to the Revolution of 1848; in England at the same time the philosophy of the identity of interests resulted in the triumph of the free trade doctrine of the Manchester School."[43] Halévy thought that the success of the English political system in avoiding revolution, in maintaining the social order, actually stiffened its resistance to the Benthamite school. The success of peaceful reform contributed to further victories for pacific evolutionary political and social change. The basic problem of modern democracy in Halévy's mind was not merely one of order, and here he most certainly hoped to correct the French conservative interpretation of the revolutionary era, but of the kind of order and stability that the English maintained, an order that allowed for change and for liberal reform.

Halévy's analysis, unlike Taine's critique of the French national character, did not preclude French imitation of the qualities of self-restraint and tolerance, which he thought were fundamental to stability and to progress, precisely because he refused to root England's stability in race, national character, or inimitable institutions. The origins of liberalism were comparable in the two nations, he asserted, against any thesis that England's liberty lay in the Middle Ages. His concern was to find the functional substitutes in England for the coercion and centralization which were the instruments of order in other states. He found them in qualities of mind, in a social ethos, in liberal virtues, all moral characteristics which were imitable and adaptable. They were, however, qualities which were not the contribution of the utilitarians to English society; he thought the Benthamites were the moving force, not the stabilizing one. They provided an impetus to reform, which went hand in hand with a moral and moralizing humanitarianism; they were the publicists exposing evils and proposing remedies according to a few simple principles which could be applied to any problem—education, public health, factory legislation, or the indigent poor. They were the public servants who made administration appear to be a science and applied their principles as though they were inexorable laws. These men, their disciples, and others of a similar cast of mind acted to create government machinery in a country in the throes of industrialization the effects of which were fast rendering the old machinery of government useless to remedy evils, when it was not an obstacle to reform. The utilitarians did this when the mentality of the political nation was dimly aware of the difficulties. And all of this was accomplished in England when France, which Halévy thought was better equipped in the machinery of government, experienced a continuing conflict between the forces of change and stability, liberty and authority.

The history of Halévy's own awareness of elements of collectivism and authoritarianism as well as liberty and individualism in the principles of philosophic radicalism is instructive. It is also important to our evaluation of his contribution to Benthamite scholarship, to the controversy building around the thesis of the administrative revolution in government, and to understanding his overall view of the forces of movement or progress and the forces of conservation or stability in nineteenth-century England. Halévy was the first to emphasize the authoritarian, as well as the liberal, strain in the utilitarian heredity, but J. Bartlet Brebner could accuse him of having almost "no premonition of the collectivist threat"[44] to liberty. Brebner, whose work launched the "administrative revolution" debate in its current form, thought the early Halévy work underemphasized the cumulative state intervention in industry that paralleled the move to free trade. Further, he thought that Halévy's view of 1832 was one of unmitigated triumph of "British liberalism, political and economic, over the domestic authoritarianism of the landed interest and the mercantilistic restrictions cherished by the trading and maritime interests."[45]

It is, of course, Halévy's contribution that he was the first to note the collectivist implications of philosophic radical doctrines, which is something that Dicey and Stephen, whose books were contemporaneous with *The Growth of Philosophic Radicalism*, did not see. Halévy's fundamental premise of the contradiction between the artificial identification of interests and the assumption of a natural harmony of interests revealed these collectivist implications. Further, he was fully aware of the potential for socialism in several of the social thinkers who drew from the same sources and expounded a similar argument to that of Bentham. His small book on Hodgskin traced this potential, but the theme was clear in *Philosophic Radicalism* as well.[46]

Nevertheless, the weight of Halévy's early work did tip the scale toward Benthamism as an individualist, democratic, and emancipating doctrine. His concluding observation, written in the winter of 1902–03, noted that within the span of twenty years after Bentham's death a new and simplified form of utilitarian philosophy dominated English life; the principles of Manchester had triumphed over the principles of Westminster. Spencerian liberalism found the meddling Conservatism of Shaftesbury and the meddling Radicalism of Chadwick equally repugnant.[47] But Halévy continued, underscoring the ambivalence he had sketched throughout the volume, Stuart Mill "was bringing forward simultaneously the objection of Liberalism as against authoritarian Democracy, and the objection of Socialism as against the philosophy of laissez-faire." Thus, "the contradiction existing between the two principles on which Utilitarianism was based was now apparent to all men."[48]

Halévy originally compared the Benthamites with the philosophes, England with *ancien régime* France, and he did see them as the individualistic and egalitarian force for reform. He saw 1832 as a major triumph of individualism as Brebner says. Nevertheless, just as he, a committed republican, admitted the problematic nature of the legacy of the Revolution, he saw a double-edged sword in Radical activity. Certainly in *Philosophic Radicalism* he thought the liberal reforming edge was the cutting one. And clearly it remained to the end most important in his thought regarding the Benthamites. In his third volume of the *History*, written in the 1920s and published in 1923, however, his narrative of the Reform Bill moved immediately from the triumph of the liberals to the Benthamite revolution in government. "The victory of 1832 was scarcely won when Radicals made a systematic effort not only to make government democratic but strong. . . ."[49] This Radical endeavor aroused the opposition of both Conservatives and Liberals, who had grown accustomed to a weak state in the previous century. Discussing the election commissioners provided by the Reform Bill itself—a measure which is not usually cited as evidence of what has since been called the "administrative revolution in government"—he stressed Bentham's "long jump" from "enlightened despotism" to democracy, saying that he had skipped all the intermediate, liberal, mixed government positions along the way.[50]

In keeping with his theme, Halévy emphasized "this new aspect which the policy of reform was assuming represented a genuine, perhaps even the most characteristic, aspect of the doctrine of the orthodox Radicals, of Bentham and his followers."[51] After all, "utilitarian philosophy was not solely, nor even perhaps fundamentally, a liberal system; it was at the same time a doctrine of authority which looked to the deliberate and in a sense the scientific interference of government to produce a harmony of interests. . . ."[52] The "Prussian" or "French" principles of administrative centralization and compulsion dominated the Factory Act as well. In the New Poor Law the parliament granted regulatory powers more extensive than England's law had ever before known. Bentham's disciples were very far from "professing that systematic dislike of any and every form of State interference which thirty years later would be characteristic of Richard Cobden and Herbert Spencer."[53]

These issues connect with some of the most important historical problems for the mid-century. They have implications for the administrative revolution question as well as the radical and democratic tradition in English politics, especially the nature of the reforming impulse of the century. Jennifer Hart has described much of the historical research which purports to describe the reforms in administration in England as a Tory interpretation of history, that is, an interpretation which eliminates the role of the Benthamites and of ideas themselves in the making and carrying out of reform. Certainly Halévy's work, whether in the early *Philosophic Radicalism* or in the *History*, stressed the role of the utilitarians and the second-generation Benthamites (Stuart Mill and his friends of the "Utilitarian Society") in the planning, writing, and administering of legislation which strengthened the state in England. They were the central figures in Halévy's estimation.

Halévy did not regard the Benthamites as laissez-faire; the very thesis of his *Philosophic Radicalism* pointed out the unrealized contradictions between their economic and political thought and actions. The works of such scholars as Jacob Viner, Lionel Robbins, and Henry Parris has reinforced his emphasis on the ideas and actions of the utilitarians as decisive in nineteenth-century reform. They have argued as well that the thought of classical economists was not purely laissez-faire, as he did when, for example, he pointed out that Ricardo could hold to his optimism because he steadily minimized disturbing factors for political or theoretical rea-

sons. Ricardo was laissez-faire on rent but not on the condition of the people question where he was a gradualist on the
Poor Law; Malthus was laissez-faire on the Poor Law because
of his population theories but not on the Corn Laws for the
same reasons; finally, Smith was not doctrinaire.

There is a strand of criticism which refused to eliminate
the Benthamites, for better or for worse, from the growth of
governmental power and Halévy's work is at the very origins
of that strand. Oliver MacDonagh's work has become the
symbol of the argument for the non-intellectual, almost apolitical (in the sense of the parties) impetus to the development
of administrative machinery. In contrast to MacDonagh the
work of Hart, Finer, Parris, and a number of others, rejects
any thesis concerning the mid-century administrative reforms
which would argue the growth of governmental machinery as
a response to particular problems rather than a coherent ideology. At the heart of the matter is a political judgment about
the nature of reform, the role of ideas in history, and the origins of the welfare state. Brebner, who was responsive to the
strain in Halévy's thought which focused on the problem of
protecting individual liberty on any utilitarian basis, saw
Jeremy Bentham as the archetypical British collectivist, as opposed to Adam Smith, the fount of laissez-faire liberalism.
The force of the work of Gertrude Himmelfarb on Bentham
and on John Stuart Mill has been to remind commentators of
this aspect of two men who are too glibly and easily assumed
to be the classic champions of individual liberty.[54]

What was Halévy's ultimate understanding of the nature
of the Benthamite legacy, indeed of the liberalism of the Victorian era? At the very moment that he wrote the pieces of the
fourth volume of the *History of the English People*, which is
the posthumously edited volume on the Victorian era, he was
working on the *Histoire du socialisme européen* in which the
central problem of his thought was the fundamental contradictions in collectivism and socialism, which had their roots
in democracy. He admitted in the introduction to volumes
two and three of the *History* that the war had made him see

many new aspects of the previous century, including the inadequacy of party as an explanation for policies in the first half of the century, the very origins of socialism in a country which had not yet made democratic reforms, and many other issues. And yet as he wrote he saw the previous century as fundamentally different from his own era, not as the origin of it. He did not see the Victorian era as the origin of the welfare state. For him the Victorian era was the high point of the liberalism of Manchester, not of Westminster. The history of England was not a study in the origins of totalitarian democracy either; it was an exercise in the history of liberty. Continental history gave lessons in the origins of radical democracy, a subject he would return to in the *Era of Tyrannies.*

Halévy's understanding of the evidence led him to argue that although utilitarian ideology could serve as the justification for tyranny, or at least for the greater authority of the state over the individual, the actual results of Benthamite efforts in the first half of the century contributed to greater freedom by destroying the vested interests and privileges of the landed classes and opening a new era of economic and political reform. Utility was philosophically neutral in respect to emancipation or subjugation, the decisive question was the particular form assumed by utilitarianism in England in this period.

In his narrative history, as in his study of utilitarian ideology, Halévy was quick to call attention to examples of the Benthamite willingness to infringe upon individual liberty and to strengthen the power of the state, but mid-century England remained for him "The Age of Peel and Cobden," not the era of Bentham and Chadwick. These aspects of English life—the individualist and industrialist ethos, Christian humanitarianism, parliamentary institutions, and historical traditions—far outweighed the impetus to collectivism in mid-century England.

As Halévy later explained it, in one of his last comments on an English historical problem, the essence of the English system of administration well into the twentieth century was the "spirit of the great unpaid."[55] To his mind this spirit of voluntary service, rather than the esprit of a paid bureaucracy, softened the harsh edges between subject and state and between the classes. The triumph of this spirit was the work of others, not of Benthamites. Some editors, who were sympathetic to the utilitarians, asked Halévy to address himself to "municipal progress," choosing to commemorate the centennial of the Municipal Corporations Act of 1835. Halévy commented that in truth the critical act in the history of English local government was the repressive New Poor Law of 1834. But that was too painful an experience for Englishmen to celebrate and too heavy an onus for the Benthamites to carry. Just as the Whig aristocracy kept their political influence virtually intact for another half century after 1832, so the gentry maintained their moral authority after they had lost administrative power when the enforcement of the New Poor Law was turned over to a professional class of bureaucrats. By a clever maneuver they gave both the power and the onus of poor relief to the central government, thus discrediting the Benthamites' hope for a strong, centralized state. For Halévy the English were as fortunate in their history of clever maneuvers as the French were cursed by their experience of confrontation. He saw the advantages of avoiding the issue, or at least avoiding the experience of expressing the issue as an irreconcilable conflict between social groups. For him, the essence of the English way was an antipathy to the state, respect for the duties of the "great unpaid," a prevailing spirit of tolerance, even hypocrisy, compromise, and self-reliance that more than countered any impetus to centralization and to collectivization.

CHAPTER THREE

The "Halévy Thesis"

WITH THE completion of *Growth of Philosophic Radicalism* Halévy turned to a project he had long planned: "a theory of progress in the modern state to be entitled, for example, England in the nineteenth century." Historians might think French history more amusing, he wrote, but "the sociologist has to consider the English point of view much the more serious."[1] In his judgment the English point of view was more serious because they had built a progressive, stable society safeguarding liberty by their voluntary obedience, by their submission to "organization freely initiated and freely accepted."[2] How had the English remained so free and yet so stable, so tolerant, so able to compromise, so liberal? Other men had found England's secret of parliamentary democracy in her navy, her national character, or her industry and commerce. But to Halévy in 1906 it seemed that many of these attributes were fast being acquired by other nations and races, with more or less success, until "representative government in fact bids fair to become part of the common inheritance of mankind."[3] But while the forms of government might be imitated, could the social morality on which they were grounded be adapted? Was it possible for the blessings of English liberties to become the common inheritance of mankind?

Halévy's answer, and one of the major themes of his history, was that beliefs, emotions, and opinions, specifically the evolution of religious ideals into an effective social ethic, exercised a decisive influence on English institutions. To Halévy the uniqueness of English liberalism lay in the fact that it had maintained its tie to Christianity, that it was permeated by morality and the moralism of evangelical Protestantism. The "Halévy thesis" traced the evolution of the evangelical movement of the eighteenth century as it inspired the Nonconformists, revitalized the established church, and won the loyalty of many of the working and middle classes away from politics or unmitigated material ends to religious enthusiasm, away from revolution, class antagonisms, and economic hardships to reform, Christian love, and self-improvement. By the middle of the century, "the religious and moral agencies" needed merely to continue their action "to maintain the balance of English society."[4] After the First World War, in the *Epilogue* to the *History*, he raised the implications for liberalism and parliamentarianism of the decline of individualist morality which he saw taking place with the rise of socialism and racism, and the "possible euthanasia of Christianity itself." Even then, he would still say

> Today [1923] as in the past everything in England is instinctive groping, mutual tolerance and compromise, the effects of that moral and religious constitution whose factors we have analyzed elsewhere. That constitution persists in its main lines unchanged and is still the source of those admirable political manners, abused, but all the while secretly envied by those who, on the Continent, whether they belong to the parties of the right or of the left, profess the creed of violence.[5]

Halévy's thesis, which has been designated a "Methodist thesis," was only half of the explanation by which he hoped to account for the "miracle of modern England," a pervasive liberal reforming temper of mind capable of reconciling antagonistic ideologies and competing classes. The other half—the evolution of a reformist temper from the conjunction of radical, dogmatic Benthamite utilitarianism with classical economics—had, after all, been the subject of his first investigation into English ways and thought. Rather than accept the obvious theory that Evangelical Christianity and non-Christian Radicalism were opposites, Halévy saw that there were many areas in which there was a regular working alliance between the two forces, represented by Wilberforce's social conservatism and Mill's secularism. He saw that there were intellectual as well as practical affinities between these apparently polar opposites. The austere hedonists, the utilitarians, made up in character what they lacked in philosophical theory. Similarly, the evangelicals' narrow intellectual vision was broadened in practice by their feeling for humanity. Halévy thought "the partial junction and combination of these two forces theoretically so hostile" to be "the fundamental paradox of English society."[6]

In *England in 1815* he elaborated upon the idea that he had first introduced in *Philosophic Radicalism*: the affinity between "the moral temperament of the Utilitarians and that of all the Puritanical sects which modern England has produced."[7] There was not an exact coincidence of specific issues upon which both groups agreed, but the area of overlapping interests was very great. Bentham and his disciples were ardent advocates of model prisons, model factories, and model schools, practical causes which also appealed to Christian philanthropists who had been "educated in the school of industrialism."[8] If political and legal reform did not inspire the evangelicals to zealous activity, and temperance or moral censorship were matters of relative indifference for the utilitarians, they were as one on anti-slavery. Bentham himself wrote "if to be an anti-slavist is to be a Saint, Saintship for me. I am a Saint." Halévy pointed to the asceticism in Bentham's moral arithmetic and in classical economics as akin to Protestant asceticism, certainly in its effect.[9]

Halévy was acutely aware of the complex relations of thought in nineteenth-century England. To him, the apparent theoretical contradictions between Malthusianism and Evangelicalism seemed less significant in practice than their common hostility to the doctrines of progress spread by atheistic humanitarians. Utilitarians and Protestants, for all their differences, were both profoundly individualistic; to Halévy, the range of beliefs beginning with the Protestant sects and moving toward the Benthamites were "a series of imperceptible transitions" of individualism. On the eve of the First World War it seemed to Halévy a demonstrable fact that British individualism was "a moderate individualism, a mixture whose constituents [were] often mingled beyond the possibility of analysis, a compound of Evangelicalism and Utilitarianism." [10] The logic of the ideas had little to do with their power. An admixture of tenets from different and contradictory origins could nonetheless move men deeply. This insight was one that on other occasions Halévy extended beyond the evangelicals and the utilitarians to the aspirations of the socialists and the emotions of the nationalists and it enabled him to see connections between the two that defied the logic of the ideas.

The "English miracle" was an awesome affair to Halévy. It was all the more awesome because in France comparable ideologies had remained irreconcilable, and French class consciousness, which was no more pervasive than that of the English, had deepened into class hatreds, which he feared could never be lessened. For Halévy the French political reality was the direct effect of the Revolution, which made factions of parties, tyrants of governments, and conspirators of opponents. The historic reality of the Revolution thus focused his vision on England's experience as well as English ideas. Not that Halévy's realization of the problematic character of the Revolution made him part of the conservative tradition. Eric Hobsbawm in appraising Halévy's work said that the insights he drew from the perspective of revolutionary France made his books as great as they are. He might have said as well that the conclusions about the dual nature of the industrial and political revolutions experienced by England and France which Marx had drawn focused Halévy's perspective. Both seem perfectly true in the sense that the problematic nature of ideas, actions, and institutions was posed more clearly for Halévy and his contemporaries than it might have been for others not schooled in the French political tradition or, more accurately, shaped by the revolutionary tradition. Hobsbawm's other judgment that Halévy's liberalism was his weakness and the cause of the failure of his work patently fails to appreciate that his political values led him to pose the questions that give his work its transcendant quality, a quality transcendant enough to still shape the work of men like Hobsbawm and Thompson and their disciples. His work is not so readily dismissed as the failure Hobsbawm would like to believe, though his answers are not as congenial as his questions.[11] His liberalism first led him to the work of the Saints and enabled him to put aside his own doctrinaire secularist views to see more clearly the social impact of this peculiarly English religious experience. His English friends might belittle the evangelicals' contribution because they were advocates of more and grander changes, "truer" progress, but as a Frenchman he was impressed by how much liberty the English possessed because they knew how to compromise, agree, argue, and obey.

Halévy was not, of course, the first Frenchman to find England the model of liberal institutions. Limiting oneself to the nineteenth century, one can still point to a number of prestigious predecessors: Constant, Tocqueville, Guizot, Halévy's uncle Lucien Anatole Prévost-Paradol, his father's friend Hippolyte Taine, his colleague Emile Boutmy, and the historian whose work he admired most among his contemporaries, Charles Seignobos. Nor was he the first Frenchman to focus upon Protestantism in one form or another as the crucial factor in the unique development of the English social ethic. His Protestant thesis was one he shared with Voltaire, Guizot, and Tocqueville, even to the extent that the aspect that they shared of this thesis was their concern for the connection between Protestantism, individualism, and liberalism rather than the more economic interest in Protestantism's bond with industrialization. (Halévy's identification of Protestantism with English liberalism, in almost a Whig fashion,

THE "HALÉVY THESIS"

and his own distaste for neo-Catholicism in France explains his concern over the Catholicizing trend in English religion that he saw in his own lifetime.) [12]

A Protestant or Puritan thesis historically served a variety of purposes for French men of letters. The French liberal tradition held that "liberty is ancient," tracing its supports to privileged orders or to the struggle of the bourgeoisie for individual freedom in the late middle ages and in the Reformation. Since the Restoration, the giants of the liberal tradition had shown a marked sympathy for the Reformation and for the French Huguenots who continued the "bourgeois" struggle for liberty that culminated in the eighteenth-century French political revolution. These origins legitimized the French Revolution, which they interpreted as parallel to the English Puritan revolution. That was the tradition of Guizot and de Remusat, Constant and de Staël.

For those who were not a part of the liberal historical tradition, for those for whom the Revolution was a break in French history, the Protestant thesis served to make England's history distinct, a thing apart from France's experience. According to Taine and Renan Protestantism had made revolution unnecessary for England. Thus Renan could confide in David Strauss that the Reformation was the most profound revolution of modern times, implying that it far surpassed the French Revolution. Explicitly, he could join English and German intellectual and scientific accomplishment to the Protestant tradition. Taine, who would not accept English superiority over the French in the realm of pure thought, nevertheless acknowledged the English genius for liberty—a genius firmly founded upon the moral seriousness of the English national character, which he persisted in calling their racial character. English Protestantism had created a social ethic which tempered modern individualism (defined by him as egoism without restraints). As Taine saw it, unbridled egoism in France encouraged the frivolity of the philosophes, which, when joined to the ignorance of the masses,

THE "HALÉVY THESIS"

brought on the disaster of social dissolution, the ultimate legacy of the Revolution.[13]

Although a Protestant thesis was quite common in French thought, obviously it was not understood by everyone to mean the same thing; its meaning varied according to one's politics and view of human nature. Halévy's first venture with this theme was his two articles on the "Birth of Methodism in England" in the *Revue de Paris*. Halévy had explained his motives for these two essays to his two closest friends. "What is Protestantism? How does it differ from Catholicism? That is all the problem I am trying to resolve à propos of Methodism."[14] He hoped to "define those two forms of Christian religious exaltation, which are called Catholic and Protestant."[15] But if that was his motivation, he failed, because his essays did not resolve the grand questions of Catholicism and Protestantism, indeed he scarcely touched upon these questions. He briefly explained his understanding of Protestantism: "Protestantism is not a weakened Catholicism; it is a different kind of Christianity; one would be tempted to call it an altogether different religion."[16] Defining Protestantism as the Pauline adherence to the doctrine of "justification by faith," he affirmed his belief that it furthered tolerance because it had an almost "superstitious awe for the human personality,"[17] which was the view generally propagated in France by the neo-Kantians, whose influence had touched Halévy himself. In all, he was primarily interested in the social implications of English religious beliefs, not in theological ones. As he expressed it, he wanted to know "how England came to be a Puritan nation and remained one in its social code to the twentieth century."

Halévy's articles were deliberately timely. He consciously aimed at a broad audience as well. *The Revue de Paris* was an intelligent and urbane journal rather than a scholarly one. At the very moment that Halévy raised the question of the social function of religion in a modern liberal society the Radicals were in the midst of a campaign to cut the ties between the

Catholic Church and the secular state in France. In the aftermath of the Dreyfus Affair, lasting to the First World War for
many of the Dreyfusards, liberal republicans set themselves
the task of building a secular, rationalist social morality in
order to secure French republicanism. Halévy was one of
these liberal republicans, though his activities were more intellectual than activist. Faithful to his pledge of "perfect sincerity," although he was not able to believe totally that a secular morale descended from the philosophe temper was
sufficient support for a liberal social ethic, he committed himself to it. In spite of a lifetime of contributions to republican
schooling Halévy was never completely secure in the belief
that it would be able to foster the social ethic of tolerance that
he felt the nurturing in evangelicalism had given to England.
He was sure that the English liberal social ethic was the
offspring of the marriage of evangelical Protestant impulses
with utilitarian doctrines and actions. This was a heritage
that Catholic France could not share, but at the same time
neither could secular and rationalist France, his own France.
Like many Anglophiles in the French liberal tradition Halévy
certainly feared that the French were too clever by half, that
rationalism, though philosophically more sympathetic, had
not as yet created a social ethic for France that could compare
with the force of English evangelical self-restraint.

The Methodist project was one Halévy had conceived
and initiated several years before he published his essays. He
began collecting documents while he was in England working
on the utilitarians. While honeymooning in Portofino he
wrote to Bouglé of his New Year's resolution to "study the
English religious mind, especially the relation of dogma to
the sociological elements of English Protestantism in the
nineteenth century." [18] He postponed his work in 1901, however, to get his study of the philosophic radicals ready for
publication (in part because he heard of Leslie Stephen's
forthcoming volumes on the utilitarians). Meanwhile, he
asked Daniel, whose interests led him to working-class movements in England, to search for crucial documents in Lancas-

ter.[19] In 1904, when his third volume of *Philosophic Radicalism* was in print, he took up the subject of Evangelicalism again: "Free finally, I have vast projects on England; and immediately, I am going to see if it is impossible to study religious society in England in the nineteenth century sociologically. I've already talked of this to you. . . .[20]

The following year Halévy was so deeply involved in this work that he begged his friends to call off their efforts to secure Henri Michel's post for him; he did not want a chair in philosophy because his science was, more and more, history. He reported his progress: "I have plunged deeper into Methodism and after a month of disgust (these exalted minds are very weak minds indeed!) I have regained my interest. And finally, I am thoroughly investigating again modern English history, virtually contemporary history."[21]

For a decade before he published *England in 1815* he investigated subjects which were essential to it. He had contemplated the work since 1896 and though he worked intensively on problems related to Methodism for at least two years prior to the 1905–06 essays, he had been working on and off on the problem of Methodism since 1900. The Methodist study had been underway for over a year when Halévy learned of two *normaliens* (Chevalier and Leger) who had undertaken research on the same subject. Halévy wrote that he might not have pursued this second part of his set of theses concerning the nature of the balance of English society if Lucien Herr had not been such a "fanatic." Herr's opinions were so secular that he had forgotten to tell Halévy of these young men, ignoring them because they were both "more or less clerical."[22] Herr may have been quite right not to tell him, although in Halévy's terms for the wrong reasons, because his study scarcely resembled their work. The implications of this investigation for his general view of England in the nineteenth century cannot be overestimated.

In the moment that Halévy hesitated, thinking his time might have been wasted in this study, he confided to Bouglé the point of his research. Admitting that he had let this Methodist study distract him from his larger project, had in fact welcomed the temporary relief from the introductory volume which we know as *England in 1815*, Halévy sketched his English problem in the sociological manner. What he intended, he said, was "a theory of progress in the modern state. . . ."[23] England had built a free, progressive, stable society on the self-discipline of her people, on a social ethic of self-improvement and individualism. Furthermore, that social ethic had been reinforced in the eighteenth century at the precise moment that the propagation of radical ideas, joined with the social discontents of a changing economy, had led to revolution in France. He had, in the *Growth of Philosophic Radicalism*, investigated the nature of English radical ideas and the unique destiny that they had in England. Now he proposed to examine the religious aspect of England's liberal social ethic.

Bernard Semmel has pointed out that Halévy's work followed that of Hippolyte Taine,[24] but if it did, it certainly followed the path to a different end. Just as the *Philosophic Radicalism* study responded to a French tradition, which discredited the ideas of the Enlightenment for their part in the origins of the French Revolution (a tradition which continues to the"origins of totalitarianism" discussion of today), the Methodist essays developed from a Protestant thesis regarding England's liberalism. In Hippolyte Taine's work the two theses had come together to explain English liberties and French radicalism; as historian of English literature he noted the contribution that the Methodist revival had made to the spiritualism and emotionalism, to the awakening of religious feelings that made England immune to revolution at the end of the eighteenth century; as the historian of the French Revolution he stressed the impact of radical ideologies on the masses of Frenchmen who were moved by their destitution to attack their institutions and leaders in 1789. It was to the joining together of these two theses that Halévy addressed himself.

Halévy's choice of a rather uncharacteristically loose

structure for the early essays, the "Birth of Methodism," makes sense once one sees that his argument raised each of Taine's points to make a correction or a refinement. The "Birth of Methodism" essays were published in two sections. They were divided into several pieces roughly held together by the central themes of the Puritan nature of English Protestantism and the causes and the effects of the Methodist movement. From section to section within those themes the principle of connection is difficult to discern, though they were not random thoughts. They are not the fullest statement of Halévy's thesis but a preliminary sketch of it which he was to elaborate and place against the economic and political background in *England in 1815*. A good portion of these essays was addressed to the revision of the misconceptions, which were the mainstays of the Protestant Puritan thesis of the French tradition, especially as propagated by Taine. Characteristically, Halévy's criticism was not a polemic directed against the great historian to whom Halévy and France were intellectually indebted. Instead, he quoted the opinions of contemporaries of the Wesleys who espoused Taine's views and then questioned them.

First, Halévy, like Taine, stressed that England had not consistently been a Puritan nation; eighteenth-century England had known as strong a rationalistic tendency as France. Unlike Taine Halévy did not see Puritanism as a function of the English "race" or even self-discipline as the "dominating faculty" of the English people. The concepts of race and dominating faculties, which he rejected totally, were Taine's stock in trade. Though the great positivist historian recognized that the English had been the leading free thinkers in the seventeenth and eighteenth centuries, he explained them as a people whose fundamental national character was marked by a tendency to "melancholia," to a seriousness of moral purpose. "The race is capable of deep emotions. . . . You can only move the men of this race by moral reflections and religious emotions. The cooled Puritan spirit still broods underground. . . ."[25] Although Halévy agreed that in the eighteenth century the English experienced an awakening of religious sentiment, he could not accept racial or national explanations. How the experience of Puritan indoctrination had been preserved seemed a more meaningful question to him.

Halévy thought Taine's contrast of clerical eighteenth-century France with irreligious England missed the enduring Protestantism of the English middle and lower classes. Taine's drama heightened the irreligiosity of the English ruling classes and intellectual elite in order to parallel the situation in France. Taine, for all his stress on the "scientific fact," was more a literary stylist than a scientific historian and this emphasis led him to dramatize the conversion of the nation by a few individuals, that is, by the Wesleys and Whitefield. Taine's admiration for Wesley was boundless: "What could such a man have done in France in the eighteenth century? At his death 80,000 disciples; in 1870 a million!"[26] But Halévy, who also believed in the power of the individual and the force of ideas, found the stress upon the few individuals "much too simple to be entirely satisfactory" as historical explanation. He thought that the Wesleys had built on the solid social foundation of the English middle and lower classes, who had remained staunchly Protestant from the seventeenth century, untouched by the irreligiosity of the ruling class. Not in these essays or later in the *History of the English People* would Halévy attempt to explain the mechanisms by which the ideas of the previous century had maintained their hold over the English Protestants; admittedly a task as difficult as tracing the filiation of radical ideas from the seventeenth-century Dissenters, Democrats, and Republicans, and one that still leaves many historians vaguely dissatisfied with the assumption of continuity. Halévy's narrative of the Wesleys' experience argued that they could make very little impact on the English bourgeoisie as long as their message was ritualist and High Church, which was to say not sufficiently Protestant.[27]

Halévy criticized the overdrawn picture of the irreverent English painted against the background of a declining established church and dissenting chapel. He denied that the evangelical revival was as great a break with the past as Taine and others had estimated. The picture of decline was based on too exclusive a regard for the leadership of the church and the society and too little regard for the middle and lower classes. The "seeds of religious renovation had existed for a considerable time within the Anglican Church, and Methodism emerged from one of these seeds." But he argued that small groups of pious men within the Anglican establishment would not have effected the regeneration of English Protestantism without the evangelical fervor of the Dissenters. The vitality of the Protestant impulse was demonstrated by the prevalence of anti-Catholic outbursts and Dissenting secessions over doctrinal issues, particularly those congregations which rebelled against Deist teachings.[28] In short, where the roots of irreligiosity were not deep, as they were not in England, Deist and secularist ideologies would make little headway; in the eighteenth century Englishmen continued to be heated by religious controversy and warmed by religious faith. By implication, of course, and Halévy intended the implication, the revolution in France was not merely the work of a few men either; the revolution, like all great social upheavals, had its roots deep in the people and therefore in modern democratic terms it had a certain legitimacy. Debating the same questions Halévy's conclusions differed markedly from Taine's. Skeptical as he was, Halévy was nonetheless a democrat, a republican, and a liberal.

Taine's model of revolution, which was fashioned from his speculations on the origins of the French Revolution, shaped Halévy's interpretation. Taine credited the Methodist revival with saving England from the horrors of a French Revolution by appealing to the spiritual longings in the English nation against its irreverent aristocracy, its native Deists, and its deprived and depraved lower class. For Taine the reawakening of the moral sensibilities immunized England against the fatal disease that struck France. He coupled a fundamentally conservative view of the role of the elite in history with a vision of the entire destiny of nations being moved by the "blind forces of the masses, by the 'mystery of crowds.'"[29] Halévy's thesis combatted this pessimistic polarization. To Taine the important question was: "Why did the working class agitation of 1738, after its violent beginnings, take the form of a religious and mystical movement whose ideal was, after all, extremely conservative, instead of terminating in a social revolution?" Halévy's comment was that "this question raises difficulties only insofar as one has illusions concerning the role that the common people play in history."[30]

Halévy too ascribed a great influence to the evangelical revival in averting a French Revolution in England, but it was not to the suffering masses that he attributed the active stabilizing or revolutionary role. He concluded his essays with an argument for the investigation of "a singularly influential class," one which had played a very small part in Taine's story, the bourgeoisie, the "middle class," "composed of those who occupy posts of command, high or low, in the economy without participating in the political leadership of the nation, without being members of the governing aristocracy." It was the bourgeoisie, he asserted, that "provides nations with their moral tone." If in 1739 this class had been moved by revolutionary sentiments, "convinced that it must instigate a movement of intimidation and insurrection against the existing social order to obtain satisfaction of its demands," a democratic social revolution could have been brought about. But the English bourgeoisie was not revolutionary, not irreligious, not republican in the 1730s; it was not, in short, the French bourgeoisie of 1789. Though the lower orders were restless, reduced to poverty and "accessible to all forms of collective emotion" "popular discontent took the form the bourgeoisie wanted to give it," a religious and conservative form.[31]

The eighteenth-century revival of English Protestantism explained for Halévy "why in modern England there are no genuine lay parties of social and political revolution." In these early essays he wanted to express the vitality of faith and good works in the social ethic despite the attack by modern rationalizing forces—the "advance of the commercial spirit and industrial civilization," the scientific spirit and critical rationalism. His emphasis was not on the transmutation of a waning faith into economic rationalism, but on the life that remained in the social ethic built on an eclectic doctrine of salvation by faith and the testimony of good works. He did not assume a connection between Protestantism and the commercial and industrial spirit or between Protestantism and a scientific, critical rationalism; he assumed a conflict. His problem is not the one that Max Weber chose for himself in *The Protestant Ethic and the Spirit of Capitalism*. (Halévy appears not to have read Weber at the time of these first essays in spite of his interest in sociology, perhaps because the publication was virtually simultaneous. He did read him before *England in 1815* and recommended Weber's discussion of the kinship of economic and Protestant asceticism, similar to Halévy's parallel between the behavior of utilitarians and evangelicals.)[32] For Halévy, a renewed faith struggled more effectively against rationalism in England than anywhere on the continent with critical differences in the political results: the English lacked the sectarian and dogmatic spirit and they neither created nor adhered to parties of social and political revolution. These political and social aspects of religion were Halévy's main interest—not unlike the emphasis of his contemporary Durkheim and others concerned with problems of "social conscience" or "social control."

By the time Halévy wrote *England in 1815* he was more confident of the context in which his "thesis" belonged. His *Philosophic Radicalism* had been well received, even in England.[33] He had investigated both working- and middle-class radical movements. His friends Graham Wallas, the Webbs, and Frank Podmore were laying the foundations of a new political and social history of the first half of the nineteenth century with their studies of working-class leaders, local government, the poor laws, and utopian socialist movements. *England in 1815* was the first of "four or five volumes" which Halévy planned and for which he had been collecting the

THE "HALÉVY THESIS"

green cartons in his study for years.[34] His theme was the Christian basis of nineteenth-century social cohesion, the way in which religion counteracted the individualistic, virtually anarchic tendencies in English society during industrialization.

The first volume was his cross in many ways. In 1906 he found the thought of writing the general themes too demanding to make a beginning. He began just the same and virtually finished by the end of 1910, only to have his manuscript rejected by Max Leclerc, the publisher. His confidence badly shaken, he wrote to Lucien Herr, the one man whose discretion and editorial judgment he felt he could rely upon. Herr had been the librarian of the Ecole Normale as well as the scientific editor of the *Revue de Paris* when Ludovic Halévy and Ernest Lavisse resurrected it; he had also encouraged Halévy five years earlier to undertake the Methodist project.

Halévy explained that the last chapters on religion, letters, and sciences were meant to explain the first two sections of his tableau, his introduction to the origin and character of English institutions and beliefs, especially the political liberalism of the English. He pointed out the areas where his book would be useful, beginning with the subjects that would most interest the socialist librarian and were most congenial to Halévy's own values and problems. They were not religious topics at all; they were the textile and related industries, the struggles between the owners and wage earners, the prejudices of each class of the nation, the economic conditions and the recruitment of the ruling elite. In these matters he knew that he had something to add to the present state of knowledge, even to the work of Mantoux and the Webbs. He also stressed that his book was unique on the question of the English Protestants and, above all, on the sects before and after the Methodist revival. On these subjects he said, "I *know* that my book contains many things that aren't found in any other book; I say this not only for French but for English as well."[35] In a more modest manner Halévy repeated this

THE "HALÉVY THESIS"

claim in his preface to the English translation of *England in 1815*. His very good friend Graham Wallas' introduction underscored Halévy's original research into utilitarianism and Methodism, drawing the attention of English students to his refusal to regard religion as sufficiently discussed "by partial compilations or chatter about Newman."[36]

The ideas he had sketched in broad strokes in the Methodist essays developed into an impressive tableau in his *History*. His vision was enlightened by his values and he thought he had the explanation of the temperate character of the liberalism and individualism of nineteenth-century England. In his early essays he had asked:

> If religious sentiment, in its essence, is reverence for the incomprehensible, could this not be seen as the mystic foundation of English liberalism? Liberalism, thus defined, would imply both the conviction that our reason meets with insurmountable barriers in its course, and reverence for, or, if you like, awe of, those things in nature which escape our intelligence. To this outlook, so characteristic of the English in modern times, French rationalism was singularly unsusceptible.[37]

His study of England convinced him that the almost stoic restraint of the English was based on Christian self-discipline and exercised a powerful force for peace and compromise, stability and social cohesion, greatness and goodness (he enjoyed reminding his English contemporaries of those Victorian words) in the face of an anarchic, atomistic economy and a highly-stratified social system.

He aimed to depict British civilization and society as a whole, showing how the different orders of social phenomena—political, economic, and religious—combined with one another and acted upon one another. His synthetic method, particularly in the first volume which is his masterpiece, was a tribute to Taine's conception of history as a description of institutions and ideas through the scientific display of the facts. But, as Gustave Lanson pointed out in his review of Halévy's first volume, Taine himself had aspired to

THE "HALÉVY THESIS"

rather than achieved his goals. Halévy came nearer to realizing a perfect blend of analysis and factuality without Taine's prejudices.[38] Sharing Taine's ideal, Halévy differed markedly in the important role he assigned to ideas. Influenced in his first works by Taine's twin hypotheses and explicit parallel of France and England with regard to radicalism and Protestantism, Halévy balked at race, geography, "style," or temperament as modes of historical explanation, much the same as he rejected any deterministic approach, preferring on principle to stress the power of ideas.

Significantly, Halévy began his major inquiry into English society *after* the French Revolution. He assessed the forces that preserved England from revolution in the aftermath of the French wars and then weighed the forces for stability in the face of the emerging industrial revolution. Thus, he shifted the problem of his Methodist essays from Taine's model of revolution to his own. Taine had argued that a great discontented mass, moved by irreverent ideas of their aristocracy, toppled their government and destroyed its institutions in France. In England this had not happened, he asserted, because the English were religious and religion was an antidote to revolution. From some of Halévy's critics it would be difficult to tell that he opposed such a simplistic view of the nature of revolution.[39]

The French revolution was foremost in Halévy's mind when he first speculated on Methodism and utilitarianism and Taine was the determinist against whom he argued. But in *England in 1815* Halévy's focus shifted to encompass industrialization and the revolutionary implications of industrial change, and Marxist determinism became his target. The model of a militant class, bourgeois or proletarian, in the midst of economic dislocation superseding the dominant social group, seizing the state or moving to share authority and enact the legislation of its class interests, did not fit the events. In Halévy's mind there was no English equivalent of the French Revolution of 1789, the "three glorious days" of July 1830, or the uprisings of 1848. It was one of the blessings

THE "HALÉVY THESIS"

of the English experience that there was no equivalent of the bloody June days either. If anything, Halévy's views led him nearer the Marxist model in his sense of the history of France than his understanding of the experience of England.

Against a Marxist model Halévy accepted a construct in which the governing classes made concessions in order to avoid the greater evil of political instability—a Whig interpretation in part. He did not accept, however, any Whig identification of urban or rural interests with party divisions nor a view of party as the vehicle of conservative or liberal policies. This, coupled with his historical method of writing from the perspective of the center of politics, discussing problems as they were perceived by contemporaries and commenting upon the factors which seemed decisive to them led him to reject a simple party analysis and to see the importance of men like Peel, the talents of the Liverpool-Castlereagh government, and the significance of campaigns that crossed party lines. Further, Halévy accepted, in part, Tocqueville's proposition that the decentralization of government contributed to liberty by making it more difficult for a minority to seize power and wield it in an illiberal manner.

In *England in 1815* Halévy began by arguing not with Taine or Marx but with Montesquieu. Point by point he contrasted the constitution of Britain that was the object of Montesquieu's affection with the reality of government in 1815. Actually his argument with Montesquieu was a rhetorical device, certainly not a sustained debate. His analytical description of the legal, administrative, political, and military structure of government, national and local, found that English liberties rested not on separation of powers but on the inefficiency of English institutions. The king was unable to exercise the control of the government that every other European prince exercised and furthermore he was popular because of and not in spite of his intermittent madness and his worthless family.[40] The administration was chaotic, corrupt, filled with men whose positions were sinecures. The judiciary so confused powers that the confusion always operated to the detriment of the monarchy, which was a *reductio ad absurdum* of Montesquieu's vision. The representative system made some response, though an imperfect one, to public opinion and to mobs, still exercising their "right to rebellion" in the large loopholes of the law. It was a "country governed without police." "To palliate the evils of such a system men reckoned on the phlegmatic temperament of the people. . . ."[41] And through this anarchy the one thread of unity, which was enough to hold society together in the revolutionary era, was the control of the navy, judiciary, legislature, and central and local governments by a single class, an unreformed aristocracy. In his theory of revolution Halévy did not need to exaggerate the evils of unreformed England, merely to indicate that stability was a delicate balance. He did not heighten into Tory terror the government's measures for social peace. He pointed out that the system was not sufficient to guarantee peace without evangelicalism, but he was sensitive to the very real potential for reform from within the constitutional system.

In the course of the century this government, which seemed so fragile in 1815, gave proof of greater stability than any other government in Europe. To account for this apparent paradox, Halévy suggested that those elements, which were capable of sowing disorder and anarchy and which were inherent in the nation's political tradition, "lost their unruly character and submitted insensibly to a discipline freely accepted." For the secret of this progressive regulation of liberty, he said, "we must seek elsewhere, in the economic organization or the religious life of the nation. . . ."[42]

In the realm of the economy there was no other country in the world in which the new capitalism had developed so greatly and with so little governmental assistance; but if wealth increased, deep industrial and financial crises accompanied it. The disorganization of the employers matched that of the workmen caught in the chaos of the early stages of industrialization. The repeal of the Elizabethan Statute of Apprentices was "a triumph by no means making for social peace. . . . Never before had the existence of workmen's associations in England been so precarious; never had their character been so revolutionary." The system of credit was far from systematic; it was as disorganized as the other elements of the economy. It would seem, Halévy summarized, that all the economic evidence pointed to the revolution that Sismondi and Marx predicted would take place. "If the materialistic interpretation of history is to be trusted, if economic facts explain the course taken by the human race in its progress, the England of the nineteenth century was surely, above all other countries destined to revolution, both political and religious. But it was not to be so."[43] From his studies of the economy he concluded that the secret of the social order did not lie there any more than it rested in the political institutions.

Several critics have asserted that Halévy's neglect of the social, political, and economic factors making for unrest in England in the period 1815 to 1850 limits the utility of his work.[44] Careful examination does not bear out this charge. A full two-thirds of *England in 1815* was devoted to political and economic institutions and conditions. This criticism is even less valid for the second and third volumes of the *History of the English People*, which are chronologically developed and confront economic and political problems much as they confronted the policy makers of the period. The very thesis of the Methodist essays assumed a connection between the severe economic dislocation of 1738–40 and thereafter and the religious revival.[45] If a criticism can be made in this area, it is that Halévy did not explain the intensity, the endurance, and by what mechanisms religious enthusiasm came to express the sufferings of the masses. He assumed but did not explain a causal relationship between the economic troubles and the wave of revivalism.

Halévy certainly grounded his work in the material circumstances, but he stressed the role of ideas and beliefs in shaping social behavior. Having described the political and economic institutions of England, he proceeded to analyze another level of reality, the "beliefs, emotions and opinions, as well as the institutions and sects in which these beliefs, emotions and opinions take a form suitable for scientific inquiry."[46] His descriptions of the religious establishment paralleled the picture of chaos and confusion in the political and social establishment. His concern was with the practical implications of the religious faith of the Protestant sects as much as their beliefs and organizations. He argued that the religious revival of the eighteenth century was responsible for the extraordinary stability of English society in the next century. In *England in 1815* the year-to-year feuds between the sects and the Establishment, which he discussed in greater detail in volumes two and three, took second place to this general effect by which evangelicalism reformed morals and manners by drawing Christian communicants inward to their own lives and souls. The moral commandments became the social codes—anarchical but orderly, practical and businesslike, but religious, and even pietist.[47]

Halévy emphasized neither the rigidity and intolerance of the Nonconformist conscience nor Methodist opposition to education and hostility to humanistic science and culture. Although he had no special admiration for the evangelical mentality, which offended his liberal rationalism,[48] he was capable of noting its contribution. He was impressed by the practical effects of the dominant religious movement for social solidarity through self-reliance, individualism, and political and social virtue. His narrative of the campaigns of the Nonconformists against Catholic Emancipation, of men like Miall, whose paper *The Nonconformist* epitomized for Halévy the narrow, bigoted, negative policies of nonconformity, shows little sympathy for their position. Yet viewed sociologically, in terms of its impact the evangelical movement evoked his deep and abiding admiration.

One of the difficulties of current historiography is that much of the attention that is given to the Halévy thesis assumes that it applies only to Methodism or Wesleyanism. The major premise with regard to Methodism as a religious movement was that it revived the Puritan religious impulse in the national consciousness. He found in England's social ethic a residue of Puritanism in the powerful sense of duty and conviction of sin as well as the tolerant individualism. He searched the eighteenth century for the conduit of this Puritanism and found it in the spiritial reawakening in all the Protestant sects: first in the Wesleyan reform movement within the established church and then in the evangelicalism that permeated the Dissenters and animated the Methodists. The unexplained questions that intrigue those interested in religious history, questions of the nature of the connection between high Anglicanism and other Dissenters, questions of doctrine, personality, and organization did not interest him very much. Perhaps he erred in thinking the Puritanism self-evident and in thinking it unnecessary to explain the mechanisms by which it was transmitted, but the centrality of the Protestant revival and the demand that its unique contribution be addressed in terms of its social and political implications commands respect.

A further problem arises from the fact that much of the present discussion of the Halévy thesis assumed the impact of evangelicalism bore only upon the "proletariat" or the laboring classes. The boldest summary that Halévy made of his thesis argued that the Nonconformist sects, strengthened by the Methodist revival, "offered an outlet by which the despair of the proletariat in times of hunger and misery could find relief, opposed a peaceful barrier to the spread of revolutionary ideas and supplied the want of legal control by the despotic sway of public opinion."[49] The second and third clauses of Halévy's summary were as important to him as the first one. They are virtually ignored by present historians. By the "opposition of a peaceful barrier to the spread of revolutionary ideas" Halévy indicated a major theme from the essays and from the *History*. A necessary ingredient in Halévy's recipe for revolution was a middle-class enthusiasm for radical ideas, specifically that portion of the middle class immediately above the laborers in skills and consciousness, which could furnish the leadership for secular, revolutionary movements, as they had in France. The Nonconformists, not just the Methodists, created an alternative enthusiasm for that all-important class. Evangelicalism, transcending religious, institutional, and class barriers, created a social ethic which substituted a moral public opinion for legal control.

Halévy's assumption of the importance of a middle class to the Wesleyan movement means that much current discussion of the Methodist problem misses his point, a fact which has not been noted by some of the social and labor historians who would be his critics. He did not claim that Methodism reached the depths of the lower classes except for a rare rural area; its potential came into play as the worker rose "out of barbarism in which the working class was plunged." One of the most successful aspects of Puritan Nonconformity, as far as he was concerned, was its ability to become a transitional creed, "a stage in the history of the English family."[50] Nonconformity transcended class, formed a social conduit by which the unskilled laborer became a skilled workman, an artisan, moved into the petit-bourgeoisie and perhaps even the bourgeoisie and from there, without the "slightest difficulty," into the Church of England. There was no comparable institution in France. He was confirmed in his thesis by a fact that critics believe undermines it, the fact that radical working-class leadership often originated from Nonconformist backgrounds. He was struck by the phenomenon of relatively little bloodshed in workers' demonstrations, even among the Luddites, when civil war had only recently been endemic in the countryside. To him risings that ended with petitions to Parliament meant that the Nonconformists had done their work.[51]

The curious status of the "Halévy thesis" of a decade ago, when Gertrude Himmelfarb postscripted a survey of the state of the question in an essay in *Victorian Minds*, has changed.[52] Then the "thesis" was treated repeatedly as though it had been superseded by historical investigation in spite of the fact that very little work had been done and that which had been could be divided roughly into two camps, those who followed the work of J. L. and Barbara Hammond, such as E. P. Thompson and Eric Hobsbawm, and those whose studies were more or less confined to the Methodist tradition, such as R. R. Wearmouth or J. H. S. Kent. At the present time, however, there is a full-blown and major Halévy controversy, for which no serious student needs the ideological implications drawn, and it has developed less as a result of any direct confrontation with the thesis and its systematic defense or refutation than as the ultimate end of a number of investigations which have bearing on the thesis. Several of these investigations, which pay special tribute to John Walsh of Jesus College, hold out the promise that we might gain a history of nineteenth-century English religious culture; other studies are more definitely expanding our knowledge of working-class culture for the same period.

The work of Thompson and Hobsbawm has inspired a number of studies on various aspects of working-class life, organization, and activities in which the effect of evangelicalism-Methodism figures prominently as a part of the grand question of the social transformation of the eighteenth century. The change from a pre-industrial culture, perhaps idealized as one in which laborers worked in rhythm with nature and in keeping with their customary rights and privileges, to an industrialized work discipline system is, at present, being documented as part of the history of the emergence of social controls legitimized by ideology, including religion. The original question for much of this work was Halévy's—why was it that England, which experienced so much social and economic chaos in the process of industrialization, did not experience political revolution? Ideology shapes the question, just as Halévy's question was shaped by the tradition of French conservatism and by Marx, but it cannot always determine the answers.

The work of two of Halévy's contemporaries, J. L. and Barbara Hammond, is widely acknowledged by men like Thompson, Hobsbawm, and George Rudé as the classic of

modern social history. *The Village Labourer* (1911) is "one of
the most distinguished products of the only era of British history until the present which took a really serious interest in
the farm workers";[53] *The Town Labourer* (1918) and the *Skilled
Labourer* (1919) are praised for their author's "profound sympathy for the predicament of the British labouring poor in the
transition to industrial capitalism" and for their systematic
use of the Home Office Papers in the Public Record Office,
still the primary source for the information we have on the
unrest following the Napoleonic Wars to the 1830s.[54] Faulted
in specific interpretations and for generally not seeing the
depth of the unrest, the Hammonds' books are nonetheless
respected and influential and if they are deemed superseded
it is for the particulars not for the overall interpretation.
Methodism, according to the Hammonds and followed by E.
P. Thompson in *The Making of the English Working Class*, was
a harsh, repressive, regressive religion which broke the spirit
of the English proletariat. The Hammonds, Thompson, and
Halévy all agree that the influence of Methodism was enormous; they disagree on their assessment of the good or evil of
that influence. The Hammonds' vision of the laborers was not
as revolutionary as Thompson's is—he asserts that between
1789 and 1832 there was in England a genuine conscious working-class revolutionary movement led by secret revolutionary groups, which the government suppressed by a full-
scale political repression, aided and abetted by the middle-
class Radicals who betrayed the workers' very real revolutionary potential. The Hammonds depicted the laborers as
isolated victims of economic forces and of cruel political leadership who allowed themselves to be seduced by Methodism
into withdrawal, social passivity, and resignation when radical and class-conscious action might have secured political
rights and trade unions to protect their livelihood. Thompson's work went much further than the Hammonds' three-
volume social history of the age of industrial revolution in
depicting a social psychology of immeasurable misery.[55] He
utilized modern psychological insights and language to argue

THE "HALÉVY THESIS"

that Methodism was actually "the psychic process of counter revolution."[56] In sum, for both the Hammonds and Thompson Methodism was a cross-current amid the forces that were strengthening the class consciousness of the new urban population. It divided the working classes, taking their energy and their money and reducing the chances for a successful political or economic maneuver.

It is difficult for writers as sensitive to the culture and life experience of the laborers as Thompson and the Hammonds to sustain such a totally negative view of the impact of Methodism, difficult to reject *in toto* working-class culture. For both the Hammonds and Thompson the attempt to render the life experience of the laborers led them to an eclectic version of Methodism—it was the chiliasm of despair, the consolation of the poor, and yet at the same time for many of them it was the saving experience. "The teaching of Methodism was unfavorable to working-class movements; its leaders were hostile and its ideals perhaps increasingly hostile; but by the life and energy and awakening that it brought to this oppressed society it must, in spite of itself, have made many men better citizens, and some even better rebels."[57]

In the most fundamental way Halévy, the Hammonds, and Thompson agreed about the effect of Methodism on nineteenth-century England—that is, that it prevented revolution. The Hammonds and Thompson regarded the transports of Methodist enthusiasm as an unhappy fact in the historical record of the laboring classes whose story they hoped to preserve. They draw a dark and passionate portrait of repressive measures of a government that worked hand in hand with Methodism as stabilizing factors in early nineteenth-century England. Halévy's technique in *England in 1815* and the succeeding volumes was to prove that the government was weak yet stable and to reason that social peace must therefore have rested in the effects of nonconformity upon the populace. But the government's weakness could have rendered it either repressive or willing to grant concessions rather than test its strength. Halévy's narrative revealed that

THE "HALÉVY THESIS"

it did both, but his general theory emphasized the role of evangelical religion, of social ethic, over government repression. Halévy's strength lay in his awareness of the fragility of government, but also the other side of that weakness that he did not have to turn the epoch into a reign of terror to show the ability of this government to maintain peace.

Similarly, the mind of the lower class did not have to be coerced and controlled to keep the peace, only influenced. The Hammonds and Thompson have perhaps joined together the factors of repression and evangelical religion too much. In his picture of the manipulation of the working-class psyche, Thompson viewed Methodism as more devastating than Halévy could have imagined—modern psychology helping Thompson to stand Halévy's Edwardian virtues on their heads. A difficulty arises then, however, in one's view of the labourer's radical tradition, which proceeds hand in hand with the evangelical impulse in that same psyche. Oftentimes Thompson's very love of the material, of the working-class culture, supplied the evidence with which to doubt his generalizations of a devastated psyche.

In view of the many areas of agreement among the Hammonds, Thompson, and Halévy, in spite of differences in style, orientation, and values, it seems that Eric Hobsbawm confronted Halévy more directly. Hobsbawm, in "Methodism and the Threat of Revolution" denied that the working classes were Methodist, categorically rejected the idea that Methodism played any part in averting revolution in the period 1790 to 1840 and argued that the failure of the masses to carry off a revolution was the result of poor organization, inexperienced and divided leadership, and government reform and repression. Halévy stressed that the threat of revolt was intermittent, tying it rather closely to the economic difficulties after the Napoleonic Wars, 1819–22, 1829–32, 1836–41, and Hobsbawm followed that timetable roughly. Both Hobsbawm and Halévy agreed that the British ruling class, wisely yielding to the pressure of the middle classes, never lost control. Hobsbawm would also insist that the ruling class yielded to the pressure of the masses led by middle-class reformers. As to economic crisis and its effect upon religion, Hobsbawm argued that it cannot be assumed that industrial workers turned toward religious sects "as an alternative to revolution or radical politics," that often workers became radicals and Methodists for the same reasons.[58] When Halévy first made his connection between evangelicalism and revolution, he connected revivalism with the economic discontent of the 1730s, perhaps following the same assumption Hobsbawm made for the nineteenth century, but thus far no one appears to have pursued this question. Basing himself on the census of 1851, a generation later, Hobsbawm claimed that working-class areas were irreligious and that those workers who were religious were Nonconformists, not Anglicans or Methodists, that those who were Methodists were too few in number to exercise any influence. As Gertrude Himmelfarb pointed out, Halévy made no claim of working-class Methodists in the 1850s, only that the "religious and moral agencies. . . . had already done their work" by that time.[59]

Because Halévy's model of revolution focused on the important revolutionary middle and upper-lower class it is in more direct conflict with Hobsbawm than with Thompson. Halévy's argument was precisely that Methodism lessened the potential for revolutionary action among the middle class and top artisans. (In terms of theoretical concerns the discussion was yet another approach to the question of radicalization of the populace, or the lack of it, which he had raised in the context of *Philosophic Radicalism*.) Thompson saw the same effect of Methodism working in repressive and regressive ways on the working class. He saw the mitigation of radicalism, not the softening of brutal life during the early stages of industrialization, not the blurring of distinctions between master and man because of shared evangelical faith. Methodism meant labor submitted to the harsh discipline of religion as well as machine, its sense of outrage drugged and dimmed by the promise of religion. Halévy's model may have led him astray because it was based on the French Revolution, perhaps even on the classic tradition in political philosophy which ascribed the stabilizing influence to the middle ranks. Research in the central records focused on the problem of a government trying to maintain order may have obscured the variety of responses in local areas to itinerant preachers and concealed congregations whose spirit was not wholly other worldly and whose impulses toward their betters not purely deferential. It may have reinforced a point of view which prized stability.

But the Leninist model Hobsbawm contrasted with Halévy's French Revolutionary one has not corrected much. For Hobsbawm there was no revolution because the ruling class knew when to make concessions and did so without Methodism to teach it prudence or political timing. Further, the working class was too disorganized to constitute a genuine revolutionary threat which would seem to belittle the potential crisis that Thompson, the Hammonds, and Halévy saw. Hobsbawm thought the working classes who were influenced by Methodism were activist Primitive Methodists in whose congregations workers learned to be good trade unionists. Contrasting with the French Revolution, Halévy thought some force necessary to teach the ruling class and the middling classes prudence, political timing, and the wisdom of concessions. Comparing with the French during the revolutions of 1789, 1830, and 1848, Halévy thought English workers much less susceptible to violence, class hatred, and radical ideology by reason of religious faith. He knew of the irreligion of the lower clases by the Hungry Forties, saw the Nonconformist sects as a buffer between the conservatism of the Establishment and the "irreligion, indeed the gross ignorance of religion, of the lower classes" virtually to mid-century and believed that religion itself was transmuted into a social ethic thereafter.[60]

It must be stressed that Halévy's thesis was not merely a Methodist thesis. The points that Hobsbawm believed he scored when he pointed out the strengths of the "old dissenters" vis-à-vis the Methodists or secessionist Methodists are not talleyable even if one dwells only on Halévy's earliest statement of his thesis in *The Birth of Methodism*. One of the best sources on the religious history of the century agrees with Halévy that Nonconformity as a whole experienced a revival, Dissent taking considerably from Methodism over the century. John Walsh, in "Elie Halévy and the Birth of Methodism," pointed out that Halévy missed the positive "symbiotic relationship between declining Nonconformity and rising Methodism" of the early years because he was too concerned with the question of the mechanism by which Puritanism had been kept alive since the seventeenth century.[61] (This Whig interpretation which assumes some continuity from the Puritan revolution to the eighteenth-century radicals which has been assumed generally by Marxists was also assumed by Elie Halévy.) But on the specific nature of Methodism and Dissent Halévy's work seems closer to the reality of the evangelical experience within and without the Establishment and throughout the middling and lower classes than Hobsbawm's

The process by which the Nonconformist conscience, mellowed and redeemed by the evangelical experience of personal salvation, transformed the society and made the English truly self-governing was the third critical clause in Halévy's summary of this thesis. It "supplied the want of legal control by the despotic sway of public opinion." This full process, which moved the Church of England as well as Dissent, shaping the entire culture of mid nineteenth-century England, was an integral part of Halévy's thesis. The "Methodist thesis" emphasized the transmutation of the sects from radicalism in the seventeenth century to deism and non-belief on the eve of the French Revolution, into respectable religious groups in the nineteenth century. Their renewal of devotion had important results for social stability, not just in the conservative politics of Wesleyan leadership but in the moral behavior of a nation of respectable subjects. Halévy cannot be said to have neglected in his *History* other factors for stability, such as the example of France (which he might be said to overemphasize), the success of reform politics, the energies and abilities of leadership at various times, chance and muddling through, and prosperity or the hope of it from the economic system, even repression and stringent measures against protest. But there is no doubt that he was impressed by the religious underpinnings of the English national morale.

Halévy thought he could see the religious underpinnings of the English national morale, the Victorian ethos in his own time. He didn't think it was the most elevated of religious thought—he compared it to the Pears soap advertisement that equated cleanliness with godliness—but its social effects were beneficial. He found this ethos in the instinctive groping, mutual tolerance, and compromise which withstood the terrible ideologies of the twentieth century,[62] in the vital force of the British labor movement after the First World War as it tried to obtain some institutionalization of wartime cooperation,[63] and in the spirit of the League of Nations.[64] It was the quality which he said almost made an Anglophile of him.

Contemporary critics who concentrate entirely on the question of revolution miss the significance of the Halévy thesis. It was tied to an evaluation of the nature of the culture of nineteenth-century England. Halévy asked not only why England did not experience a revolution; he was concerned as well with the nature of the Victorian social and moral reformation which is avoided in so much of the controversy about the thesis. In the largest sense, he posed the following questions: How did the values of the various classes of Englishmen change? How were the new ones internalized to make political peace and stability possible and to make industrialization work? What was the process by which religious ideas and moral reform permeated this culture and continued to affect behavior long after Christian belief was undermined? How and when, if ever, did the working class, or any other class, withdraw from this culture? Even in the last years before his death, with the prospects of another war before his eyes, symbolized by the swastika on the flag flying over the

THE "HALÉVY THESIS"

German embassy in London as he passed on his way to the archives, he could feel England as a land of peace. He would not have called for a post-mortem on the strange death of liberal England.

Unfortunately much of the controversy about the "Halévy thesis" has not addressed itself to questions of this order, though it seems that Thompson's broad general scheme of inquiry proposes to ask and answer some of them. Though Halévy was the *philosophe manqué* he was a scientific historian and a number of the questions that he posed or implied in *The Birth of Methodism* are still to be answered satisfactorily: How did Puritanism survive? How did evangelicalism originate in the established church and reawaken Puritanism from within Anglo-Catholicism? What was the connection between economic adversity and the reawakening of faith? What was the religious history of the nineteenth century? Whom did the Methodists attract and why? What motives prompted the Methodist mission to the poor and how effective was that mission? Was Methodism a conservative, stabilizing force in the eighteenth century, in the nineteenth century? Was there a Methodist Revolution, an English aspect of the democratic revolution? What was the effect of this same religious movement abroad in the colonies? And there are many others relating to the basic thrust of Halévy's inquiry into order and stability or to reform and change.

But contemporary critics quite rightly have sensed that Halévy's thesis—certainly his history of nineteenth-century English political culture—constitutes a radical rejection of economic determinism, providing us with the major work, addressed point by point to an investigation of an alternative interpretation of the interplay of the forces of class conflict and politics. It is not surprising that Halévy's work and his formulation of the problems have remained central to the historiography of this period. What is surprising is the willingness even of Halévy's champions to rest their arguments on his bold, general, and popular statement of his thesis—the early Methodist essays—rather than his much more subtle

THE "HALÉVY THESIS"

unravelling of the threads of religion, ideas, and culture, through English society that is his *History of the English People*. Only the crudest polemics can appear self-congratulatory scoring points on some over-simplified view of Halévy's thesis. The others find themselves drawn more and more into the enormously complicated problems of religion and popular culture and its function in Victorian political stability, just as Elie Halévy was.

There is no doubt that Halévy's conception of the good society was one in which there was a minimum of external authority over the individual and a maximum of self-discipline. This was one of the fundamental precepts of his liberalism. For him the dominating fear was not John Stuart Mill's tyranny of the majority. For him it seemed that a foundation of social stability and political liberty required a degree of voluntary submission by the individual, even if unconsciously, to social pressure, perhaps to conformity. Once fulfilled, this requirement permitted existence of a free society, one with a minimum of state controls and the maximum of individual freedom.

CHAPTER FOUR

Studies in Socialism

ELIE HALÉVY devoted half of his scholarly life to the
problems of European socialism. In France his reputation
rests upon the volume which his students and friends as-
sembled from his notes and lectures on aspects of European
socialism given at the Ecole Libre des Sciences Politiques
every two years from 1901 to 1937. This volume, *Histoire du
socialisme européen*,[1] together with a collection of his essays
and lectures in *Era of Tyrannies*[2] are his most frequently cited
and most popular works in his own country. Yet neither is
the sort of finished scholarly history that Anglo-Saxon
admirers of *England in 1815* or *The Growth of Philosophic Radicalism* associate with his name.

When one recalls Halévy's central problem in *England in
1815:* "why is it that England has been the most free from
revolution, violent crises and violent changes?" one sees that
the internal logic connecting his early study of socialism and
his earliest English studies was a question of revolution, a
dialectical problem of liberty and stability, reform and revolution. To answer this question of revolution versus reform he
began what was to be the multi-volumed case study of English history in which he tested, among other hypotheses,
Marx's predictions about capitalism, industrialization, and
revolution. The *History of the English People* and the pieces
that reflect his study of socialism are contrapuntal works;

they may, in fact, be seen as a dialectic of liberty and authority, a study of liberalism and socialism. The unfinished and random nature of the publication of his work on socialism obscures this insight somewhat, but English history and European socialism, the two courses that Halévy taught at Sciences Politiques, were linked: "the first was the subject, the second the polemical target of much of his life's work."[3]

Halévy's corpus is divided into two movements but the two movements were composed simultaneously. His first investigations of socialism developed side by side with *The Growth of Philosophic Radicalism*, the Methodist essays, and *England in 1815*. They led to the biography of Thomas Hodgskin and the early essays on Saint-Simonian thought. The socialism studies appear to be an aside from his central concern with liberalism, but they gain ascendancy with the Great War.

As we have seen, Taine and the other critics of the French Revolution set up the first model of revolution that Halévy used, a model which contrasted the destructive effect of Enlightenment rationalism on the French national character with the beneficent heritage of England's religious revival in the mid-eighteenth century. *Philosophic Radicalism* and the Methodist essays both responded to Taine to say that rationalism and reform, even democracy, did not always have the effect of heightening class conflict and revolution; they had not done so in England. Further, Halévy asserted that the unique blend of religious enthusiasm and utilitarian rationalism had created an individualistic, liberal society with admirable freedom, tolerance, and flexible attitudes toward progress and change.

In *England in 1815* Marx was on trial as well as Taine. England was, after all, the nation from whose experience of industrialization and class conflict Marx had supposedly drawn his laws of industrial development. His economics was drawn from the classical economists and he had proposed a theory of historical development to socialism, the evidence to support the theory purportedly drawn from the English political, economic, and social response to industrialization. On several levels Halévy thought English history in the first generations of industrialization just didn't bear out the Marxist interpretation of history, not even for the same society in the throes of industrialization in the exact epoch upon which Marx built his science. The polemic with this Marxist interpretation of history would run through the first three volumes of the *History of the English People,* the research for which was completed before World War I.

His original methodology, the history of ideas, structured his approach to "isms" (a *normalien* trait with little precision, he was known to joke). He came to believe that socialism and democratic liberalism had developed from similar intellectual roots and that both ideologies contained a contradiction between their desire to emancipate and their will to organize society. This message ran as a subtheme through *Philosophic Radicalism* in the contradiction that he saw between the artificial and natural harmony of interests of the utilitarians. It would be the import of Halévy's first contributions to Saint-Simonian studies as well. There were, of course, other roots to socialism—statism and authoritarianism—which gained importance in his work after the Great War but he thought these had little to do with democratic liberalism, except that they might destroy it.

His emphasis on ideas and intellectuals was itself a polemic with Marxist or any other kind of determinism. Although he did not deny the importance of the social infrastructure, he was convinced that politics and ideas enjoyed a certain autonomy in men's lives.[4] His master historian was Thucydides. He thought politics were not merely the reflection of the relations between conflicting social classes (or the rationalizations of the class interests of historical participants). As a historian and as a philosopher Halévy opposed Marx, but, as we shall see, he was more fascinated by other currents of socialism than Marxist ones. He was increasingly drawn to the history of social classes, organizations, and economics rather than ideas, though there is a sense in which he remained more attracted by ideas, especially original ones, in socialist questions rather than actual political power or influence. This is apparent in his estimation of the Labour Party or of syndicalism.

Both his *History of the English People* and his investigations of socialism were parts of Halévy's attempt to comprehend the drift of the twentieth century toward democracy or caesarism. Even before the war he was sure that socialism held the secret of the future. "But I can't decipher the secret and I am past any position of saying if socialism leads us to a universalized Swiss republic or to European caesarism."[5] The war deepened his sense of urgency, leading him to write the *Epilogue* to the *History of the English People* and to formulate his most pessimistic prognostications regarding socialism. But before or after the war he was troubled by recurring doubts and had relatively few moments of optimism.

Like so many of Halévy's intellectual interests, his socialist studies reflected the shifting sympathies of the Dreyfusard generation; his conclusions and values were always his own. He had as an adolescent expressed an interest in "socialism, that great, powerful and formidable doctrine that we can not appreciate in France"[6] and he was, like his father and brother, deeply sympathetic to the social problem, but his scholarly involvement does not seem to have developed until the Dreyfus years. Many of his friends were attracted to socialist movements, their contributions to "socialist" studies marked a surge of interest, and their names are a roll call of the most influential French commentators on the subject— Georges Weill, Durkheim, Sebastien Charléty, Charles Andler, Bouglé, Maxime Leroy, Charles Rist, Charles Gide, Hubert Bourgin, Daniel Halévy, Georges Sorel, E. Dolléans, and Guy-Grand.[7]

Halévy himself dated this flowering of interest in socialism from Durkheim's course on socialism at Bordeaux in 1895 and 1896, which he said was the moment of the shift of the intellectuals from democratic radicalism to socialism.[8] Emile Boutmy's addition of a course in the history of European socialism at the Sciences Politiques was a response to this current of interest. His choice of the young Halévy as the man to teach it drew on his talents for both political and social theory and history and gave him an opportunity. He undertook several studies for this course, returning to little-known sources (both English and French) and making brilliant and unorthodox insights. He published articles, reviews, and *Thomas Hodgskin* in his first years at Sciences Politiques. He participated in many conferences at the Société Français de Philosophie and he served as the main contributor to the "Vocabulaire technique et critique de la philosophie" for definitions of social ideologies and descriptions of social movements.[9] His friendship with Bouglé deepened as they shared strong interests in social movements and ideologies. Later, after the war, their reputations as authorities on modern social movements well-established, Halévy and Bouglé contributed studies of Sismondi and Proudhon to the series *Réformateurs sociaux*, in which the finest scholars of the Third Republic edited the works of the most important French social thinkers. Their edition of *La Doctrine de Saint-Simon. Exposition, Première Année, 1829* remains today the definitive edition upon which other works and translations are based.[10] The edition kept the thought of Saint-Simon available for the generation of the 1920s and 1930s, a vital alternative to Marxism in France. Finally, with the 1930s their interests and collaboration were institutionalized when the Centre de Documentation Sociale was founded at the Ecole Normale Supérieure with Bouglé as its head and their young colleague Raymond Aron as secretary. Throughout, from 1901 to 1937, with only the break for the Great War, Halévy trained generations of students at the Sciences Politiques on the history, problems, and interpretations of socialism.

Other commentators on socialism have attributed the enthusiasm of French intellectuals to broader trends, specifically to the marked leftward turn the Dreyfusard agitation took in the months after Zola's conviction. This leftward turn has been credited to Jaurès' political skill in joining the majority

Socialists with the Dreyfusards for Radical or republican reforms against the opposition of the "orthodox Marxists" led
by Jules Guesde.[11] Jaurès was a man of considerable political
skill—he had begun as an Opportunist in party—but his
humanist, intellectual socialism, and personal attractiveness
exerted a powerful force over those who were not Socialist
party adherents. French socialism from its origins to Léon
Blum had maintained the force of its eighteenth-century philosophe origins, in a passion for justice and happiness, for a
rational organization of society. It exerted in Halévy's time a
powerful appeal, almost religious, for humanist intellectuals;
it could also constitute a formidable drive for organization of
society, economy, and politics. Further, the first decade of *la
belle epoque* was not a time of rigid sectarianism and the conversion to socialism of many Dreyfusards did not cut them off
from their fellow republicans nearly so much as the leap into
faith of a "neo-Catholic" did.

French socialist thought and working-class movements
were both in a state of flux and as late as the 1890s working-
class organizations in France were not at all dominated by
Marxist doctrinaires. Guesde and other leaders who aspired
to Marxist orthodoxy can hardly be said to have concerned
themselves with doctrinal issues and, in fact, there were very
few sources available to them in French upon which to base
dogmatic discussion.[12] (In fact, it may be said that French intellectuals, even those of the Left, did not seriously wrestle
with Marxist doctrine until the Second World War.) It is
somewhat of a paradox that in France the men who first made
scholarly investigations of various aspects of socialism—men
like Durkheim, Daniel and Elie Halévy, Charléty, Leroy, Rist,
and Gide—were liberal or radical, that is left of center, in
their politics. (Though it may be paradoxical it is certainly in
keeping with the fact that the most productive dialogue with
Marxism has generally come from without, from philosophical idealists, rather than from other Marxists.) These liberals and radicals have been characterized as establishment
figures; they were certainly part of an intellectual and social

elite. In their scholarship there was an obvious desire to contribute to social peace as well as to learning, a hope that the
social question did not have to be resolved by blood and
iron. There were gaps in their empirical understanding of industrialization in France, but their intentions were generous.

The emphasis of the scholarship of the first flowering
was definitely on theory and on the democratic, voluntarist,
and associationalist aspects of early socialists. More than national pride attracted these men to early French socialism.
French socialism was more congenial than the tradition that
they thought of as German—Marxist, bureaucratic, and statist
socialism. They thought French socialism was more sympathetic because it was humanist, fraternal, and *solidariste,* calling for cooperation of the classes and social groups of society
to make social reform. There was a democratic radicalism in
the French tradition which was not integral to socialist ideology itself, a point that can best be made by contrasting the
ideas and values of Durkheim and friends with the German
"socialists of the chair" Schmoller and Adolf Wagner.

This French non-sectarian republicanism and socialism
was symbolized by the spirit of the *universités populaires* in
which bourgeois students tried to "go to the people." Students, workers, socialists, and liberals discussed politics, economics, and socialism in an informal environment.[13] Daniel
and Elie both supported the *universités populaires,* both hoping to lift the public's apathy they had experienced during
the Affair. In the first flush of his non-denominational socialism Daniel began a book in which he hoped "neither to propose a solution nor to convince, but only to describe . . . the
elements of material or moral civilization that exist in the
working class." He wanted to "help some people to feel that
the people aren't barbarians and that they have among them
the possibility of civilization very different from ours, but
most acceptable, if not superior. . . ."[14] Elie's private judgment of his brother's history was dilettante, admiring faith
for its own sake like a neo-Catholic.[15] The same hope and
new faith inspired Léon Blum's *Les Congrès ouvriers et socia-*

listes françaises (1901). Even Elie, never much of a religious "enthusiast," was committed to these *universités* and in the 1920s regretted that his youthful cause had not developed along the same lines as the English workers' extension courses.

In all, left republicanism and socialism met frequently and shared much in the first years after the Affair. The *Revue de Métaphysique* published some of the leading minds in France on such questions as the crisis of liberalism, progressive taxation, the ethics of socialism, the social role of the cooperative movement, strikes and the right to work, and revolutionary and reformist syndicalism.

Most of Elie's close friends remained liberals, democrats, republicans, and anticlericals, but not without a little envy of the socialist faith. Isolated scholars, like Bouglé, fighting apparently losing battles with anti-Semitic leagues in the provinces, admired the confidence and unity of the socialists. The socialists never seemed to despair of their faith and besides, they shared many republican values.[16] For those who did not become socialists, the half-way house of *solidarisme* furnished them with political shelter.[17]

Between 1896 and 1914 *solidarisme* was the doctrinally fragile program of piecemeal economic and social reform of the Radical (later the Radical-Socialist) Party. One historian has called it the official creed of the French government in the period prior to World War I.[18] *Solidarisme* joined together a wide range of political views; perhaps, as Halévy thought, more by slogans than by program. Some, like Léon Bourgeois or Charles Gide, found in *solidarisme* what they felt was lacking in the French Revolutionary republican tradition: fraternity rather than individualism; voluntarist and government cooperation rather than laissez-faire; the duties, not merely the rights, of man and citizen. Others thought the bourgeoisie had not fulfilled the promise of the revolution and had worked only for itself. For many *solidarisme* was an attempt to steal the socialists' thunder. Unwilling to accept class warfare as it was practiced by bourgeois and Marxist alike, republicans could urge the transformation of the politically democratic state to a social democracy by encouraging mutualism—trade unions, cooperatives, and educational and friendly societies. They advocated maximum hours legislation, the regulation of working conditions, and minimum insurance programs for workers; some even advocated the progressive income tax, though most regarded that as the confiscation of private property, which *solidarisme* wanted to preserve.

To Halévy's mind they corresponded roughly to Liberals of the Lloyd George Churchill stripe but with less concern for legislation and more interest in the statement of program. Alain was one of the leading spokesmen for the Radical party during its *solidariste* period, contributing a regular column to a Rouen paper for years. Bouglé was deeply involved and ran for the Chamber of Deputies against Halévy's advice. Halévy did not participate in Radical *solidarisme* with Alain and Bouglé. He had a difficult time expressing his political views in slogans and he thought the criticism of liberal republicanism was legitimate. But he voted *Bloc des Gauches* even while he was convinced that their candidates were moral and intellectual mediocrities. Jaurès' political style was more attractive than drab Radical politics, he wrote, but "I would like to die under a liberal and republican regime. Why doesn't Jaurès defend the Republic or better, why does he take such a complicated, revolutionary manner of defending it?"[19] He joked, "I remain non-socialist, republican, even Tammany. . . ."[20] After all, the moral worth of the independents was too low for anyone to believe in them. In spite of the fact that he was genuinely concerned about social problems, that he supported all the *solidaristes'* reforms, and that he agreed with their expressed desire to separate social amelioration from the class-bound and ideology-ridden politics of the Republic, his antipathy to political life was too great for active participation. His moral principles and his realistic evaluation of the political temper told him that *solidarisme* was a dream and socialism was the reality. He wrote to Bouglé: "Your program of liberal *bismarckism* is almost as utopian as his [Jaurès]. His advantage over you is that there exists in France and in every country in Europe an organized socialist party while *solidarisme* exists only in the thinking of some French professors. In this sense, if your goal is to create a French *solidariste* party, you are more utopian than Jaurès."[21]

Halévy might have felt at home with the *solidaristes* in their goals and their intentions, if not in their critique of liberal republicanism. He admitted that he was always suspicious of class wars. "Because of civil war, class against class, the French Revolution was not the reform it wished to be."[22] He agreed with the *solidaristes* that class warfare in France had made politics there a clash of rhetoric, a field day for demagogues, and little else. Questions of social reform, political democracy, and elementary civil liberties had been lumped together, condemned and ignored by many of the political elite of the Third Republic. He and the *solidaristes* made the same criticisms of the socially callous policies of French political parties. For Halévy class strife in his country, in contrast to the English experience, meant very little had been done in the preceding century to lessen the want of the many. Herein Taine's comment that a genuine historian doubts the perfection of his own civilization and lives as gladly out of his country as in it applied to Halévy. The English had accomplished much that the French could imitate in terms of political and social reform, or so he thought.

Before the outbreak of the First World War, despite his liberal skepticism, Halévy was hopeful for a future of democratic social reform and a democratic society, much more hopeful than he would ever be again. He thought that a new industrial society was emerging from within the confines of the old one and that there was hope of industrial democracy if this new system loosened old class rigidities. He wrote an article for the *Revue de Métaphysique* in which he hoped recent trends in the economy might develop new political institutions as well. Later, in the thirties, he was to date his attempt to re-evaluate the nature of socialism at around 1910, when he began to question if he had not, under the influence of the Webbs, overemphasized the illiberal aspects. But, in fact, that re-evaluation had begun several years before, when he hoped that the new liberalism of Lloyd George might reconcile socialism and liberalism;[23] that there was in modern society a potential for democratic and liberal socialism, not just for statism. He thought it was ridiculous for non-socialists to claim that the democratization of industrial society was impossible; new forms of industry and of association might develop. "In any case, one must avoid posing the same antithesis between liberty and socialism as was made forty or fifty years ago between liberty and democracy. Liberty universalized is democracy, and when democracy universalized extends from the political to the economic domain, there is only one word to designate that—socialism."[24]

Before the war Halévy, and men of liberal political opinions like him, avoided or tried to avoid setting up any antithesis between liberty and socialism. Socialism meant social welfare measures and state intervention in the economy to regulate competition between big industry and big labor. At the close of his 1906 essay on "Saint-Simonian Economic Doctrine" he foresaw "a new industrial world emerging" in which economic competition would be more and more subjected to rules. The state would intervene to guarantee "to everyone the enjoyment of a certain basic right to a minimum of leisure, health, education, and assistance." Like the Saint-Simonians, he looked on society "as an association, not for the abolition of competition, but for its organization."[25]

He thought the day-to-day politics of French socialists and social parties unpromising, however. Despite his sympathy with attempts to solve the social question and ameliorate working-class discontent, which he thought was well founded, he disapproved of socialist leadership. "Socialists" aspired to universal human freedom as he did, but they proposed programs which he thought would end only in the greater regimentation of life and the bureaucratization of society. Halévy had little patience with arguments of ultimate ends, in this case the final emancipation of labor; he much preferred a politics of specific goals, such as the progressive income tax and social security. He thought a democratic reorganization of industry and of governmental administration was essential to the real improvement of the lives of French workingmen. He was disgusted by what he believed to be a socialist policy which refused to compromise or to accept the task of rationalizing industrial practices and organization. He thought socialist demands were merely lip service and that their deliberately utopian character betrayed a preference for leading a mob to educating a people or reorganizing an economy.

It is certainly true that before the war socialist parties in the Chamber were not exemplary, but then neither were those of the non-socialists. Halévy was not happy with either of them. His feelings about the socialists, or at least ideologues, journalist or "normalien" socialists, were clear in a bitter exchange with Victor Basch at the Société Française de Philosophie.[26] Two of Halévy's prejudices coincided here: one, his preference for immediate measures of social amelioration, for empirical politics, and for straightforward political behavior. Basch called for a total and drastic change of France before true democracy could be achieved. Although he had voted for the Radicals' social program he scorned it, justifying his vote on the grounds that the pensions would produce an immediate improvement in the conditions of the working class and simultaneously bankrupt and ruin the democratic regime. When he added some intellectual musings on the decadence of democracy as seen by classical thinkers, perhaps for the benefit of his audience, the combination of opportunism and polarization politics with a smattering of classical learning drew Halévy's fire. Halévy defended the democratic future, social legislation, and the potential for social peace within the democratic future. Halévy, whose own apprehensions for liberty and individualism in the democracy gave an almost stoic tone of resignation to his private thoughts, confided to Bouglé his disgust with Basch's vision and practice of politics and his anguish that "we have come to this and that the French are as incapable as a hundred years ago of interesting themselves in the methodical organization and the progressive amelioration of the society that exists and which is a civilized society."[27]

On the eve of the war Halévy was convinced that in France the socialists did not want a program of amelioration. And if they didn't want it in France where were they sincere in their desire for amelioration as opposed to drastic transformation? They chose a program of nationalization because it was the easiest policy for the entire party, though, he thought, a sterile one for France. Instead of devising specific pieces of legislation and participating in good faith in the political life of the nation the socialists advocated a single measure and total change. "All the efforts that they [the socialists] ask is to elect a representative with a mandate to demand the socialization of the industrial regime, and awaiting the day when they can do that, they carry on relentless criticism of the abuses of the present regime."[28] Halévy concluded that the real objection to socialism was the political incapacity of the working classes in France, which were capable only of electing a revolutionary candidate or sacking a factory, inspired more by an urge for revenge and a feeling of impotence than by any desire to reform society. For a new industrial world to emerge, it would require hard-working men to strengthen those economic institutions that were necessary for the future—the trade unions, co-operatives, and municipal and state-run social enterprises. The socialist party leadership gave few signs of providing that kind of leadership.

Once again the alternatives seemed to be posed by England and by Germany. In England Labourites and Liberals had been able to make reforms and yet preserve the essence of parliamentary and liberal politics. In Germany the bureaucratic state system, the strength of which he had perceived in 1895, dominated even the socialist movement. This perception, the actual expression of the contradiction that he saw in socialism, remained the leitmotif of all his reflections on the subject: the tendency in socialism toward authority and bureaucracy, the German way or German socialism, versus the impulse to emancipate. The war would convince him that socialism must ultimately end in bureaucracy and controls. But even before the war he thought frequently that the future might make his concern for English liberalism and French republicanism irrelevant.

> What is socialism after all? In England what they call the Labour Party is a party of *mutualistes* and the principal theoreticians of socialism are the Webbs, thanks to whom I am being presented tomorrow evening to Balfour. All this scarcely resembles the social revolution that Griffuelhes dreams about—and Jaurès . . . But on the other hand at times I ask myself if England, with its "liberal" method is not as *demodée* as France with its revolutionary phraseology. Everyone is looking to Germany anyway.[29]

Before the war grim prophecy did not dominate Halévy's approach to socialism. He was, after all, a teacher and scholar of modern socialism. He approached the history of socialism through the study of ideas, orthodox and revisionist, and he placed the ideologies within the context of contemporary liberal or conservative thought and events, just as he did his study of English thought and institutions. He focused on the entire range of pre-Marxist origins of socialism, contributing to the restoration of the historical reputation of Marx's predecessors and contemporaries. Further, his emphasis on pre-Marxist socialism bore the stamp of everything he did—insightful, original, often paradoxical—and had the effect of resurrecting obscure but original thinkers who made a critique of industrialization in the first half of the nineteenth century.

As he came nearer to his own lifetime—after Marx and *Capital*—Halévy was more concerned with socialist internationals, trade unionism, government intervention in the economy, general trends within the socialist movements and in industrialized society in Western Europe than he was with socialist theory *per se*. He ranged very wide; his definition of socialism was broad enough and vague enough to include comment on all the above developments under the heading of socialism. After the war, the authoritarian aspects of socialism and its junction with extreme nationalism gained weight in his thought, no longer balanced by democratic elements.

A glance at the *Era of Tyrannies* and the *Histoire du socialisme européen* indicates the somewhat unorthodox nature of his definition of socialism. It also indicates a consistent approach over forty years. Although he became less and less concerned with the history of ideas and more impressed by economic and social conditions of the twentieth century, Halévy's working definition remained the one he gave in his course outline, one which he had formed by the period of his earliest work, 1900 to 1903. By any orthodox definition he included ideas and men not generally considered socialist, and on these questions the orthodox—one might almost say the Marxian—definition of socialism, "utopian" or "scientific," prevails in historical thinking. For Halévy socialism was simply and broadly state activity in the economy and in the economic life of its citizens, an open and liberal opinion at the turn of the century when he insisted that socialism was a fit subject for rational discourse. In 1936, however, such a definition was in itself an invitation to polemics because it made strange bedfellows of current ideologies.

Many of Halévy's contemporaries had just as inclusive a definition of socialism. Certainly it was common in British circles, liberal and conservative, corresponding to their use of the word "collectivism." On the continent, Werner Sombart, for example, defined socialism as a critique or attack upon the capitalist system, "the intellectual embodiment of the modern social movement to emancipate the proletarian class;"[30] Ludwig von Mises, in his polemical work *Socialism: An Economic and Sociological Analysis,* discussed much of the same diversity of movements under the general heading "Particular forms of socialism and pseudo-socialism."[31] But to contemporaries who were socialists it was surely contradictory, if not wrong-headed, for Halévy to lump Bismarck and Napoleon III and Tory social reformers together with socialist theorists and party leaders, both utopian and Marxist. The German historicists and mere critics of utilitarian social policy, such as Tories, Chartists, and Thomas Carlyle, as well as critics of capitalism or bourgeois society such as Sismondi or John Ruskin were included in Halévy's definition.[32]

Catholic in his willingness to include many sectarians, heretics, and others who do not appear to be believers in the first place, Halévy then confined his subject to an economic doctrine. "An economic doctrine above all, modern socialism affirms that it is possible to replace the free initiative of individuals by the concerted action of groups in the production and distribution of wealth."[33] For the "Vocabulaire technique et critique," a project of the Société Française de Philosophie, Halévy and Charles Andler, the noted French Marx scholar and Halévy's friend, contributed a definition in which socialism was "the doctrine according to which one could not count on the free play of individual interests and initiatives in economic matters to assure a satisfactory social order. Therefore, it was judged desirable to substitute for the actual organization, a concerted organization which would lead to results not only more equitable but more favorable to the fullest development of the human personality."[34]

Halévy and Andler distinguished among the many doctrines aptly called socialist on the basis of three separate criteria: (1) their attitude toward the use of the power of the state for the realization of their aims; (2) their attitude toward revolution as the means of establishing socialism; and (3) their program for future socialist states. By these criteria there were socialists who rejected the use of public power to constrain individuals economically (including most advocates of free associations, *mutuellisme*, collectivism, anarchist communism, contemporary cooperatives). These socialists opposed others who would utilize either the democratic or bureaucratic forms of state power (municipal and state socialism). There were evolutionary or reformist socialists as well as those who asserted that a new economic order could be established only by force or revolution. Finally, there were socialists who proposed to describe in great detail the particular form of the future socialist order as well as socialists who rejected program as a matter of principle, such as Sorelian syndicalists and anarcho-syndicalists. In all of Halévy's thinking on this subject there was a basic and explicit distinction between the democratic and aristocratic impetus to state action. He was convinced that there were non-democratic, paternalistic, bureaucratic forces leading toward socialism just as there were democratic ones. The French republican was particularly sensitive to paternalistic statists, such as Rodbertus, Adolph Wagner, and Carlyle, who contributed to a strain of "socialism" by their criticism of individualism, democracy, and laissez-faire capitalism.[35]

Fundamentally, Halévy accepted a liberal democratic view of state power; it had inspired his study of philosophic radicalism and indeed his study of England's history as a liberal society. The liberal Halévy rejected the stress on the state; the democratic Halévy rejected aristocratic paternalism as a force for socialism. His sensitivity to these two strands can also be seen by contrasting his approach to socialism and that of his friend Charles Andler. Andler appended a note to the definition of socialism, a note of his own, not one shared by the two of them. Andler thought democratic theory, which had its origin in the defense of the individual against collective oppression, was both emancipating and destructive. The true socialists, he said, aspired to more than a defense of the individual or the equitable remuneration of his work (i.e., to more than individualism or equality); the socialist's goal of fraternity was a positive affirmation of liberty, not merely a negative one. Andler's stress on "positive" liberty was a common one among French socialists at the time. He shared it with other *normalien* socialists such as Lucien Herr, Jean Jaurès, and Léon Blum. This emphasis on fraternity was the vital humanist impulse to Andler's Marxism, an impulse drawn from philosophe origins as well as Saint-Simon and German idealist currents as much as it was drawn from positivist Marxism propagated in that era. As we have seen in our examination of French intellectual currents which contributed to Halévy's investigation of the philosophic radicals, this critique of democracy and individualism as historically and potentially destructive or "negative" had a long and esteemed tradition in French social thought. Halévy's ideal of individual liberty did not require transcendance of political and economic justice to an affirmation of fraternity, did not require transcendance of the individual in fact. For Halévy the critical issue was the fact that in its very origins socialism joined two strains of social thought, one libertarian and the other statist, a source of ambiguity in the history of socialism which he thought was still unresolved in our century.

From the beginning Halévy saw Marx as the dominant figure in socialism, not for his intellectual originality, but for his historic role.[36] In his judgment Marx had organized socialist ideology into a "system of genius," an incomparable doctrine for propaganda drawn from French and English social critics, from Hodgskin, Proudhon, Sismondi, Pecqueur, Saint-Simon, and Owen. After *Capital* "there is nothing more than the political history of socialism."[37] In his opinion only Georges Sorel and the anarcho-syndicalists made any significant theoretical contribution to the history of socialism after Marx.

Marxism's lack of originality did not prevent it from becoming synonymous with socialism, so much so that few remembered there were socialists in France and England before Marx began to write. The prestige of Marxism was so great that all the revolutionary parties traced their origins to Marx, even when they had moved far from his teaching. The greatest part of Halévy's scholarly work on socialism revived the pre-Marxists, but he did not think that scholars had lessened the identification of socialism with Marxism a whit, not in the mind of the public or among the intelligentsia.[38] True to this thesis Halévy shifted after Marx from questions of doctrine to the development of labor movements, socialist parties, and state economic activity, a shift which his friends faithfully recorded in their collection of his course for the *Histoire du socialisme européen.*

In view of the primacy of theory, ideas, and values in Halévy's treatment of socialism and the centrality he ascribed to Marx in the history of socialism, it is unfortunate, yet significant, that he left no extended discussion of Marx. Every other year he focused his course on the historic role of Marx, repeated to a new generation of students that the power of Marxist doctrine as a political ideology lay in its philosophy of history, specifically in its economic determinism, not in its faulty economic analysis. Yet all that remains of his interpretation of Marx are four chapters in the *Histoire,* a dialogue on historical materialism with Georges Sorel (also dating from the turn of the century) and scattered other comments in other works. His interpretation in the two early lectures echo his discussion with Sorel and his small volume on Hodgskin and an essay on the distribution of wealth.[39] The editors of the *Histoire du socialism européen* thought his approach to the theory of value in the lectures was very different from his teaching of the same subject in the 1930s; there is some evidence in his notes that he would have revised it had he lived to finish the book. This is unfortunate because Halévy regarded the political economist Marx as the true Marx, which is to say that Halévy's Marx was the "positivist Marx" or the "late Marx," the one whose thought dominated international socialism of the period.

Both the early and late Halévy was convinced that the power of Marxism lay in its philosophy of history rather than its economics and he insisted that as a philosopher Marx had to be struggled with in the volume which he himself considered his major work, in *Capital.* There Marx was revealed pretending to escape the difficulties of Ricardian theory of wages and values—"at the moment of its birth the political economy of Karl Marx was peripheral."[40] It was to the critic of the classical economists that Halévy looked for his understanding of Marxism as a social theory, which is clear in his discussion with Sorel, his chapter on the class struggle and the evolution of capitalism, and his comments on Marxist predecessors. He pointed out that Marx shared Ricardo's psychology, accepting the egoistic motive, or more exactly the economic motive to appropriate wealth, as the fundamental motive force of humanity—in contrast to Sismondi or Proudhon and a number of others. Halévy, who was well grounded in German thought, was skeptical about the connection in Marx's thought between the Hegelian dialectical apparatus and the labor theory, which he saw as borrowed from Hodgskin and other Left Ricardians from the context of English political economy. "If Marx had been a Frenchman at the time of Proudhon, he would have spoken in a juridical language in order to announce a new era, predicting the reign of justice; if he had been English, he would have spoken the language of utilitarianism, announcing the future harmony of interests. But he was German, still speaking the language of the philosophers of liberty, announcing "the integral development of the individual," "the free development of each with the free development of all." [41]

Raymond Aron, who knew Halévy well in the 1930s, judges that he would not have been "very much interested in the philosophical subleties" of the Hegelian origins of Marx's thought. He suspects Halévy thought these metaphysical origins tended to obscure the essential nature of Marx. [42] The younger Halévy had been very much interested in just those subleties, but he had been moved by his reading of Hegel's *Philosophy of Right* to write that "all contemporary German civilization is founded in it." [43] Halévy's emphasis on the statist elements of socialism was so much stronger than his concern for class conflict or alienation or a number of other features that one might almost say that the nemesis of Hegelianism oppressed him more than the specter of Marxism. He had grasped at the statism implied in much of the German philosophical milieu. He judged that the impact of German social thought, that of List, the historicists, Lassalle, and even Marx, was to build the power of the state; [44] it was his judgment in his youthful article on the German educational system and it remained his bias into the thirties, twenty-five years after he ceased to pursue purely philosophical questions. When Aron knew him then, Halévy was overwhelmed with a reality of state power that he had not fully comprehended in his most pessimistic apprehensions of the authoritarian tendency in socialism. The Great War had moved this authoritarian tendency to the center of his thought.

For Halévy the essence of the Marxist critique and its power over the minds of his contemporaries lay in its determinism, in the materialist conception of history. Marx saw in the evolution of the "forms of production the necessary and sufficient condition of the total evolution of the human race,"[45] a belief repugnant to Halévy. He thought Marxism was most vulnerable to intellectual attack precisely there in its historical materialism, which he thought quintessential Marx. This conviction is evident in his exchange in 1902 with Georges Sorel. Sorel was the leading French spokesman for what was then a new movement among French and Italian intellectual socialists who were re-examining their ideological heritage in response to developments in their national labor movements and to a certain metaphysical dissatisfaction with the "positivist" Marx. The revisionist trend within Marxism and the vitalist philosophy of Henri Bergson unsettled a number of these men, including Daniel Halévy. Croce's interpretation of historical materialism with its stress on Marx's metaphysical roots seemed a liberation to Sorel, Péguy, the younger Halévy, and others like them. In a meeting of the Société Française de Philosophie Elie Halévy's position was an ironic one in that he, the "liberal," found himself defining the "orthodox" Marxist viewpoint against several interpreters who claimed to be "Marxist" as they revised the terms of discussion. The discussion revealed both the broad way in which Marxism was understood to encompass widely divergent intellectual socialist views and the attraction of Sorel's theory.

Sorel proposed as his thesis an approach to "historical

materialism" that emphasized the role of ideas or propaganda in the shaping of the consciousness of the working class.[46] He argued that Marx and Engels intended historical materialism as a living attitude of men active in a social movement and that they had never given a systematic exposition of it so that their successors must not be bound by it as if it were a dead doctrine reducible to abstract theses. The paradoxical nature of Marx's antitheses tossed off in the heat of polemical battle were no longer the correct expression of his thought, the essence of which was the propagation of the socialist idea. Sorel believed that the class struggle existed because ideas "ennobled the struggles of the workers!"[47] Perhaps, but, according to Halévy, this was not Marx.

Halévy argued that Marx had, in fact, presented in *Capital* a monistic explication of the consciousness of a class in terms of the material and/or economic conditions of life.[48] Marx and Engels gave definite expositions of historical materialism, according to which the evolution of the forms of production and exchange is the necessary and sufficient condition of the juridical, political, moral, and religious evolution of mankind. Sorel's stress on the "solidarity" of theory and practice actually reversed the relationship between the two that Marx described. Halévy objected that Sorel's emphasis on an equal and reciprocal action between the elements—the spiritual and the material, the theoretical and practical— would have been inconceivable for Marx. Sorel's use of the concepts "theory" and "practice" made them the exact reverse of Marx's meaning. Of course, Halévy agreed that they were men of action and champions of party. Certainly the socialist politics of their time explained their bias toward the language of action which "is almost necessarily the language of spiritualism and of arbitrary freedom."[49] But Halévy claimed that in *Capital*, Marx's most systematic and philosophical exposition of his thought, he wrote an essay of unitary explication of the conditions of material and economic life which formed the consciousness of a class. Sorel's combing of texts of political and ephemeral writings to justify his stress on activism, on "revolutionary consciousness," was not true to Marx, the philosopher.

Halévy's point was more than a matter of intellectual integrity, more that a refusal to "revise" Marx under the pretext of interpreting him. He was convinced that Marx's historical materialism was wrong as a science of society. He spent a great part of his life and historical work proving or trying to prove that materialism did not explain the actions of men, that the crude positivist understanding of the relation of "superstructure" to the mode of production propagated as Marxism at the time was inadequate as social theory. Other parts of Marxist doctrine might be true and most certainly Marxism held powerful sway over the minds of men, but the whole could not be said to be a science of society, which was the claim made for it by its adherents. Perhaps the Sorellians had a better understanding of the shaping of revolutionary consciousness but it was not Marx's understanding of it. Halévy judged that Marxism was incomparable for its potential for propaganda and as an activist movement and that this power rested on its fatalist or determinist philosophy of history which described the evolution of industrial society and predicted its inevitable end.[50] Marxist ideology was not a science of society in his opinion, but its impact would not be reduced in any major way by the intellectual refutation of its political economy. As he commented extensively in a review of a philosopher's attempt to refute Marx that one had not done justice to Marx to see him as an economist, that he had to be approached as a historian, specifically as a philosopher of history. Marx's power lay in his theory's ability to capture the imagination as a critique, as a history of the evolution of the processes of production and the repercussions of that evolution on the society. And Halévy thought that power would not be diminished for most by all the abstract criticisms of Jevons, Menger, or Walras against the labor theory of value.

As Halévy posed it, the question of socialism was: "Are there in modern society forces that push toward the dehumanization, toward the socialization of economic production?

If there are not and to the degree that there are not, then socialism is false. If there are and to the degree that there are,
then socialism is true."[51] Although Halévy thought some of
the precursors of Marx were even more incisive social
theorists than Marx, he knew scholarship would not reduce
the power of Marx over the minds of his contemporaries. He
thought there were others more inspiring of a humanist view
of man and the future, but there was no comparable movement through which a socialist could act to protest dehumanization and embourgeoisment. He wanted to keep open the
lines of communication between liberal humanitarians and
socialist ones, but after the war he became more and more
pessimistic about the prospects for these openings. So long as
socialism was a "social fact," a genuine response to the very
real conditions of modern industrial society, then Marxist
ideology could serve an activist movement.

Given Halévy's interpretation of Marx as a powerful sys-
tematizer of the social and economic thought of others and
his belief that Marxism was much more a powerful ideology
than a contribution to our social thought, one ought not to be
surprised that the works he published on socialist topics deal
with the origins of socialism. Before World War I he published works on Thomas Hodgskin and Saint-Simon, an essay
on the question of the redistribution of wealth in the classical
economists and socialists, and made extensive inquiries into
industrialization and unionization in England and France and
the response of intellectuals to it. After the war he continued
his work on the origins of the doctrine and the history of
labor and socialist movements. His estimate of Marx's indebtedness or ideological strengths did not vary, but his sense
that English liberalism and French Jacobinism might both be
demodée grew stronger across the years. Socialism might not
necessarily or logically end in Marxism, and more flexible,
liberal, and democratic institutions might ameliorate the conditions of the masses, but pessimistically, it seemed to him
that the economic, political, and social realities of modern in-

dustrial society, especially those arising from the war, reinforced the ideological appeal of Marxism.

The pre-Marxist origins of socialism were of critical importance in Halévy's thought, but he drew away from the popular view, which was made even more popular at the time by the socialist-Dreyfusard alliance, that socialism was left-wing republicanism. Several historians of socialist thought trace the Marxian antecedents to the French Revolution and in a number of cases to the socialist legacy of the eighteenth century in Rousseau, Mably, and Morelly.[52] One might have expected Halévy would do the same in view of the fact that his early interest in English political and economic thought arose from a desire to study the reformist impact in England of revolutionary French ideas. But Halévy explained that he began his course with 1815–48 because he regarded modern socialism as an economic doctrine originating mainly in the industrial revolution and the poverty which accompanied it. Socialism hoped to resolve "the paradox of the modern world—the pauperism which was born in mechanization." ". . . [M]odern socialism is an historically original phenomenon . . . [differing] profoundly from ancient conceptions which seem to us today to be more or less socialist."[53]

Halévy, like Durkheim, excluded eighteenth-century social doctrines as primarily agrarian in spirit, more "communist" because closely linked with the ancients rather than the moderns. The emphasis of the "communists" on social harmony through a moral change in the individual meant that the economy was a peripheral concern rather than the heart of the society. Unlike Durkheim, who tended to separate moral responses from socialist activity altogether, Halévy included thinkers whose response to industrialization was primarily moral (for example, Proudhon, Carlyle, and Ruskin). His line of division was whether their quarrel was with industrialization or with human nature.

Halévy did, however, see a profound influence on the socialist movement, not socialist doctrine, by the French Revolutionary tradition. A number of republican characteristics which were not inherently or logically socialist had been joined to the socialist tradition by historical circumstances. For example, the egalitarianism of the Jacobins of 1793, which might or might not be socialist, had stimulated the socialist movement. Or the revolutionary hopes arising from the discovery that mankind could move quickly and totally from one regime to another and that it was capable of heroism, generosity, and altruism animated the socialist cause as well as the republican. Republican rationalism inspired socialism with the belief that the age of reason was at hand. Finally, revolutionary internationalism found new strength in socialist propaganda. An heir to Eighty-Nine and Forty-Eight, Halévy emphasized that the principles of 1789 were neither irrevocably nor inherently a part of the socialist tradition.[54] As he pointed out, there were socialists who were not egalitarian, notably Saint-Simon and Charles Fourier. Christian socialism, which preached a corporativism that idealized the Middle Ages (in itself a reaction against the French Revolution) certainly was not rationalist in its outlook. Further, Christian socialism and corporativism, while constituting a critique of the French Revolution, were important elements in Third Republican solidarism. There was, and perhaps always would be, a current of socialist thought as nationalistic as it was socialist; certainly the influence of Lassalle on the Bismarckian state socialism was strictly national and deliberately reacted against the radical internationalism of 1789. *Solidarisme* claimed to be completely French, just as Fabianism asserted its uniquely British character. No one of the elements of the Jacobin tradition was a fundamental tenet of socialism; any one could be joined to a socialist program. Halévy's point remained that socialism as an ideology arose as a protest against industrialization, regardless of its intellectual or organizational antecedents. Significantly, perhaps even ominously, though it arose in the same era as classical economics and democratic radicalism, socialism nonetheless was another species, not merely a left-wing republicanism.

Halévy's first work on a socialist topic grew directly out of his study of the utilitarians, the weight of the argument and the style of analysis placing this book squarely in the line of *Philosophic Radicalism*. Originally Halévy intended to write only a hundred pages or so of homage to Thomas Hodgskin, a forgotten worthy, but when the "short notice" was finished it was too long and too complex for a journal.[55] The style was virtually a direct, chronological narrative of his life and ideas with long extracts from works no longer in print. The forgotten man, who made the same criticism of Ricardo that Marx would make and the same critique of Bentham that Halévy would make, assumed an importance great enough for the French scholar to write a full-length study during a period of immense activity in his life. He was at that moment in the middle of his third Bentham volume, which he was rushing to completion because Leslie Stephen had just published his *English Utilitarians*. He had just married Florence Noufflard, was preparing his course on socialist thought, editing the *Revue de Métaphysique*, and participating regularly in the Société Française de l'hilosophie. He wanted to make his study of the nature of the "English religious mind," "a study on the reciprocal relation of beliefs and social forms,"[56] centering on the Methodists. Yet Halévy put aside these other interests to write this book.

Halévy's first enthusiasm for the eccentric working-class Radical was for the man who invented the Marxist theory of surplus value—that is, as one of the precursors whose intellectual achievements were incorporated by the master synthesist, Marx—but as he pursued Hodgskin it was his libertarian and individualist protest against *étatism* or collectivism joined with his working class sympathies that appealed to the young scholar. Hodgskin was, after all, a radical anarchist, the vigorous opponent of the authoritarian strain in Benthamism, as much the precursor of Spencer as of Marx. His thought bore little family resemblance to the statist programs of such British socialists as Sidney and Beatrice Webb, whose enthusiasm about this *English* progenitor of socialism neglected the essence of his thought.[57] Hodgskin focused on many of the same problems that Bentham did, on vital questions of reform, the economy, crime and punishment, and yet his answers differed markedly from those of his utilitarian friends. Hodgskin began his work in the search for a philosphical justification of the right to punish and ended by denying the efficacy of and the right of punishment and thus the rationale of legislation. He called into question, in short, the basic assumptions of the Benthamite calculus and the utilitarian movement.[58] Similarly, the implications that he drew from the labor theory of value, when he thought to apply it as a law of society, differed markedly from the application that Marx would make.

Hodgskin was the first man to point out the equivocal nature of Benthamite thought which Halévy believed to be fundamental to the understanding of English utilitarianism and social reform. Equivocal because it combined authoritarian and libertarian strands, the benevolent legislator with the "invisible hand" of laissez-faire economics and the optimism of the natural harmony of interests of Smith with the pessimism of Malthus and Ricardo, this ambiguous doctrine had spawned all manner of movements in England. Beginning with the libertarian aspect of Benthamite thought, which borrowed heavily from Godwin and Smith, Hodgskin developed its logical conclusions on progress and on law, economics, and society. Accepting the thesis of a natural harmony of interests, Hodgskin concluded that there was no need for positive law nor, for that matter, for government. He merely extended the Benthamite explanation of the origin of "sinister" laws, as a defense of private interests, to all laws. If Benthamites attacked monarchical and aristocratic systems of government in order to propose parliamentary democracy, as in James Mill's *Essay on Government,* Hodgskin carried the logic of the argument a step further and denied any need for delegates. Similarly, Halévy pointed out that Hodgskin took his political economy from the Ricardian labor theory of value, with which Ricardians justified profit, and in applying it literally and logically, he emerged with an egalitarian doctrine. The fundamental characteristic of Malthusianism, as of Benthamism, was a belief in the inevitable persistence of poverty because the limitless growth of population could not be matched by the productivity of land. But Hodgskin's optimistic faith in the natural harmony led him to believe that "as men increase and multiply, there is a constant, natural and necessary tendency to an increase in their knowledge and consequently in their productive power."[59]

Hodgskin's rejection of Benthamite general principles rested on the necessary identification of interests by the supreme legislator or legislature. Hodgskin condemned Bentham and Mill for refusing to admit the existence of natural rights and for positing that law and the law-giver gave rights their significance. Hodgskin accused them of having lifted

> legislation beyond our reach and secure[d] it from censure. Man, having naturally no rights, may be experimented on, imprisoned, expatriated or even exterminated, as the legislator pleases. . . . Filmer's doctrine of the divine right of kings was rational benevolence, compared to the monstrous assertion that 'all right is factitious, and only exists by the will of the lawmaker.'[60]

Hodgskin's critique of Benthamism clearly posed the difficulty in reform through the agency of the beneficent legislator or administrator. If individuals had no fundamental inviolable rights, what would protect the individual and all his differences from the reformers' passion for organization?

In *Thomas Hodgskin*, the article that grew out of hand as he wrote *The Growth of Philosophic Radicalism*, Halévy posed the conflict of liberation and organization in the radical tradition and in the socialist tradition, a conflict that was rarely apparent to adherents of the doctrines. He thought that histo-

rians erred when they reduced Hodgskin merely to a prede-
cessor of Marx. The founder of the Mechanics Institute was
not merely a man who missed his opportunity to become
"the theorist of the nascent English socialist movement."[61]
As Halévy saw him Hodgskin was a libertarian socialist
whose practical program did not differ much from Ricardian
laissez-faire. "He was the first—before Herbert Spencer—to
found a free trade philosophy on the criticism of the Benthamite philosophy of law."[62] Hodgskin's anticapitalism was
subordinated to his anarchism. Hodgskin always fought
against every intervention of government and of law and
especially opposed such interference in the distribution of
wealth. He also rejected the "communism" of Owen, Saint-
Simon, or the Moravians because it merely continued the
rights of property in other forms. But he and Percy Ravenstone had made the critique of "fetishism" of the economics
of Mill and MacCulloch that Marx would borrow and in this
respect he was Marx's teacher.

That the English "socialist" tradition developed from
such unlikely origins as Hodgskin was one of Elie Halévy's
pet paradoxes. English socialism was not simply a branch of
Marxism. For that matter, despite the Marxist hegemony over
socialist môvements at the end of the nineteenth century,
Halévy refused to consider the socialism of any European
movement as merely a simple branch of Marxism. But the English labor movement had not succumbed at all to the Marxist
domination that characterized European parties; the Marxist
Social Democratic Federation was a pitiable group, he
thought. For Halévy the labor movement joined together several very English traditions: one, the nonconformist, another,
an ingrained parliamentarianism and a vigorous radicalism.
The intellectual origins of English socialism were similarly
unique and grew out of two traditions: one, religious and
aesthetic as well as humanitarian, a protest in the name of
both beauty and justice against oppression and exploitation,
symbolized by Ruskin, William Morris, and Carlyle; the
other, also opposed to class conflict and seeming to conciliate

parliamentarianism and social democracy, the bureaucratic or administrative socialism of the Fabians Sidney and Beatrice Webb.[63] This Fabianism, which proposed a reconciliation of socialism with bourgeois democracy, between the greatest good for the greatest number and a more rational science of administration, without violent revolution, dominated Halévy's postwar attention to British socialism. He typically referred to the "German" or statist socialism of the Fabians when discussing British socialist theory, except for some interest in Guild Socialism which reflects both his intellectualist bias and his French national concern with syndicalism. What is more amazing than his relative neglect of the nonconformist and aesthetic British socialist currents (though he first called attention to them) is his lack of interest in other English utopians, given his penchant for theory.

It has been said that Halévy was anxious to show Marx's indebtedness to Hodgskin, either to belittle Marx's intellectual contribution or to show that because Hodgskin's theory was unsound, perhaps Marx's was as well.[64] This view misses the point. The question for Halévy was a greater one than the truth or falsity of Marx's teaching, which could be better handled in economic debate or in philosophical, nonhistorical discussion. Halévy's interest was rather in the peculiar drawing together here, as in Benthamism, of divergent elements of thought, elements which incorporated biases or prejudices in defiance of logic and yet molded them into powerful doctrines. Why did Marx and Marxism see capitalist economic production according to Ricardian labor theory long after other economists had rejected that theory? Halévy thought the answer to this question lay in the realm of the history of ideas rather than in the ideas themselves. He thought the active propaganda and the simplicity of the teaching of "an intransigent group of Ricardo's disciples" had fixed the labor theory on the Marxists. Halévy pointed to the fact that historically the working-class theorists, the democratic opponents of Mill and MacCulloch, had seized the Ricardian labor theory of value and refuted his political econ-

omy by a form of *reductio ad absurdum*. Marx had adopted
their tactic, making himself, or at least his "science of society" "the victim of a universal obsession of the generation
that preceded him."[65] Why Marxists should remain victims
of that obsession was another question.

Halévy's general problem in *Thomas Hodgskin* was the
same as in *The Growth of Philosophic Radicalism*—the influence of a doctrine in history. It was a problem in the history
of ideas, just as Benthamism was, and all the more problematic because the body of ideas was based on an economic
fallacy. He thought it was also based on a misreading of history and a shallow materialism, but all the more a problem in
the history of ideas. The answer to the problem of the success
of an ideology, in this case of socialism, lay in the history of
ideas, in the conditions and the social ethic of contemporaries, as Halévy indicated to Bouglé: "I read Pecqueur. Have
you read Pecqueur? All that Marx wrote on capitalist concentration was copied from Pecqueur. *The success is a mystery.*
Because, why does the worth of the theory return, and will it
always return, to Marx? *I have tried imperfectly to resolve a
problem of the same genre with Bentham"* [italics mine].[66] The
important question with respect to ideology was neither its
originality nor its validity. Hodgskin and Pecqueur were
original thinkers, but the historic role was Marx's. Later, after
World War I, Halévy would have a certain impatience with
many purely intellectual considerations of origins and
theories, pushing them aside for the political, social, and economic realities, but as a young man the ideas of the early
nineteenth century exerted a powerful attraction in part because socialism and liberalism were closely interrelated and
because they both joined peculiarly contradictory tendencies
within their doctrines.

Halévy thought the contradictory tendencies of much of
the social thought of the revolutionary era of 1780 to 1848
were joined and held together by belief and emotional commitment. He drew his deepest insights—one might say his

premonitions—into the nature of socialism and modern society from the conflicting tenets of Saint-Simonian socialism. He addressed the Saint-Simon problem at least twice in his life: first, in 1907–08, when he wrote two essays on Saint-Simon's economic doctrine, essays which he had planned since at least 1902, and later, in 1924 when he and Bouglé edited and wrote a long introduction to *La Doctrine de Saint-Simon*.[67]

Halévy's early essays, which were a return to his grandfather's interests, are remarkable for the fact that Halévy confined himself to Saint-Simonian economic doctrines, a conscious decision to rescue the historical Saint-Simonian teachings from the two generations of oblivion or misrepresentation they had suffered. Of course, the analysis of Saint-Simon's economic views was merely one aspect of his total view of society and its evolution, but Halévy's focus on socialism narrowed the scope of his concern, enabling him to omit the mystical, Christian, or religious foundation of Saint-Simonian thought, discussing merely the influence of the theocratic school on the prophet's authoritarianism. In itself this approach was a rescue operation of Saint-Simonian thought. Charles Andler had just verified Marx's debt to Saint-Simon in his introduction to his translation of the *Communist Manifesto*. Contrary to Marxist polemics, which dismissed Saint-Simon as utopian, Halévy found that his economic thought had evolved from liberal reformism, classical economics, and specific administrative schemes of the Napoleonic and Restoration regimes; his thought was, in short, very much a reflection of the actual politics and thought of his period and not the half-baked notions it was popularly held to be.

Saint-Simon's thought was rooted in the era of Bentham and Hodgskin, the "early years of the century when, in the words of Saint-Simon himself, 'the Revolution had made Frenchmen enthusiastic about politics.' "[68] Halévy traced the gradual evolution of Saint-Simonianism from fundamentally liberal precepts to an implicit socialism just before his death in 1825. His point in the first essay was that the liberals who associated with *Censeur européen* and the Saint-Simonians of *L'Industrie* had in common their view of history, politics, and economics and that they remained unaware that there was one vital area in which they did part intellectual company. That was the area of social reorganization. To the liberal social reorganization meant the suppression of privileges and corporations to make it possible for the individual and the economy to be free. To Saint-Simon it meant replacing the political and military leaders of his society with its true leaders, the men he called *industriels,* which included writers, intellectuals, philosophers, scientists, as well as financiers and entrepreneurs. To Halévy it seemed that the authoritarian elements that came to dominate Saint-Simon's system followed naturally from this goal of social reorganization. The *industriels* would administer government and the economy according to goals of increased production; rationalization of society would end its domination by politics.[69]

Then, in the second essay, Halévy followed the doctrine in the hands of Saint-Simon's disciples until they preached a "complete socialism." For him then the main point was that Saint-Simon's doctrine was not an explicit socialism; that, perhaps without his knowledge, his system rested on a principle opposed to the fundamental principles of classical political economics that he still considered his own. Others had affirmed a socialist principle without adhering to socialism. Hodgskin, for example, was a working-class democrat whose political thinking was anarchist. Without being a socialist, even a utopian one, he had devised the labor theory of value. But in Saint-Simonian doctrine there were "latent" elements of socialism; his willingness, for example, to use the powers of the government to "industrialize the constitution," "to bring about a transfer of property favorable to the growth of production." Industrial society, as Saint-Simon conceived it, was functionally hierarchical and each member was rewarded according to his rank. His "producing" ability determined his rank; he was to be chosen by cooptation rather than by

election. Like Bentham, Saint-Simon was no democrat. Like
many critics of the Enlightenment, he thought popular sovereignty to be merely a "negative" revolutionary idea used to
destroy the evils of the *ancien regime.* [70]

But Halévy reasoned that modern socialism was an essentially democratic doctrine. Therefore, one would have to
conclude that Saint-Simonianism was as little socialist as it
was liberal "unless, at the same time, it [was] opposed on
equally essential points to the social doctrines of Adam Smith
and J. B. Say." [71] Did Saint-Simon make a critique of essential
elements of Smith's doctrine? He thought he had indeed; for
example, Saint-Simon regarded economic phenomena from
the perspective of the producer rather than the consumer who
he considered nonproductive, consuming the labor of others. This was a definition borrowed from the physiocrats. He
understood competition as competition for the distribution of
ranks and rewards, which more faithfully reflected contemporary French society than Adam Smith's ideal of free commercial competition. For Smith the egoism of individuals would
bring about the harmony of interests, but for Saint-Simon
professional emulation, the force of moral sentiment or social
enthusiasm or some form of religious sentiment was essential
to the creation of a harmonious and "positive" society.

As Halévy saw it, Saint-Simon's implicit "socialism"
played a unique role in the history of modern socialism because it grew almost imperceptibly out of liberal doctrine. [72]
Saint-Simon's vision of a central organization of industrial
labor and a planned distribution of social wealth was fundamentally socialist and was his original contribution to social thought.

Halévy's interpretation that the germs of socialist doctrine were present in Saint-Simon's thinking broke with the
common opinion of his time. Generally, the disciples were
held responsible for turning Saint-Simonianism into "socialism," but Halévy thought the Saint-Simonians were responsible for condensing and systematizing the doctrine, not
for contributing its socialist elements. They had refined

Saint-Simon's philosophy of history, positing a progressive view in which the human race inevitably evolved from disparateness to unity, from the exploitation of one another to the subjugation of nature. In order to facilitate the industrial development of the world that Saint-Simon envisioned, they proposed to restructure the economic and social institutions of man. To make property as socially productive as possible they sought to alter the laws governing interest and inheritance.[73]

Halévy pointed out that the Saint-Simonian principle of reward as it was understood in the twentieth century—"from each according to his capacity; to each according to his work"—was not an exact rendition of the doctrine of the disciples. Bazard and Enfantin, the leading Saint-Simonians, recognized the right of the individual to consume freely the value created by his own labor but not the right to command another's labor or to be idle. The only right conferred in the formula was the management, use, and exploitation of property, the use of tools, the right to work, but not the right to enjoyment of the produce. Their meaning was evident when they said:

> Since everyone is rewarded according to his function, what today is called income is no more than a stipend or a pension. An *industriel* no more owns a firm, workers and equipment than a colonel today owns a barracks, soldiers, and arms; yet everyone works enthusiastically because the man who *produces* can love glory and can have a sense of honor as well as the man who destroys.[74]

Halévy's contemporaries assumed that an inequality of function necessarily created an inequality of needs. But the latter inequality ran counter to the Saint-Simonian prophecy of a future in which all antagonisms were suppressed through a world association of individuals who fulfilled tasks that were not so much unequal as they were different. If everyone had learned to love the occupation that he had chosen, why was there a need to add "to each according to his work"? Halévy pointed out that Saint-Simonian thinking was a profound change in the idea of competition, but that his disciples did not believe they could eliminate competition altogether. Their hope was that in the future competition would be in "things" and not in persons; competition would turn man against nature to subdue it for the benefit of all mankind, not man against man for private profit.

Halévy thought the Saint-Simonian critique of competition was prophetic. He also found himself sympathetic to it and hopeful for changes in society which were in line with that critique. In *La Doctrine de Saint-Simon* he thought he had found the most faithful representation of the thought of the group and their master as it had crystallized from 1825 to 1829 and it was no accident that he thought this period the most fertile and inventive one for French socialist doctrines. There French social thought had confronted problems basic to the modern era and speculated on solutions he might find congenial. During those years the Saint-Simonians presented a new definition of the state as a government of things and not persons, a new sense of property as something that must be socially useful and must be utilized by those individuals or classes capable of exploiting it for the public good, and these utopian socialists conceived of a new idea of religion as the expression of the collective ideal of a people, an ideal that united men with or without a belief in a deity.

Halévy's discussion of the Saint-Simonian critique of competition indicates just how sympathetic he was to the idea of society in which property was socially useful and the state regulated it for the general well-being of its citizens. Classical economists, he said, were right to make the idea of competition central to political economy, but they were certainly wrong to believe that it was a simple idea. Competition could be beneficial as well as harmful. Above all, "economic competition presupposes rules; it is not the same thing as the struggle for survival that assures the victory of the strong by the brutal extermination of the weak; it precludes violence; it even precludes fraud."[75] He thought the Saint-Simonians had wisely seen that the "unlimited competition" of European industry of their time was a transitory stage. The Saint-Simonians had foreseen the growing syndicalization or cartelization of industry developing after that transitory period. Finally, they had predicted the steady growth of the public sector of the economy.

Halévy's critical estimation of socialist theory usually was closely tied to his evaluation of the adequacy or inadequacy of it as an explanation of social realities, that is, the political and economic facts of workers' movements, industrial developments, and organization. Therefore, his prewar evaluation of the Saint-Simonians is noteworthy for its measured optimism and coincides nicely with the mood of his essay on the redistribution of wealth. He concluded on the Saint-Simonians with a prophecy of his own of a new industrial world emerging with new rules to regulate competition and to ensure cooperation or the organization of competition.[76] He took hope from the fact that without governmental intervention institutions were developing that might be the making of a new industrial world. This, he said, had been one of the blind spots of the Saint-Simonians: they had not foreseen the democratization of industrial production along with its concentration; they had not been concerned that the state, which performed increasing public services, would be democratic; they had foreseen the cartel but not the trade union. In those hopeful days before the war Halévy thought the remedy for the possible degeneration of the system lay in its democratization, which was taking place not as the result of state control but as the effect of state regulation. Democracy pressed the state to regulate for the public good the competition of gigantic industry with giant labor.

The war would change all that. Whereas before the war he was hopeful for the democratic potential of socialism and of society, afterwards he became increasingly apprehensive that the war had strengthened the socialism of controls and of statism. Saint-Simon seemed all the more relevant to postwar problems, but the potential statist future seemed more likely than a democratic one and the virtues of the rationalization of industry paled before the prospects of excessive control. In his only postwar publication related to Saint-Simon—the long introductory essay to the edition of *La Doctrine de Saint-Simon* (1924)—he confined himself to general observations about the seeds of authoritarianism in the origins of socialist theory. He did this at the very time he was making a study in worker-management sociology, which seemed hopeful about the prospects for social peace and changes in the economic and political structure that remained at the end of the war. In theoretical terms, however, he was pessimistic not just about democratic socialism but also about liberalism, which he thought he saw decay to a merely intermediate position between two conflicting movements, both of which would strengthen the power of the state—"caesarist *étatisme* and democratic *étatisme*," as he would designate these movements at first sight—a corporativism with capitalistic and Christian tendencies and a syndicalism with emancipationist motives.[77]

Halévy was not the only one who re-thought Saint-Simon after the war. There was a vogue of Saint-Simon among intellectuals in France and Germany. They saw him as the prophet of technocratic revolution, of a restructured economy that would alter the political and social system to create the new industrial society. There was a flurry of books and articles on "technocracy," *industrialisme*, and schemes for economic growth and redistribution of wealth through banking and credit.[78] There was a certain practical interest stimulated by the fact that the organization of industries into federations during the war continued to try to control contracts, fix prices, and regulate labor relations. The Comité des Forges or the Confédération Générale de la Production Française seemed to fulfill some of Saint-Simon's predictions. In England, too, there were a number of industry-wide experiments to "reconstruct," including those aimed at reducing home competition.[79]

Immediately at war's end Halévy examined "The Whitley Councils" and then two years later he addressed himself to the problem of worker control.[80] In general Halévy seemed to operate as though he believed that the chief practical influence of ideas came after they had hardened into dogmas and that their adaptability as dogma depended on their applicability to specific conditions. Was Saint-Simonianism applicable to the postwar situation? Was Marx? The ordeal of the war had revealed some strengths in British attempts to insure social peace and changes in the economic and political structure. Halévy was favorably impressed for the moment by the vigor of democratic socialism. The war had revealed gaps in the social structure, reforms that had to be made, but it had also taught that Britain and France could rely on cooperation between the classes to a degree that no one would have believed possible before the war. At the edge of a Europe torn and dislocated by war and Bolshevik revolution "a British statesman [could] consider his country finally cured of the disease of political revolution and rioting."[81] Nonetheless, the changes were quite revolutionary; "I have a feeling that things in England are revolutionary but it is without red flags and gunshots."[82] But cured of the disease of rioting and revolution did not mean the success of the Whitley Councils, which, Halévy asserted, were attempts to obscure the class struggle that is the essence of every trade union and every organization in which trade unions participated.

In fact, what he observed over the five years following the war convinced Halévy that the movement for "industrial democracy" or "worker control" was destined to fade away because it did not "correspond to the deep needs of the proletariat in large-scale industry."[83] Neither did the management's flirtations with "neo-Saint-Simonianism" contribute to worker control, at least not as then conceived. The aims of the working classes were the improvement of working conditions and their standard of living; they were not interested in running firms, or improving productivity or cornering a market by protection or any other scheme that management had in mind. These activities militated against the legitimate and quite separate interests of the workers. Worker-management

organizations would only contribute to the workers' un-
easiness and discontent and end by depriving them of their
legitimate spokesmen—that was the lesson that Halévy took
from the experiments that the British had devised. Although
in Germany, France, and Italy the question of worker control
of industry was a part of militant trade unionist demands in
the 1920s and in spite of the fact that the Tenth Party
Congress in Russia (1921) had faced the demand by the
Workers' Opposition for worker control, Halévy thought the
movement was transient, reflecting worker resentment of
wartime controls and the lag in real wages. Workers' demands seemed limited actually. A policy of taxing the rich to
protect the workers' standard of living would undoubtedly
have satisfied working-class voters had not the cost of living
risen continually, wiping out their gains and eluding their legitimate pursuit of a share of the prosperity. The exaggerated
attention that was paid to questions of worker control by
ideologists was merely another example of the mistranslation
of legitimate and deeply-felt practical needs and resentments
into socialist demands.

Halévy published only two long essays on socialist
thought after the war: one, the long introduction to *La Doctrine de Saint-Simon;* the other, a short biography and study of
Sismondi, placing him in the context of classical political
economy and drawing a filiation of influences and ideas to
Proudhon, Louis Blanc, and Marx. Both of the essays were a
response to contemporary problems, an attempt to point out
the relevance of early nineteenth-century thinkers to the
problems of the postwar epoch.

His brief study of Sismondi was part of a series on
seminal economic and social thinkers to which Bouglé contributed a volume on Proudhon. There was an air about the
series of renewal of the commitment to the non-Marxist origins of socialism that had characterized these same contributors' work at the beginning of the century when Halévy had
done his Hodgskin and the original Saint-Simon essays. His
choice in 1933 of Sismondi, a pessimist who had a century

earlier predicted the crisis of overproduction and underconsumption, was on the surface an attempt to write about a thinker whose work was most relevant to current conditions, but the essay itself shows the same fascination with intellectual leaps by men whose liberal principles would not allow them to call for state intervention that had operated in the Hodgskin. In his prewar Saint-Simon essays there had been a theme of the ties between these early socialists and liberal classical economics.

Sismondi had argued that the probable outcome of modern economic society would be the concentration of capital in the hands of the few, overproduction and the glutting of the market, and the poverty of the working class. As poor in solutions as he was rich in theories, his proposals tended to look to the past or to call for regulation and restriction; both remedies incompatible with his liberal principles. Halévy's extensive comment in Bouglé's session in 1912 on Proudhon stressed the individualist, anarchist Proudhon, whose origins were in Enlightenment juridical thought. He thought Proudhon's critical work was *La Justice dans la Revolution et dans l'Eglise.* He had little interest in interpretations of Proudhon drawn primarily from 1848 and after and thought even Proudhon's legacy was directly to individualist moralists of the working class and intellectuals.[84] Current concerns distorted several thinkers' socialism in his opinion, particularly Proudhon or Saint-Simon. But in the case of Sismondi, the war speeded up the process he had predicted and Halévy did not know whether the solution was to go back, as Sismondi recommended, or forward to some new form of state socialism, which he abhored, but "Whatever the issue of our troubles, there, it seems, is how the problem must be posed: it was Sismondi, not Jean Baptiste Say, who formulated it for the first time, more than a century ago."[85]

When in 1924 Halévy returned to Saint-Simon, he saw the germs of twentieth-century politics of the Right and of the Left in his socialism. Saint-Simonianism left its traces everywhere. "Hardly a party or an ideology had not borrowed something from the doctrine, or at least from the phraseology, of the Saint-Simonians, the true heralds of the entire century."[86] Saint-Simon's political influence fed two quite different streams of social thought—the social conservatism of Comte and Littré and the revolutionary schema of Marx. In 1924 the hopes that Halévy had had for the evolution of a democratic socialism—Saint-Simon had ignored the potential of democratic forms—receded with the impact of the war. He saw that, on the one hand, Saint-Simon's teaching had attracted all those with an instinctive aversion to modern individualist society (Carl Rodbertus, Thomas Carlyle, and the conservative Comtists) who Halévy called "the extreme right wing of Saint-Simonian positivism,"[87] including men such as Charles Maurras. This Right Saint-Simonianism had rejected the prophet's predictions of a universalist new Christianity. Halévy argued that this wing had joined nationalism and statism to their vision of a new industrial society. He queried whether Guizot had been wrong to see socialism in Napoleon III's humanitarian but statist social measures. Was not the "Saint-Simonian on horseback" as legitimate an heir to Saint-Simonianism as the revolutionary republican socialism of 1848? Napoleon III's measures had precious little to do with the republican tradition of the preceding generation—the era of Buonnaroti and Louis Blanc—and with the Marxism of the next, but were they any less socialist?

On the other hand, the lineage of left Saint-Simonianism was as much a story of strange bedfellows as the descent on the right. Halévy drew a direct filiation of ideas from Louis Blanc to Lassalle to Bismarck. Had not Saint-Simonianism fed Marx and his followers the fatalistic science that "taught them that the transition from one state of society to a higher state was always accompanied by violence."[88] Was this not Saint-Simon's law of progress, that organic societies are replaced by new ones because internal contradictions between classes or social forces end in the destruction of one society and its replacement by another? Saint-Simon and his followers were opposed to violence, expecting their analysis to aid men rationally to avoid the consequences of these contradictions, but Halévy wondered if Marx was unfaithful to Saint-Simon's fatalism. One might query Halévy, pointing out Hegel as sufficient source for Marx's fatalism, but for Halévy the fatalism was as disturbing as the violence in socialism whatever its source.

The true failure of Saint-Simonianism lay precisely in the fact that, like Hegelianism, it could spawn such dissimilar children, some of whom would destroy their own heritage. It was Halévy's premonition that he perceived a genetic similarity. After all, class antagonisms, war, and crisis had not disappeared, he pointed out. The destructive Jacobinism Saint-Simon had detested had returned, as destructive and as negative as in its first appearance. Europe had not reached a final state of organization in which these horrors had disappeared. But the nature of the antagonisms had changed: the conflicts were no longer between individuals in a system of free competition, now they were between rival state systems. Finally, Halévy drew the conclusion that modern socialism is a doctrine with a double aspect: a doctrine of emancipation, which aims at the abolition of the last traces of slavery remaining in industrialism, and a doctrine of organization, which to protect the freedom of the weak against the strong, needs a restored and strengthened power in the hands of the state. The contradiction was present at the very source of socialism and it remained alive in the legacy of Saint-Simonianism. The war only made the conflict more apparent.

CHAPTER FIVE

The Ordeal of the World War

LIE HALÉVY was almost forty-four when the First World War began. He had dreaded the coming of a general European war since his trip to England during the Boer War. He had not had much faith in the devices liberal men of peace rely upon to resolve the conflicts that lead to war—arbitration, international law, and an international language.[1] Neither had he been a pacifist. His estimation of the realities of European power politics had restrained his anger at the military even during the struggle for Captain Dreyfus. Like his master Thucydides, Halévy held individuals responsible for wars, all the individuals who made up public opinion, not conspirators or a clique of leaders. Yet, however individual, personal, or even petty the specific pretext for war, the outcome would dwarf the origins.[2]

He hated war and all the irrational passions of men that were allowed, even encouraged, to surface in war. He feared the impact of any war that would escape from the cage of European alliances. He understood the destruction that would inevitably follow the unleashing in war of the revolutionary potential of militarism, nationalism, class and national hatreds. He immediately grasped the fact that the extension of state bureaucracy that would inevitably take place during the war would have far-reaching implications for personal and political liberty. He also knew from the beginning that this was no short war, but like the Peloponnesian struggle one which would last a lifetime of ten, fifteen, or thirty years. He was led by the experience of the World War to stress the statist and illiberal forces at work in the history of this century. His understanding of the dynamic relation between war and revolution, nationalism and socialism and liberalism set new priorities for his postwar work. The events of the four years darkened his hopes for the liberal, democratic, and parliamentary institutions in which he believed and cast a shadow over his postwar reflections on socialism.

But the year 1914 was not a turning point in Halévy's life; it did not change his conceptions of contemporary history, only his emphasis. The Great War did not try his values and find them wanting. In fact, his basic beliefs provided the perspective, the intellectual distance, that gives a timeless and philosophical quality to the problems that he raised in relation to the war and to the judgments that he made. A profound pessimism permeates his wartime correspondence. Not for an instant did he succumb to an enthusiasm for the conflict that many intellectuals experienced. In spite of his disgust with the brutalities of the twentieth century, the tempest fascinated him even as it oppressed him.[3] His letters, especially those to Léon, became the expression of his innermost thoughts and moral resolution.[4] They move freely back and forth from his characteristically critical and frank comment on daily events to his abiding ethical concern to comprehend the direction of the social movements of contemporary history.

Intellectual independence and objectivity of a sort were not states of mind easily won or maintained in the midst of national and party passions unleashed in war. In a sense, Halévy chose isolation from Parisian intellectual and political life. Relieved that the Sciences Politiques did not require that he teach—"higher education this year seems the most ridiculous of sinecures . . ."[5]—he increased his spiritual distance

THE ORDEAL OF THE WORLD WAR

from Parisian intellectual life by finding war duty first in a village, Rochecorbon (Indre et Loire), and then in a hospital in Albertville in Savoie. As long as the war continued he would not engage in research, nor would he write on the war or on any other subject, nor would he maintain the daily contacts with Bouglé, Léon, and Brunschvicg, all of whom remained in Paris. He would not join his cousin René Berthelot or his friend Chartier (Alain), who had volunteered for combat duty at the front. Although his wife and her brother's family were near him during most of the war, he was separated from his brother Daniel who served in Pas de Calais and in Paris. Several times during the war Halévy resisted the efforts of his friends to secure a political or diplomatic position for him. He said that his "true friends" in England and in France had no influence, and he could not play the role of an agent. He would die of boredom or of disgust with the idea of all the half-lies he would have to tell. "If I must serve a function related to the war, let it not be an intellectual one or a quasi intellectual one! Let it be concerned only with the realization of material ends! Let's keep our intellect intact for the day that we can give it complete liberty!"[6]

Distance preserved his patriotism from the exasperations of Paris, from the hateful quarrels between the parties, conflicts he had always feared were endemic to French political life. His friends wrote to him of the intrigues and the currents of opinion which charged the intellectual and political atmosphere in the capitol. He was intensely critical of the war effort expended in the offices and salons of the Parisian elite. But in Albertville he learned of intrigue behind the scenes only from letters. He read Parisian newspapers sporadically, relying on foreign papers, particularly the Swiss. His physical isolation worked together with his skepticism in such a way that his constant thoughts were upon the forces that had brought about the war and the world-wide slaughter that the war permitted rather than various strategies for victory or party conflicts. Only the physical exhaustion of his medical duties and the presence of his family in Albertville alleviated this somber mood. Distance left Halévy alone with his own bleak thoughts on the realities of the war, alone without the relief or distraction that many men found in keeping abreast of the daily news of politics and battles. Relief was not what Halévy sought in the first months of the war; he wanted a duty that had to be done.

One must proceed without illusions, Halévy wrote to Léon, because "we have before us ten to fifteen years or thirty years of war."[7] "The second, the last part of our lives will scarcely resemble the first,"[8] he predicted. The insane destruction of mankind masquerading as a crusade of rival cultures would make any peace only a truce.

> This war or this set of wars will last a long time. If it can't last a long time with the armies constituted on the type of armies that we have now, they will change the types of armies. If the armies fall to half of their effective strength, they will battle with half-armies. If they must ruin themselves, they will ruin themselves. The questions which have been raised this last summer are those which could not be resolved in a dozen months.[9]

Men deceived themselves with illusions of greater causes than their selfish ones, and such illusions only served to intensify their passions.

> If war is the law of humanity, let us accept war. If universal peace is our ideal, let us say "down with war!" Without reservations! But to believe that universal peace will happen through a crusade is totally an illusion. War can only lead to peace through the exhaustion and horror that it inspires.[10]

The sadness of a fatalist was deepened by the anguish of the pessimist who saw the men around him evade the implications of their thoughts and acts and deceive themselves with the hope that the war might be turned into a movement for peace or into any other thing but what it was.

"One must do what must be done" is the theme of his correspondence from the very beginning of the war. War teaches the philosophy that it is able to teach, the art of living from day to day and of accepting the necessities of each moment, he wrote to Léon. Each must do what he had to do: Chartier had gone to the front; Léon must resurrect the *Revue de Métaphysique* as soon as he was able; Halévy must make himself fit for the duties of war. There were 50,000 wounded to be cared for after the first engagement of the war and he must make himself an orderly. It was "the work of a domestic but useful, and the conversation of the trooper is much more sane in these times than correspondence with intellectuals." [11]

For the moment, however, he was repelled by the bitter campaign against German culture in France. Was it a movement of deep feeling in Paris or a superficial and passing overreaction to the outbreak of the war? he asked Léon. He would not believe that he could not hear Wagner, read Hegel, nor admire Nernst, the chemist, and Klein, the great mathematician. His first reaction to the fact that the last two had signed a manifesto of ninety-three intellectuals in defense of Germany's invasion of Belgium was to remind Léon that there had been no French intellectuals to resist Napoleon's wars either; but second thoughts recalled with some pride that Chateaubriand and Madame de Staël had resisted Napoleon. Perhaps Léon was right in believing that the Germans were a nation of lackeys. But Halévy was more interested in the great Germans who had not signed the manifesto, men like Simmel, Hugo von Hofmannsthal, Richard Strauss, Hilbert, and others. He thought about writing something for the French press to call attention to the absentions but knew it might only force these Germans to take a second stand. That was more than one could ask of another man's courage. [12]

Léon and he owed it to France to refuse to allow the excuse of the war to suppress indefinitely "all French culture," particularly the contribution made to it by their *Revue*. In the midst of chauvinist passions the most pressing problem was not to become the slave of an exclusive nationalism. It was, of course, second nature to Halévy to think of the *Revue* when he was anxious about the strength of French national character. They had created the *Revue* in the belief that critical intellect and moral rectitude could fortify French culture and public life. The *Revue*, like his other commitments, had been his personal affirmation of the primacy of the public mind in the life of the republic. He did not think, however, that the efforts of idealists like himself had uplifted the public spirit sufficiently above class antagonisms and material concerns for it to meet an arduous test of faith. His deepest fear was that should the state of siege of 1914 be relaxed France would not have the moral endurance to continue the struggle. And France must continue and must survive! He was repelled by chauvinist rejection of German culture, but that did not mean that his pride in French intellectual culture faltered in any way. France was the one nation in Europe with "a civilization to rival Germany." All the others were dominated by German thought or incapable of fostering a genuine culture. [13] But he had always feared the French public spirit to be too weak, too divided by political and social conflict to safeguard the ideals and institutions that he cherished most deeply.

His prognosis for liberal republicanism in France was a bleak one, as one can see in his grim summary of French nineteenth-century history.

> Twice the country was governed by honest men—during the restoration and during *l'Ordre Moral*. Twice by low and cynical intriguers—under Louis Philippe and during the Third French Republic. Twice the country was fully and unanimously satisfied—after the *coup d'état* of 18 Brumaire and after the coup of December 2. And I am neither a legitimist nor a Bonapartist. Do you understand? [14]

He was convinced that the war had not healed any of the wounds in the French body politic. In the first months of *l'union sacrée* he had feared that all the infirmities of the French political mind, of the national morale, were only temporarily alleviated. Political life in France was too precarious to survive the "battle without end in time and space," [15] to survive political anarchy. France could not bear that degree of anarchy without killing itself. The English could bear "anarchy better than any other people, despite zeppelins and submarines . . . because at the sign of chaos a great adventurer can always rise out of Parliament to express the national will perfectly." But in France "the dictatorial power required by the military situation of the country [could] only be created outside of Parliament and as a consequence against Parliament. . . ." [16]

In a note to Léon from December 1916 Halévy suggested a convenient fiction which he thought captured the political reality in France. Suppose the Senators and the President were killed virtually simultaneously and the emergency made it impossible to follow the elaborate constitutional procedures of the Third Republic. The assumption of executive authority by a Director or by the president of each of the chief agencies of the administration would create, at once, a highly centralized and democratic government, one which would be too popular for the Chamber to resist. Even England had come to regard certain parliamentary customs as encumbrances in the middle of the war. In France, where the true obstacles to reform were the Presidency and the Senate, how much more vulnerable were parliamentary institutions! [17]

The end of parliamentary institutions in France was not imminent in 1916, Halévy thought, but the danger was there if the generation of national wars which threatened European politics materialized. [18] The danger to parliament was at least two-fold: the probable spread of cynicism toward representative government, which would be the result of sterile parliamentarianism in a crisis, and the increase of centralization and bureaucratization, which was inevitably brought on by the war. Halévy was sure that the political leaders of the French parliament could not break their habit of opposition, their ritual of destroying ministries with no other ambition or policy than taking the place of the ministers. The majority of the Chamber was more concerned with rooting out and preventing corruption, protecting the small propertied citizen, and supervising the bureaucrats than with reform or efficiency in pursuing the war. Halévy thought parliament's incessant control of the wartime bureaucracy had the effect of making it torpid and inert when it ought to be active and intelligent. When deputies and their friends burningly denounced the bureaus, he remarked, one regretted that the bureaus had no way to attack the parliament for its lack of foresight and its weakness.[19]

Cynicism itself was an evil and one of the most dangerous results of the failure of liberal institutions during the war. One could not, as adversaries usually did, generalize from the abuses of French parliamentarianism, to all representative forms of government. When Halévy proposed the topic "De la sterilité du regime parlementaire en France" for the *Revue,* Léon understood him to mean "De la sterilité du regime parlementaire," to which Halévy replied, "It is not at all the same thing and scarcely has anything to do with war. It was a problem before the war and will pose a question again after the war."[20] Neither the British, nor the American, not even the Italian political system resembled the French. "It might very well be that the evil is not susceptible to political reform and is part of a kind of general weakness of our civilization against which all reform of the constitution would be powerless. But, before giving oneself up to skepticism, one must try everything. . . ."[21]

Trying everything meant strengthening the executive vis-à-vis the legislative branch of government. It might save parliamentary government in France. But trying everything was a dangerous gamble, because the cards, at least French ones, held the possibility of a Bonapartist future as much as the prospect of a Jacobin Directory. The only constitutions that were truly favorable to liberalism were complicated constitutions;[22] that applied to France just as much as to England. The only times that were truly favorable to liberalism were peaceful ones.

Alain said the historian was sad because he was a fatalist. Halévy was not a fatalist, but his pessimism was so deep that all his wartime letters are as profoundly sad as they are moving. His medical duties were rigorous enough to satisy his desire to be useful and active. Carrying out his war service to the point of exhaustion in a provincial town made it possible for him to avoid the political intrigues and gossip of Paris. He could respond to the demands of duty, obey the commands of national loyalty, and yet hold himself aloof from the propaganda of war.[23] He felt that silence was best. "In times of war, if pacifist eloquence sounds false, the eloquence of belligerence sounds falser still. A single writer pleases me right now and that is Joffre. The rest is, or ought to be, silence."[24] By its nature scholarship was radically international, incapable of being organized for Allied or Central Powers. He cautioned Léon that they should not try to mobilize science in the service of national causes, but rather should imitate the Vatican and defend their religion as well as the Catholics did by continuing to exist above nations.[25] He grimly observed that during the war the true intellectual life of Europe had been forced to live in prison camps. Their *Revue* must not take part in the campaign of national hatred that was being carried on by each of the belligerent powers.[26]

The *Revue*, however, ought not to be silent. It was imperative that an independent voice be heard in France during the war as it had been before the war. For France to maintain the uninterrupted publication of a consistently serene and impartial review would be a challenge to Germany. "It is essential that it [the *Revue*] contain, in as great a number as is possible, articles of pure philosophical speculation. . . ."[27] The *Revue* did not have to take on the look of a patriotic pamphlet. "Bernhardi and Maurice Barrès must not make Europeans forget either Plato or Descartes."[28] It was one thing for the *Revue* to deal with the literature of the war, with parliamentarianism during the war, or with socialism and the future of democratic socialism after the regimen of the war; after all, Halévy had never shied away from relevant topics and these were but a few that he proposed for discussion in the *Revue* under the rubric of "practical questions." But it was another matter entirely if an issue were devoted solely to questions of the war.

There were many difficulties of publication during the

war. Not the least of these difficulties was the fact that there were few dispassionate metaphysicians living and writing philosophy in the heat of battle. Halévy's unwillingness to undertake his usual commitment to editing made him sympathetic to Léon's publication problems. But understanding did not mean that he accepted Léon's intellectual and organizational activities outside the *Revue*. What was the point of reviving the Société Française de Philosophie, if everyone was an idiot?[29] He doubted the utility of Léon's attempts to organize scholars from the Entente nations, because the Entente was not held together by spiritual or moral values, only by the political interests of the moment. When Léon took up duties as a cultural liaison to the Americans, Halévy was quick to remind him of his obligations to the *Revue*. At that moment, in 1917, when French morale had sunk to a very low point—Halévy thought it even lower than the morale in any other belligerent country—there were other more pressing duties. So long as they had in their hands the "instrument with which to struggle against such decadence," they ought to use it.[30] When Léon took up again the anticlerical campaign which was one of his life-long commitments, Halévy, the secularist, warned him against an excess of anticlericalism if he were truly concerned for the national morale: "The true French danger isn't the clericalism . . . the true French evil is apathy, indolence, negligence of duty. . . ."[31] And it was this French apathy that he, Léon, and the *Revue* must combat with all their efforts if they hoped to strengthen the national fiber.

The *Revue* must turn every adversity to an advantage in furthering the life of the mind in France. If there were no works of pure metaphysical speculation, then why not commission something on ideological movements? Why not a series on the philosophy of war literature that was revealed in each of the belligerent states? Perhaps they should do something on the concept of civilization that each of the belligerents believed itself to be defending. The question of the influence of the war on socialism merited a study. Halévy was sure that the effect would be unfavorable to the democratic or liberal forms of socialism (syndicalism or trade unionist movements) and conducive to state socialism. He was convinced that "the state of war directly favored state socialism and by reaction revolutionary or anarchist socialism."[32]

Why not put together a special number on the repercussions of the war on the organization of Europe, particularly on the economic systems? Or one on the political transformations of democracy during the war—on the "insensible evolution" of democratic governments under the pressure of external events?[33] There were a number of problems which deserved attention that had been put aside during the war: for example, educational reform, or the question of the nationalities in postwar Europe, or the new balance of power that would be established with or without arbitration, or a League of Nations, all would be a worthwhile project for the *Révue*.[34] As for the peace conference, Halévy had a half-dozen problems he wanted to pose for League of Nations enthusiasts from the point of view of a skeptic. Did the principle of nationalities mean that the League would have the right to interfere in the internal affairs of states to insist that new states be created for the minority nations? Would the just peace that everyone called for mean that each nation would be accorded what it wanted, that is, independence? Could there be any practical equality between states? Were the rights of small nations to independence as sacred as pacifists said they were? Would the League intervene in terms of obstacles to immigration or tariffs or colonies, or would the last problem remain outside the jurisdiction of the League?[35]

In the last months of the war Halévy was recalled to the Sciences Politiques to take up teaching again. At Sucy he worked without pause, not stirring even for the air raids. He threw himself into the "most urgent task," which was to "work to draw together again the ties of European civilization. . . ."[36] He was convinced that a new era in world history had opened on the day that the war began and that Jaurès was assassinated. It was madness to believe that the factions and parties could return to the prewar politics or that even nations could resume prewar policies. He was, therefore, a "convinced Wilsonian," musing that it was the wisest position to take and that the risks of taking it were absolutely nil. Of course, the American "didn't have angel's wings under his presidential overcoat" but until the "new order" he wrote, he would remain Wilsonian.[37]

> I ask for a quick peace and no annexations. And that's that for politics. But when I say that I am less nationalist than ever, my preoccupations are a great deal less political than intellectual. I ask that a religion of patriotism not be allowed to establish itself, more exclusive, more tyrannical, more bloodthirsty than that of any church. I want there to be some scholars, some professors, some 'mandarins' to conserve intact the center of European culture. I ask that the French forget the existence neither of Kant, nor Hegel nor Goethe; that they look for those Germans (Swiss republicans, southern Germans, etc.) with whom it is possible, without dishonoring themselves, to revive relations. We can't spend the remainder of our lives—which begins to grow shorter—in these idiotic questions of races, of languages, and of frontiers.[38]

His commitment to conserve a center of European culture shaped Halévy's postwar role. He was also committed to conserving liberal, democratic, and parliamentary institutions. In the drastically changed and changing world of postwar Europe this liberal historian found there was much that he wanted to conserve of the past.

The broad outlines of the topics that Halévy proposed for the *Revue* were those problems he thought crucial in the postwar world. More and more his own schedule of research and publication returned to the origins of the war, the political and economic transformation of democracy under the impact of the war, and the effect of the war on socialism and revolution. When he returned to the *History of the English People* he admitted quite frankly that he saw the diplomacy and the economic problems of reconstruction in the nineteenth century in a new light, that the war affected volumes two and three.[39]

He was deeply conscious of an obligation to do what he could to sew the fabric of European civilization together again. He deliberately cast himself in the role of go-between for England and France, a special, self-imposed task of explaining English policies to the French and the political behavior of their French allies to his English friends. As part of this new role he intensified his critical efforts to expose illusions, myths, or ideologies which he felt stood in the way of genuine understanding among the allies and the peoples of Europe. He dug deeply into the problems of the origins of the war, in part to be able to clear away the rubble of simple explanations and simplistic definitions of national interest in the popular mind. Halévy believed the simplifying ideological explanations of aims and interests had exacerbated the public's "disinterested and fanatical emotions" and pushed politicians to aggressive policies.

As Melvin Richter has pointed out, Halévy himself became a veritable symbol of the entente cordiale.[40] In many respects, this was more true after the war than before it. The scholar, who refused a position in the Secretariat of the League of Nations because it would interfere with his work and who had always left the numerous social obligations of the *Revue* and the Société Française de Philosophie to Léon, now initiated and maintained contacts in England with men of all parties and many occupations.[41] Each year the austere historian-philosopher, whose rigorous work schedule led him to put aside every honor and shun social occasions in France, spent the several months that he and his wife, Florence, were in England freely mingling with English friends. They saw his old and dear friends Graham Wallas, H. A. L. Fisher, Ernest Barker, G. P. Gooch, the Hammonds, the Webbs, as well as many political and intellectual figures. He frequently spoke before English meetings in the interwar years. He taught in England. He published several pieces in the *Revue de Paris* and in *History* that were written for intelligent, educated French and English readers, rather than for scholars alone, and they clearly show his intention to be a spokesman, if not a symbol. His increasing stature meant his actions as a scholar and teacher reached a broadening audience. In addition, he accepted a commission to work with Pierre Renouvin and Sebastien Charléty in collecting the official French documents on the origins of the war.[42] Accepting it could only take him away from the *History of the English People* and he ran the danger of being a part of the war propaganda effort he had avoided for the duration of the hostilities. Refusing it would not release him from the self-imposed duty of the citizen-scholar to use his science to comprehend the revolutionary forces at work in the war. His commitment to truth would save his work from being a part of the war effort after the peace.

An essay review that he wrote marking the end of the war underlined his commitment to action as a scholar and teacher. In a review of John Morley's *Recollections*, Halévy's tribute to Morley, the "last of the great Victorians," was also his epitaph for Victorian liberalism.[43] Morley's resignation at the outbreak of the war, when, in Halévy's judgment, liberty and universal civilization were at stake, symbolized the denouement of the Victorian era, an era "so serious and so charitable, so full of faith and capable, all the same, of so much tolerance."[44] The pessimistic despair of Morley, the austere free thinker, the moralist of democracy, pacifism, and liberty, the statesman in Ireland and in India, the last man of the Benthamite tradition, expressed the disintegration of the stoic virtues of an era. Halévy too had despaired, but he had not thought it possible to wash his hands of responsibility. In the Victorian era he thought two strong currents—the sentimental and the rational—had come together to create a powerful stream of reform. Among the Victorians both currents had included the strengths of stoicism, exemplified in men who possessed the stoic virtues and who were at the same time great men of action. Several Benthamites had been such men, and it was their capacity for rational reforming action that had first attracted Halévy to the philosophic radicals. He had seen the stoic behavior underlying the hedonist principles of the Benthamite disciples as he had seen the discipline beneath Methodist emotional indulgence. Facing the postwar world Halévy rejected Morley's despair, reaffirming the philosophical ideal of stoic action.

Halévy's role as intermediary between the publics of the once cordial allies was not a popular one. As he indicated much later in an unpublished exchange with an editor of *The Spectator*, he felt that one must go against the trend and speak the truth, attempting to allay the fears and distrust between the two peoples, because there were plenty of others who were willing to raise the public's political temper.[45] To speak the truth, even if it meant going against the trend, was his way. To attempt to allay the fears and distrust between the two peoples was a new challenge. In England, he criticized English policies and explained French behavior of which he was sharply critical. In France, he explained English policy calmly and patiently and used his sharp wit to puncture hackneyed ideological clichés and French national prejudices.

Implicit in Halévy's concern to fill this role was his fundamental assumption that the true interests of the Western democracies were bound together just as they were held together by their common principles and institutions. The assumption grew stronger in the interwar years, although in Halévy's honest estimation the prospects of understanding did not brighten. The democracies could be divided as easily as they were joined by a public opinion inflamed by distrust and misunderstanding, reacting to ideological clichés rather than rational self-interest. The true danger to peace lay in the public's willingness to sacrifice its real interests to great causes, to ideological clichés, simple ideas which, by their nature, were revolutionary ideas imposing themselves to the exclusion of and by the destruction of all other principles and traditions. By doing violence to the complexity of things, simple ideas worked against peace.

THE ORDEAL OF THE WORLD WAR

For the first postwar meeting of the French and British philosophical societies at Oxford Halévy spoke about "The Nationalities Problem."[46] He sought to restore the complexities of a principle that was fast yielding to the dominant simplification of liberal ideology. Surely the most popular liberal formula for a lasting peace in 1920 was the "self-determination of peoples." Halévy believed in the principle and had from his youth extended it to include the Irish and colonial peoples subjected to the French and English as well as Poles or Czechs or Alsatians. But at Oxford he questioned the programs for peace that liberal Europeans naively espoused without recognizing that they included several inherently, or at least potentially, contradictory principles.[47] Halévy, the Wilsonian, voiced his doubts in England, the home of the greatest enthusiasm for the League of Nations and for the slogan of national self-determination. Wasn't there a contradiction between self-determination and a League of Nations that implied, to some degree at least, the limitation of sovereignty in order to keep the peace? Was it possible to maintain a durable peace if the concept of national self-determination alone was maintained to the neglect of other principles, particularly those of natural frontiers and of European equilibrium? These companion principles were too easily dismissed by the current liberal ideology. Surely the principle of national self-determination could be the cause of war if it alone were allowed to govern the relations between states and peoples.

The nationality problem was not the only issue in which ideology and reality were dangerously far apart. France was faced with a rapidly dwindling stock of good will among her allies. Public opinion in France was scarcely aware that France had few staunch allies in Britain.[48] The French, who had never understood England or English public opinion very well, undermined their diplomatic position as they operated with an image of England that was merely a figment of their own ideological imaginations. Too many Frenchmen made the mistake of attributing an ideological motive to the diplomacy that had resulted in the Anglo-French Entente. They compounded the error by assuming that this ideological motive remained in force after the war. Some made this error because they hoped that antagonism to Germany was the inevitable conflict of rival capitalist nations; some did so thinking the foreign policies of democratic, liberal states were compatible with one another and incompatible with those of the autocracies. Even if the assumption were correct, Germany was no longer an autocratic state. Halévy warned that before and after the war England had several alternatives in world politics, that historically England's most characteristic position was diplomatic isolation. France was not so fortunate. Should England return to that policy of isolation, what would the French do? It was a question that plagued his cousin Philippe Berthelot in the foreign office. In England public opinion was turning against France, thinking the French insatiable and vindictive in their relations with Germany. Halévy could not drive home his message forcefully enough: public opinion was the force to be reckoned with in any modern democracy, but especially in England.

He hoped for a little realism in the place of national prejudices. The conditions that had caused Britain to join the Entente and later the war no longer existed. Germany no longer threatened to upset the European balance of power by virtue of its naval and colonial power. Further, the Austro-Hungarian and Russian Empires were in ruins. In short, in all the areas of most vital concern for the English the threat in Central Europe had disappeared, a fact that few Frenchmen bothered to remember. From a British point of view only France remained overmighty on the continent. The English did not perceive the French postwar grandeur to be the illusion that many Frenchmen feared it to be. "Downing Street visibly looks, if not for allies, then for friends against France, even if they be in fascist Italy . . . ;"[49] the French deceived only themselves if they believed that ideological differences could keep the English and the Italians or the English and the Germans permanently apart.

THE ORDEAL OF THE WORLD WAR

Halévy insisted that the French must found their policies on a realistic estimation of England's economic position in the postwar era. He did not mean by this the ridiculous political charge of the French Left, a crude, vulgarized Marxism, that British capitalism having defeated Germany now would destroy France's economy. Neither did he mean the kind of glib economic analogy to the period following the Napoleonic Wars. The current passion for comparing Versailles with the Congress of Vienna and the Concert of Europe was misleading and it was a seduction that he resisted in the second and third volumes of the *History of the English People*, which were published in 1923.[50] England's unemployment problem in the nineteenth century had existed at a time when English industry dominated world markets; now England desperately needed trade with anyone, even with the Bolsheviks. If the French demand for reparations or collective security threatened the possibility of improved world trade, English policy was necessarily anti-French. The French interest, whatever it might be—reparations or collective security—must be made perfectly clear to England.

In the-aftermath of the war it was imperative that Frenchmen understand the true significance of the crisis in Europe. Few French leaders other than Clemenceau were prepared to admit that Europe was no longer the center of world affairs. To achieve a lasting peace France must win the support of America and England, because France's apparent hegemony in Europe was an illusion; Germany's power was the reality. The survival of republicanism in France and French adherence to the League of Nations would win the support of the Anglo-Saxons, if France did not dissipate their good will. How many times in the last half century had it seemed impossible that France could save republicanism? And yet out of all the warring nations only France and England of the great Western nations had preserved themselves without the excesses of Leninism and of "Mussolinism." The League was an institution that was dearer to the hearts of the English than to the French in 1923, when Halévy wrote that the French must join with the British to strengthen it because the day would come when France would have to go to the League for more important problems than reparations.[51]

The question of the origins of the war was not a purely intellectual problem for anyone in postwar Europe; it was a question charged with political implications for the present and for the future. These problems were a test of Halévy's belief that rational critical analysis of contemporary history, rigorously applied, could break the hold of prejudice and ideology on the mind and passions of the public. All his life Halévy fought an economic determinist interpretation of history, affirming the importance of individual action, of personal and group ethic, and of ideas and beliefs. All his life he rejected history by *littérateurs*, because it propagated the belief that history depended on the intimate detail that decided the actions of single powerful individuals or that a few simple ideas sufficed to explain complex problems. Determinism deprived man, citizen or statesman, of his responsibility for failures of policy between states; popular history ignored great forces and problems and with respect to the war lulled public opinion with feelings of false security. Halévy's critical history was his only way to create the necessary intellectual conditions for a realistic estimation of interests and policies. It was his political science.

The paradoxes and contradictions of history had always fascinated Halévy—he was inclined to find them in history—but there were times when paradoxes existed not in the events but in the minds of those who read back the present into the past.[52] There is a scrupulous attention to the events in the essays and reviews on the origins of the war which he wrote between 1918 and 1929. Written in response to specific problems and interpretations he eschewed the technique, which he had used so brilliantly in the past and would use again in "The World Crisis, 1914–18" and in the "Era of Tyrannies," of seizing upon the inherent contradictions to reveal some fundamentally ironic or tragic aspect of the collective forces in history. He used the narrative, chronological

THE ORDEAL OF THE WORLD WAR

method to organize his *Epilogue* volumes (as well as volumes two and three of the *History of the English People*) and in the apparent flow of events he allowed his themes to emerge.

In his essays on the causes and events that led to the war, at least nine of which were important statements, he stressed several themes specifically addressed to correcting popular prejudices of the English and the French about each other's role in precipitating or influencing the outbreak of the war. The dominant message of Halévy's essays was his belief that public opinion was the single most powerful force behind shifts in policies and diplomacy. Halévy rejected any interpretation that regarded the Anglo-French Entente as inevitable or the Franco-German conflict as irreconcilable. He stressed the failure of personal diplomacy—that of Chamberlain, or Edward VII or Baron von Eckardstein or William II—to smooth over rough relations between the nations when public opinion was aroused. In addition, he denied that economic causes were a major consideration in the minds of policy makers immediately before the war, pointing out that colonial conflicts had been alleviated in the decade before the war and that the mercantile groups in every major state vociferously opposed the war. Halévy did not write a systematic exposition of the causes of the war. He did make extensive criticisms of the interpretations advanced by others, critiques based on his research for the French commission of the documents of the war and on his experience of England and France on the eve of the Great War.

He wrote two long critiques of Baron von Eckardstein's "indiscreet" memoirs to drive home his point that in a democracy public opinion dominates the conduct of statesmen and of foreign affairs.[53] These memoirs revealed that in the 1890s England had had an alternative to alliance with France and Russia and that the alternative was much more popular than Frenchmen in the 1920s were willing to believe. There was an almost symbolic confrontation between Salisbury's policy of isolation and conciliation and Chamberlain's aggressive imperialism in 1898. By 1919 men had all but forgotten

Chamberlain's attempt to join the "Teutonic races" in a triple alliance, and Halévy reminded his readers that had Chamberlain not been rebuffed by German opinion England's policy would have been quite different. English leaders of opinion had not opposed the naval and imperial policy that Chamberlain's alliance implied, they had merely responded to the rebuff. The confrontation, the atmosphere of aggressive imperialism, and the hostility to France were souvenirs of Halévy's stay in England during the Boer War. He distrusted the politics of empire. His antipathy to Chamberlain, to imperialism, and to the Boer War had inspired a little book, *L'Angleterre et son empire* (1905), in which he had described the course of the foreign policies of Gladstone, Disraeli, and Salisbury to the advent of a full-blown imperialist policy.[54] His distaste for demagogic imperialism, as profound as Thucydides', and his appreciation of the global nature of contemporary history date from that era. After the war he chose to share the realism and moral disgust inspired by that experience.

In France it was commonly believed that the personal influence of Edward VII had brought about the rapprochement between England and France. Halévy reminded the amateur diplomatists that as late as the turn of the century the Prince's imperialism predisposed him to a German policy. Edward's enthusiasm for French night life and racing was dampened by the recurrent anglophobia of the French press. His friend Dilke was pro-French, but his closest friend was Rosebery, the pro-German imperialist. Even if Edward VII had tried to influence the Cabinet to a pro-French policy such a move could have been successful only with the support of ministers and public opinion. Then, in 1902, William II's visit to London called for an outburst of bad humor, a moral insurrection of the press. Halévy saw it as anger directed against the routine of the bureaucracy and against the German policy, an irresistible pressure of the public upon reluctant ministers. The Cabinet's only desire in the face of this outburst was to loosen Germany from the Triple Alliance. In fact, however,

THE ORDEAL OF THE WORLD WAR

the incident worked to rigidify the Alliance and to increase naval expenditures, thereby heightening British-German hostilities with the most unfortunate results for world peace. The Anglo-French Entente was not at all inevitable: it had not been inevitable in the past, nor was it in the present.

Halévy was also irritated by diplomatic historians who thought the Great War was the result of perpetual antagonism between the Teuton and the Gaul, a mere renewal of the Franco-Prussian conflict. Halévy challenged his friend G. P. Gooch's Creighton lectures on Franco-German relations with the remark that an Englishman discussing continental affairs gave the general impression of a man sitting behind the window of a highly respectable house looking down in sheer contempt upon an unseemly quarrel in the street. He proposed to offer the view of the man in the street, a continental, a Frenchman and a French democrat.[55]

Like so many other diplomatic historians, Gooch erred because he did not note the interplay between domestic and foreign policy. In France, though not in Germany, constitutionalism and parliamentary government were vital institutions that made public policy. Under the Third Republic when Gambetta, Ferry, and Hanotaux pursued a colonial policy there had been a Paris-Berlin détente abandoning the *revanche*. In actual fact, at the turn of the century the powers of Europe appeared united in common antipathy to Britain in Asia and Africa, not divided into two hostile camps, one of which included Britain. *Revanchisme* had not dominated French politics: in fact every election from 1870–71 to the eve of the Great War was a resounding vote for the party of peace. Gooch had stressed Franco-German conflict, emphasizing the influence of Maurras before the war, but Halévy countered that the ultra-pacifism of Gustave Hervé was far more influential than the *revanchisme* of Maurrasian intellectuals. He argued that diplomatic historians who saw in the 1912 election of Poincaré a move away from Caillaux's policy of reconciling colonial conflicts with Germany ignored the domestic issues. The issues of the "Chamber without a soul" were anticlericalism and the income tax, not questions of foreign affairs. Poincaré's election was not nearly as significant a symbol as the fact that the French sent a delegation of two hundred parliamentarians to the Berne interparliamentary conference for peace and Germany sent a mere forty.

Halévy's impassioned reaction was motivated by more than his antipathy to a thesis of inevitable conflict which absolved, by implication, individual men of their responsibility. As a self-styled go-between for England and France and as a French patriot he was acutely sensitive to Gooch's analysis because it played down England's role in European politics. Did Gooch suggest—what was common hindsight view in England—that France ought to have tried harder to remain friends with all states? Then Gooch had forgotten that it was Germany that determined to break the Russo-French Entente. And he had forgotten that in those days Britain made alliances only with faraway nations like Japan. Did Gooch propose isolation as an effective foreign policy for France when even England was unwilling to take that path before the Great War? And, by implication, did Gooch and other Englishmen regard France's postwar policy as insatiable and as a continuation of French and German age-old hostility in which England had no interests? [56]

Despite years of concern with the origins of the war Halévy never wrote his frank estimation of the causes other than England's role. At least one critic thought his *Epilogue* was written to take the British to task for forgetting so quickly their role in precipitating the war, emphasizing as it did the importance of the naval race with Germany in shaping English public opinion toward military preparedness. It certainly was true that Halévy saw part of his job in all this discussion of the origins as the remembering one, a difficult position in both countries. It was Halévy who remembered the connection between internal difficulties and foreign affairs, and he was quick to point out that the English documents on the origins of the war indicated a people who, if not apathetic to Balkan affairs in 1912 and 1914, were so preoccupied with Ireland and social unrest that all other interests were excluded for the moment.[57] The breakdown of the Irish conference in 1914 pushed the Austrian ultimatum to the side in the papers and out of the notes of the Cabinet as well. To all Europe the sight of the English leaving for a four-day bank holiday on the weekend of the Austrian and Serbian mobilization was incomprehensible and the English irresponsible. Halévy, the go-between, reminded his countrymen that despite Britain's preoccupation with its own affairs, it had followed immediately when France declared war. It had thrown its interests and honor with the French in the face of the threat from Germany. He asked Frenchmen if France had had England's alternatives during those summer days of 1914, facing the threat of revolution, how long would France have hesitated?[58]

With so great an emphasis on the importance of public opinion it is no wonder that Halévy was so sensitive to historical revisionism with regard to the origins of the First World War. To lose England's public favor was to lose France's best ally. And in France the underestimation of England's ability to choose neutrality or to throw its weight on the side of Germany was widespread. But Halévy's stress on the interplay of domestic and international forces was greater than a Frenchman's concern with alliances. He became convinced more and more of the connection between social and national revolution and war in this century.

The two entangled themes that dominated Halévy's thinking in the postwar era were the relation of social and national revolution to the war and the implications of the war with its attendant statism for a democratic and liberal society. In a general fashion he continued his work within the concentric circles he had traced for Bouglé in his youth—"a theory of society, a theory of modern democracy or a history of England or something else entirely in that line of thing"— but in the postwar period his attention was drawn more and more to the convulsions of contemporary history. Once he finished the second and third volumes of *The History of the English People* in 1923 he devoted the last decade of his life to the investigation of contemporary history, whether of socialism or of England under the rule of democracy. The general implications for modern society of revolution and war held together his exploration of progress in a democratic society and his second major work, the unrealized history of European socialism.

The Rhodes Memorial lectures on "The World Crisis, 1914–1918," drew together apparently disparate lectures and articles that he had done on war and on nationalism and socialism. He saw the war as the great convulsion of the twentieth century that had not yet subsided, a convulsion brought on by the fever of national and class fanaticisms.

All the great convulsions in modern history combined the forces for war and the forces for revolution, Halévy said in 1929. In the main, massive dislocations such as the First World War, the French Revolution, or the Protestant Reformation were not caused by economic problems; the true sources of such catastrophes lay buried in the deepest human passions. In a few bold strokes, he sketched the outlines of a picture of class conflicts and of socialism, which in the years before the First World War had rigidified into a movement dominated by a single doctrine aiming at the revolution of European society. Among the socialists the German Social Democratic Party had emerged as the most powerful party in the most powerful state. But for all its revolutionary rhetoric it was a party that pursued a policy "not so much of revolutionary action as of revolutionary expectation, a policy of waiting."[59] The paradox that Halévy had seen as a young man visiting Germany still seemed central to his analysis of the role of socialism in the German Empire. His argument was a fundamentally liberal one, which saw Wilhelmine Germany as the most highly industrialized and apparently democratic power that was, in reality, subject to a political regime dominated by feudal and absolutist remnants in a modern state. Furthermore, Halévy noted that the Social Democratic

THE ORDEAL OF THE WORLD WAR

party, the one that stood for democracy, simultaneously stood for social upheaval, a fact that, he thought, would have explosive consequences for world history.[60]

Halévy emphasized, however, that despite the authority of the German Social Democrats in the prewar socialist movement, Germany was not the center of the world revolutionary movement. Here Halévy's bias toward doctrine, especially original doctrine, led him to say that any shrewd observer could see that France and Russia were Europe's true centers of revolutionary activity. The Second International and especially the German Social Democratic Party did not direct revolutionary activity, as opposed to doctrine or organization. In France the rise of an anti-parliamentary syndicalism, which called for direct action against the state and against capitalism, captured the loyalty of both workers and intellectuals. The syndicalist movement had spread to Spain and Italy where orthodox Marxism had always had a difficult time and had even reached England and the United States. In Russia, where a revolution had already occurred in 1905–06, terrorist activities tried "to throw the whole society into a state of constant panic, dislocate the machinery of government, and prepare the advent of universal liberty through universal anarchy."[61] Halévy reminded his audience that on the eve of the war in every country diplomats and statesmen feared the beginning of revolution would spark war, as it had in the French Revolution, or social upheaval that would spread throughout Europe, as it had in 1848; but as it happened the outbreak of the war "threw the revolutionary peril into the background."[62] The forces for war were still more powerful than the forces for revolution in 1914.

Pushing aside the question of the war guilt of individual nations, Halévy challenged the economic or materialist conception of the war's origins with a few well-chosen facts. Between 1904 and 1911 French and German capitalists were able to resolve their conflicts, but the Krupp-Schneider agreements broke down in the face of the resistance of the French nationalists, "who thought it too international, and of the

THE ORDEAL OF THE WORLD WAR

French socialists, who thought it too capitalistic."[63] Halévy rephrased Norman Angell's argument that ties between capitalist enterprises in the great states actually made for peace. He even ventured that there was much to be said for the system of "armed peace" between 1870 and 1914, that the three "unholy allies" of the nineteenth century had understood correctly that "revolution and war are two very closely allied notions." They had formed their system of mutual insurance against both notions.

Despite the alliance systems that had split Europe in two, Halévy argued that the three autocratic courts of Eastern Europe managed to preserve the general peace in the first and second Balkan Wars because they knew that "peace was the safest course for the preservation of monarchical order in Europe."[64] In his estimation ambition for material or military power took a poor second place to the power of ideology, the revolutionary movements of national liberation, as the force that pushed the great powers to war. From the East, movements of national liberation were let loose by the revolution in Russia following the conflict with Japan, rapidly spreading to China, India, Persia, and Turkey. Halévy insisted that the dissolution of Turkey by the Young Turks inevitably raised the possibility of the dissolution of Austria. These were the collective forces pushing toward war. "The Great War was a war for the liberty of the peoples from its inception," he argued. Once the revolutionary principle of nationality began to dismember the Austrian Empire "nothing short of a miracle could prevent its developing into a general war."[65]

Halévy's aim in his third Rhodes lecture was to approach the history of the war in a new way, stressing the interaction of class and national conflict. Dividing the war into two parts, broken at 1917 by the Russian Revolution, he interpreted the struggle in the West as a struggle for nationality, whereas the German-Russian conflict of 1914 was merely a rivalry of imperialisms.[66] He assumed that had Germany been able to maintain its triumph of 1914–16 in the West it would have broken down in the face of national rebellion. Similarly, Aus-

tria-Hungary would have disintegrated following the withdrawal of German troops, victorious or vanquished. The
principle of nationality was so powerful that even the Germans could appeal to its force against the British and French
in North Africa and against the British in India and Ireland.
In Belgium and Russia the Germans were able to divide the
populace by an appeal to nationality.

By 1916, however, this war of rival nationalities was
stalemated and it took the entrance of the United States and
the exit of Russia to drastically alter the balance of power. Although Halévy insisted on the importance of American entrance into world power politics, he concentrated, in this
essay, on the impact of the Russian Revolution, which bore
out his thesis of the inextricably entwined nature of war and
revolution. At the beginning of the war it seemed as though
revolutionary aspirations were submerged in the hopes of national solidarity. But though revolutionary ardor was
dampened working-class leaders who participated in the national efforts of their respective countries succeeded in furthering the cause of socialism. Halévy was one of the first historians to call attention to this fact, pointing out that the war
economy came to be the model for socialist organization. Socialists hoped that the interventions and consolidations of the
economy achieved by an emergency government would be
continued. They could then achieve a "permanent regime of
state socialism combined with syndicalism without the horrors of revolution, if not without the horrors of war."[67]

But in the "socialist" stream there had always been at
least two rival currents joined together: one, an attraction to
organization to make the productive and political forces of society more efficient, and the other, a libertarian resistance to
organization whether it was capitalist or statist. During the
war, workers who felt oppressed by conditions in spite of the
greater benefits that they received, joined with pacifist elements protesting both the war and the leadership of the war.
It did not matter to them that some socialists participated in
the organization of victory. At the same time, there were

those whose position was symbolized by Lenin at Zimmerwald, who remained true to Hervéist propaganda of the syndicalist period before the war. They aimed for the revolution of the future, a revolution carried out by workers and soldiers against both capitalism and war.

In the Rhodes lectures Halévy assigned to the Russian Revolution a role that differed significantly from the part he believed the idea of revolution played in the history of the socialist movement or in the era of tyrannies. In the drama of the war of nationalities "the Russian Revolution had acted as a solvent of imperialism for the benefit, not so much of Communism, or even of socialism, as of nationality." Its immediate impact on the war was to demoralize the war effort of both the Allied and the Central Powers and to make possible the United States' entrance, so that "the war could be fought on the democratic lines of President Wilson's Fourteen Points." Halévy commented that Wilson's program "to a certain extent, directly or indirectly, consciously or not, was influenced by the new Russian formula of 'a peace without annexation or indemnity." [68] Events in Russia also inspired the revolt in Germany that ultimately led to peace and to a republican and socialist government. In Austria, following the Russian collapse, the national and social revolutions combined to bring about the collapse of the Hapsburg Empire. The battle of Vittorio Veneto, Halévy asserted, was merely the breaking up of the Austrian army into its component national elements to promote the social revolution in Vienna and Budapest and the national revolution in Prague and Zagreb.

Halévy underlined the inevitability and spontaneity of the dissolution of the Hapsburg Empire in the last weeks of the war. In 1929 many English liberals, as well as a number of Central European publicists, rejected the Versailles Treaty, regarding the creation of independent nations from that empire as a serious mistake. Halévy reminded his audience that a revolutionary treaty had been written to end a revolutionary war based on the principle of nationality and recognizing states created according to that principle. The realization of the aspirations of nationality at Versailles "represented the triumph of everything that the liberals of the nineteenth century had fought for."[69]

Halévy's "World Crisis" lecture was a pivotal work that drew together his investigations into the domestic problems of modern European states and his research into the origins of the First World War. Once again he stressed the power of ideas to move men to act often against any simple economic definition of their interests. Particularly significantly, he conceived of the crisis as world-wide, realizing that the postwar period was a new era in that power had shifted from Western Europe to include America, Russia, Japan, and Britain's Empire. Stressing the world-wide significance of the crisis, nonetheless he expressly denied that imperialism, in any Leninist sense, had been the cause of the war. He denied economic causation in both his *Epilogue* and in the Rhodes lectures, emphasizing the enormous revolutionary potential of anti-imperialism and of colonial nationalism. He saw Russia's defeat by Japan in terms of its revolutionary potential for colonial peoples. He saw revolutionary nationalism in the colonies as such a powerful force that he ascribed the origins of the war to the uprising that spread from the revolt in the East, a dual revolution against both the West and native governments.[70] As a matter of fact, this theme so dominated his thinking that he subsumed his discussion of the day-to-day negotiations in July and August of 1914 in the *Epilogue* under the heading "The East and the Principle of Nationality," leading Charles Seignobos, whose writing of contemporary history was more restrained, to give Halévy a geography lesson of the Balkans in an otherwise very favorable review of volume six.[71] Halévy saw contemporary history as universal; even before the Great War he stressed the interconnected destinies of Europe and the rest of the world.

Halévy's anti-colonialism had always made him particularly sensitive to the issues of imperialism and national revolution among colonial peoples; even before the war he had stressed the enormous impact of European expansion on the political and military systems of the rest of the world. Yet, when he was a young professor, the conflicting values of peace and national self-determination had bothered him. He had written to Bouglé from Ireland:

Why aren't they [English and Irish newspapers] interested in the uprising of the Bulgars? The conquest of the Far East by Russia? the absorption of the Touaregs by the French? All these events diminish the importance of the acts of the Combès ministry. . . . They raise again a problem that I can't resolve. . . . You say to me that, as professors and not soldiers, our function is to preach peace and not to conquer nations. But the problem remains. In preaching peace are we going to realize the peaceful federation of that crowd of misformed beings, great and small, which we call modern nations; or indeed, in discrediting war, to prepare for the absorption of all the weak and tired nations by those capable of dominating all the others? *Ireland wants to be a nation.* . . . What moral value does that present for an apostle of universal peace? [72]

It is difficult to understand Geoffrey Barraclough's charge that Halévy was blind to the costs of colonialism for human freedom and happiness unless Barraclough had forgotten the *Epilogue*. [73] His further point that Halévy's exclusive concern with the crisis of European liberalism blinded him to the fact that the death of laissez-faire liberal individualism might mean the beginnings of freedom for millions of non-Europeans plainly ignores the nature of Halévy's liberalism. His anti-imperialism was not built on a theory that the liberal laissez faire individualism presupposed colonialism. In point of fact, he believed the opposite, that colonialism or imperialism developed hand-in-hand with the extension of a demagogic democracy and statism. Halévy's thinking was much closer to the radical individualism of a man like Hobson, who reasoned that the preservation of liberal democratic government required an anti-colonial foreign policy precisely because imperialism strengthened the authority of the state and of the militarist social groups within the state and was therefore detrimental to democratic liberalism.

Fritz Stern has pointed out that the Rhodes lectures "reflected the happy glow of the Locarno spirit" that would be extinguished within the year.[74] Halévy did, after all, remark that the failure of the revolutionaries to turn the nationality struggle into the class struggle marked the end of the world crisis. The events that signalled the true end of the war were the failure of a communist rising in Italy and the retreat from Warsaw by the Bolsheviks. On the whole, in 1929, he thought the European political results of the war had not been as disastrous as he had thought they would be from his station in Albertville. He was able to see that the war had been conducted for the liberation of nationalities and against imperialism, and that to a degree something had been accomplished. There was still labor unrest to appease and oppressed nations to liberate, but Germany's defeat allowed the "states of the season" a springtime and a respite for England and France.

For the time being it seemed to him that class antagonisms were buried beneath national fanaticisms.[75] His analysis of the anti-imperialist struggle of the colonial world was connected to the spread of democracy and national liberty. For all his perceptive comments about Lenin and Wilson competing for world popularity he did not foresee anti-colonialism as the force joining nationalism and socialism that it has become in much of the world since the end of World War II. The situation of 1917 seemed to Halévy to be one in which the Bolsheviks had seized power by riding on that horse of national antagonisms. Bolshevism had been successfully contained in Russia as in 1917 he had thought it would be. Furthermore, he thought that socialism, which had been a disruptive force before and immediately after the war, had been acclimated in the democracies.

Although he made much of the socialists' statism, the Labour Party had taken up the tasks of the Liberal Party and much of its foreign policy. Once again England's social ethic had restrained a potential destructive force—"modern English history thus proves that it is possible to extirpate class and party fanaticism."[76] (What the implications of this blend of Liberal and Labour were for the decay of England's liberalism he could not yet say, as he hinted in the *Epilogue*.) In France the socialists had survived their confrontation with the communists, and Leon Blum's leadership seemed to promise some continuity with the Jaurèsian tradition of democratic socialism. With the emergence of fascism and Leninism, Halévy's thoughts of Jaurès sound almost nostalgic, underlining how many humane values the men of their generation shared.

But the "happy glow of Locarno" was not very bright in Halévy's "world crisis." He saw national fanaticism as more formidable than class fanaticism. There is a small glow indeed when this liberal doubts there are a hundred willing to die for the League of Nations, to substitute a fanaticism for humanity for the fanaticism of nationality.[77] He knew Italy well and was much more aware than his contemporaries, particularly than his English friends, of how much cause for alarm, for moral repulsion, there was in Mussolini's experiment. But fascism did not seem to be an ideology for export.

He did not despair of democracy until he saw the paralysis of the democracies and the socialist parties in the depression and in Hitler's seizure of power. Then, convinced that war was inevitable, Halévy would look back to 1914 as the beginning of the era of tyrannies when the combined forces for war and for revolution threatened to end parliamentary, liberal democracy.

CHAPTER SIX

The Era of Tyrannies

I N NOVEMBER 1936, just a few months after Léon Blum took office in France's first socialist ministry in the Popular Front, Elie Halévy led a conference on four controversial propositions, which he grouped together, viewing the twentieth century as an era of tyrannies. His observations about the inherently contradictory nature of socialism and its kinship with communism and fascism were out of step with the political march of the moment. They continue to spark angry words and intense feeling. He asserted that communist and fascist regimes had many features in common. Both systems arose from the World War and from a socialist critique of capitalism. Both rejected liberal and parliamentary democracy.

He did not claim that socialism, communism, and fascism were the same, but in the politically charged atmosphere of 1936 that fact was not immediately apparent to many in his audience. To those who had chosen the Left as the best defender of their political ideals against the threat of fascism the comparison itself was, if not a slap in the face, then at least a sound shaking. Those whose sympathies lay on the Right, and there were a few who participated in the session, either misunderstood Halévy's liberal democratic position, mistaking its criticism of socialism for their own, or thought his sympathies too much to the Left. Today there are those who dismiss him as a precocious cold warrior, a man unable to reconcile himself with the end of a world of privileges for his class. The politicised atmosphere of this conference persists.

To begin the discussion Halévy returned to his theme that from its very origins socialism suffered from an internal contradiction: on the one hand its supporters thought it the logical outcome, the fulfillment of the democratic promise of liberty, equality, and fraternity of 1789, a liberation from the subjection of labor by capital; on the other hand, socialism, reacting against individualism and liberalism, proposed compulsory organization.[1] He offered three historical examples to illustrate his points. First, he asserted that socialism was organizational and hierarchical in its earliest form, an insight he had drawn from his study of Saint-Simon. Second, he argued that in the reaction to anarchy in 1848 the authoritarian principle in socialism took over in Bonapartist caesarism, which he thought comparable in some respects to Mussolini's fascism. Finally, he stressed that the origins of German social democracy incorporated both Marx and Lassalle, the radical internationalist with anarchist and communist aspirations for humanity and the nationalist creator of Bismarck's "social monarchy." These assertions were familiar to an audience that knew Halévy's thought on socialism. There were many in this group who did. His historical examples were, in fact, the same ones that he had drawn upon in his introduction to the 1924 edition of *La Doctrine de Saint-Simon.*

The second section of Halévy's communication opened with the first formulation of his thesis that the era of tyrannies had begun in August 1914, when the inherent contradictions of socialism were forced into the open by the major convulsion of World War I. The belligerents extended state control to the means of production, distribution, and exchange with the support of the leaders of workers' organization. According to Halévy, that extension of control realized syndicalist and corporativist goals under state aegis. Further, state control reached beyond the economy to thought control in the forms of censorship and what Halévy called "the organization of enthusiasm,"[2] or positive support of the state. The development of similar structures and methods in all the belligerents, whether democratic or autocratic, characterized the new era. During the war, Halévy had pointed to these developments which he thought would strengthen the illiberal forms of socialism over the democratic ones.

Halévy asserted that postwar socialism derived more from the wartime regime than from Marxist doctrine. This was a new hypothesis. He commented that paradoxically many adherents of socialism in the postwar epoch became supporters out of hatred and disgust for war. They then espoused a program of prolonging the revolutionary wartime regime in peacetime. As he had pointed out in "The World Crisis" the Russian Revolution was, at the outset, a national rejection of war. But it consolidated and became organized as "war communism." The Bolsheviks' tactics inspired him to formulate another paradox, one which angered some of his listeners: "Because of the anarchical collapse, because of the complete disappearance of the state, a group of armed men, moved by a common faith, decreed that they were the state: in this form Bolshevism is, literally, a 'fascism.' "[3]

His fourth and last observation stressed that "fascism" was a reaction against socialism which directly imitated Russian methods of government. He admitted that he took the "corporatist" experiments of fascism more seriously than did other anti-fascists because he saw them as the expansion of state control collaborating with, rather than opposing, elements of the working class. There was, he remarked, an internal contradiction in European society itself, in that conservatives called for unlimited strengthening of the state with severe reduction of its economic functions, while socialists demanded the limitless extension of the state's functions with an unlimited weakening of its authority. Between these polar opposites there was a compromise position which he provocatively called "national socialism."[4]

Halévy's statement of his thesis was very brief, fewer than 750 words. He was, in fact, immediately criticized for his brevity.[5] Yet a lifetime of historical and philosophical investigations and attitudes was packed into a few general symbols, such as socialism, which took on a multiplicity of meanings, confusing the issues but also illuminating them in a manner not unlike Tocqueville's use of "equality." He was much more explicit with regard to other concepts. He chose the term "tyranny" over the current one of "dictatorship" because he intended to call to mind the ancient Greek tradition of arbitrary rule without a foreseeable end. Furthermore, in Aristotle the tyranny frequently developed from the conditions of a degenerate democracy or a war, implications which he accepted.[6] To him the word "dictatorship" signified a provisional regime, which left the normal rule of liberty intact, in that it was assumed the society would return to that state at some future date. He noted that none of the regimes to which he referred as tyrannies assumed that the governmental form was an emergency measure lasting only for the time of troubles.

It may be remarked that he did not make some characteristics of the ancient tyranny his subject, for example, motives of personal aggrandizement of the tyrant. He did not emphasize aspects of the regimes that were his subject that he was particularly sensitive to, such as single party systems or the widespread use of terror. He intended this classic conceptualization—tyranny—for its facility as a model. He was deeply moved by the brutality of the tyrannies, some of which he had seen first-hand in Italy and in the Soviet Union, and he was outspoken and active in the defense of individuals who were victims of political repression in all of them.[7] The fact that this master of ideology skimmed over ideological defenses—monolithic parties or dictatorial state control, for example—in the midst of a discussion of the implications of socialism for this century is significant indeed. His emphasis here was on the importance of war and the anarchy arising from war in the creation of governments by armed bands of men. It suggests that in this discussion he believed the fine points of theory to be less important than the absence of any real counter power to the Bolsheviks' or the fascists' seizure of power. In the discussion Halévy indicated an unusual impatience with theoretical exchange in several places.

Halévy thought he had found the phenomenon of totalitarianism in the socializing tendencies of modern life, which he saw in contemporary ideological movements and in the overwhelming extension of the power of the state during the war. His argument was basically two-fold: one, that the intellectual origins of communism and fascism were rooted in "socialism" and that they, therefore, shared many features; and two, that the experience of this century, including both the war and certain trends of modern industrial society and government, reinforced these intellectual affinities, which in turn reflected these realities. Socialism was essential to Halévy's definition of the modern tyrannies, as was the importance of the war. He limited his discussion to those states which made some appeal, demagogic or not, to socialist principles, that is to Germany, Italy, and the Soviet Union. He also limited it to those states whose foreign policies and powers held the threat of war. He preferred to leave Spain aside saying its fate was not yet clear, and he said that he would not speak of the Balkan tyrannies. They offered nothing new, he said, except that in 1936 they could claim that they had raised themselves to the level of German civilization by their autocratic and barbarous practices.[8]

There was another socialist tradition, libertarian and rationalist, democratic and anti-statist—one that Halévy had tried to preserve some memory of—but it took second place to the authoritarian and bureaucratic extension of state power in his observations of 1936. There was an ironic element in the fact that Halévy, whose early publications on socialist origins tended to concentrate on non-Marxist, non-statist figures like Hodgskin, or critics of capitalism like Sismondi and Saint-Simon, would be the one who insisted on the authoritarian heritage. These early studies had pointed to the liberating impulse in socialism, but after the war he was oppressed by the tyrannical aspects of socialism. When others preferred to stress the democratic, anarchist heritage and to reject the statist, irrationalist and especially nationalist traits of twentieth-century social movements as aberrations, inauthentically socialist, Halévy claimed a legitimate place for these mutations. There was a surfeit of ironies in this session of the Société Française de Philosophie. Halévy, who had resisted the Marxist domination of socialist thought because of its bureaucratic and authoritarian aspects, found himself in the position of placing Marx, because he was internationalist, humanist, and anarchist, in the democratic tradition in opposition to the authoritarian, nationalist strain represented by Lassalle. In the 1930s the dominance of nationalistic authoritarianism put Marx in a new perspective in Halévy's view, just as the postwar "socialist" politicians made him nostalgic for Jaurès.

It is difficult to establish the issues to which Halévy preferred to address himself in the discussion that followed the presentation of his hypotheses. Obviously the hypotheses were his issues, but in the discussion the role of war in ushering in the era of tyrannies took second place to doctrinal tendencies. It was his style to pursue the logic of his argument relentlessly, so that his responses to the points made by the other participants have the quality of forcing consideration of the validity of his insight rather than the balance any written thesis might have had. Further, the debate moved in directions other participants chose. Much of the discussion related to the validity of the communist-fascist parallels and to his definition and interpretation of socialism. His old friends Brunschvicg and Bouglé raised points that he preferred to handle briefly; that is, a purely philosophical one and then with Bouglé specifics of historical interpretation with regard to 1848 and Bonaparte III. Yet in Halévy's responses one finds his life-long concerns, views he had held for a long time, and insights he had come to only relatively recently. The consistent themes are, of course, the importance of socialism in the twentieth century and its contradictory nature. Another motif of this conference was his fear that war threatened the destruction of political liberty and perhaps the life of independent democratic states, even of democratic socialism as his generation knew it. The comparative optimism of "The World Crisis" had gone; his view of the war was no longer one in which the nationalities had indeed fulfilled the liberal program of national self-determination and kept the promise of liberty to the politically subject peoples of the world. Now August 1914 opened the era of tyrannies, promising the destruction of liberty as he had known it.

Halévy's discussion of socialism confused and outraged many in his audience. His interpretation was equivocal though fertile, but that November day in 1936 when French socialism was in crisis, when prominent Bolsheviks had been purged and executed, when fascist states readied for war, Halévy had great difficulty sharing his insights. In his mind socialism was an ideology, the tendency to centralization and concentration of authority in the hands of the state, and a mass movement of the working class. Socialism might and did include collective ownership of the instruments of production, a planned economy or an economy in which the state manipulated the price mechanism, provided supports, subsidies, social legislation, or sponsored the cartelization of industries, and modern collectivist ideology. Without distinguishing among these aspects of state authority, his definition bordered on equating all growth of the authority of the state, or *étatisme*, with socialism. In the debate he discussed a variety of phenomena as modern socialism, frequently shifting the ground of his argument. He spoke of socialism as a philosophy, as a political and economic trend toward concentration and collectivization, as the aggrandizement of state power, and as a historical movement with complex associations between socialist and nationalist developments.

While his sense of socialism and his contrast of it with liberalism undoubtedly heightened his sensitivity to common traits among the totalitarian regimes, it was also the source of considerable misunderstanding. As he had noted many times, the Marxist domination of socialism was so pronounced that men had forgotten there had ever been any other kind of socialism, as was borne out when one of his listeners, René Maublanc, demanded that he distinguish between false socialism and Marxism, the "only true and living socialism."[9] His further comments and those of others indicated that there were many who had forgotten that there were Marxists other than Soviet ones. Those who were unwilling to differentiate Marxism and Leninism were antagonistic to Halévy's grouping together of bolshevism and fascism by common characteristics arising from socialism and war.

He intended to probe the implications of socialism in terms of both the ideological developments and the structural characteristics of modern society, but this may have been obscured for some by his bias toward ideas. He argued that one could approach the phenomenon by a discussion of ideology; he meant to discuss "socialism" or "tyranny" much as Durkheim and Tocqueville had addressed the tendency in modern society to "organization" or to "democracy." But, as he had once said to Bouglé, didn't these words ending in *ism* give *normaliens* a sense that they understood and had learned something when they had nothing concrete? Hadn't he found it necessary to do history rather than the history of ideas from intellectual dissatisfaction with this mode of analysis? The power of ideas as dogma, especially if they applied to real interests in definite conditions, was even more impressive to him in socialism than it had been in liberalism, and he defended his approach:

> Ideas stylize and schematize events. Nothing I can think of seems more useful for an understanding of events than such schematization. *When we see what success a doctrine like the Marxian doctrine has had, it is because it expresses certain striking features in economic development better than anything else, because it answers certain deep needs of the working masses.* How can we deny its utility, insofar as it helps us to understand those striking features and those deep needs?[10] [Italics mine.]

When queried by Max Lazard regarding his intellectualist approach he recast his formula:

Since its beginnings, the working class movement has suffered from an internal contradiction. On the one hand, we can see it as a movement of liberation, as a rebellion against the factory system, against the subjection of labor by industrial capital. But, on the other hand, to protect themselves against this oppression, the rebellious workers are obliged to seek out a new compulsory organization, in place of the outworn institutions that revolutionary liberalism has destroyed.[11]

But was his thesis intact, as he thought, with this rephrasing? His cousin René Berthelot raised the very objection to his thesis that he had raised to his *Philosophic Radicalism*, that of the specific historical circumstances that had required the multi-volumed *History of the English People*, scarcely volumes of allusions and isms.[12] Would his theses have applied to the two countries whose histories he knew best—Great Britain and France? Or to the one that he was unable to pursue at the length he wanted in this conference—the United States?[13]

But Halévy intended to discuss all the aspects of socialism implied in his many variations on the theme. When Brunschvicg's preliminary remarks as chairman threatened to direct the discussion toward the philosophical question of historical materialism by recalling the Sorel-Halévy exchange of 1902, Halévy abruptly opened the debate to all aspects of socialism, not just Marxian, and not just theoretical or ideological ones. In fact, he tended throughout to direct the discussion away from theory to the reality of the moment. It was a session aimed as much at current politics as at general theory. He threw the discussion wide open by asking for comments, not only about the tyrannies he had described— their potential for decomposition, for survival, for expansion—but about his view of socialism itself.[14]

As we have seen, Halévy devoted half of his life to questions of European socialism, problems of ideology and of working class and intellectual movements and parties. His first understanding of socialism derived from theory, from Saint-Simon who incorporated in his doctrine contradictory impulses to liberate and to organize some authority capable

THE ERA OF TYRANNIES

of improving the "lot of the most numerous and the poorest class." This conflict resembled the one between artificial and natural identity of interests that he had found in the origins of utilitarianism. Halévy admitted that the internal contradictions in socialism might also be present in the idea of democracy, but he thought that the radical democratic stress on the equality of individuals, rather than classes, distinguished political democracy from socialism. Radical democracy was a different movement, perhaps an inherently more liberal one, though in the Jacobin legacy there was also an ambiguity of democracy and dictatorship.[15]

Furthermore, conditions in the nineteenth century had provided liberties despite the shortcomings of liberalism and the merely political nature of the radical democratic program. *The History of the English People in the Nineteenth Century* was, after all, a history of liberty, stability, and even progress. The comparison with France that was implied throughout the work was a comparison with another liberal democratic state, but one which had developed in political and social conditions threatened by extremes of caesarism and anarchy. The historical conditions of the twentieth century did not seem to promise comparable benefits of either liberty, stability, or democracy. He was fearful that even France might succumb to the illiberal forms of socialism,[16] but there were other states which shared even fewer liberal characteristics with England than France. There was a sense in which Halévy always regarded Russia as another world than Europe, but what was striking to him in the 1930s was that Italy and Germany, which were comparable, had taken the path that they had. To Halévy's mind these historical conditions seemed to reinforce state authority, ultimately vitiating the emancipating impulses of socialism, because war had misshaped socialism into tyrannical regimes. For him socialism as a Hegelian perversion, that is, as statism, had always been the enemy, one to which he was particularly sensitive since the last decades of the nineteenth century when Prussianism was dominant and his liberal attitudes were formed.

THE ERA OF TYRANNIES

From his earliest comments on socialism Halévy connected it and the militant nation-state in a profound way. In the first decade of the twentieth century when he had first discerned the contradiction in socialism and in democracy between the desire to liberate and the desire to organize, he was a champion of the regulating state, the state as guarantor of individual liberties and social reform. He had argued for the French reforms against the church in the aftermath of Dreyfus on the grounds that the state strengthened the liberties of the individual vis-à-vis the group, whether it was family, church, or industrial organization. In "Les Principes de la distribution des richesses" in 1906 he had refused to make an easy opposition of socialism and liberalism, looking forward to new democratic forms of industrial organization that would make economic democracy a possibility. Had he relinquished his faith in radical democracy, in democratic socialism, and returned to the laissez-faire liberalism that he had rejected as too narrow a sense of liberal? The First World War and the threat of another war so altered his emphasis toward the authoritarian aspects of socialism that, while it gave his observations and work a peculiarly prophetic air, it also distorted his sympathies for socialism.

Since the beginning of World War I the connection between socialism and the militant nation-state had grown stronger in Halévy's thought. The theme of the *Epilogue* was the inexorable trend toward the power of the state in this century. In it Halévy saw a decadence of liberty in Britain after the retirement of Gladstone expressed by the union of social reform and unprecedented military budgets and imperial postures. He had witnessed the growth of the remarkable influence of the state in the control of the economy even before the war. He asked the socialists, to whom he had posed this dilemma before, "How could the state be strengthened without running the risk of militant nationalism?" To most liberal socialists the risk was morally offensive, but they continued as if their domestic policies had no international implications. Other socialists were so passionate in their desire to organize that they admitted to dilemma and Halévy thought his friends the Webbs were prime examples of the social imperialists. He might have posed the reverse of the question to conservatives had his attention not been focused on the dilemma of socialism in our century; certainly, his musings on the question of state power in the 1930s at Chatham House borrowed Spencer's prophetic description of a "new Toryism" of protection, socialism, and militarism.[17] He knew the answer to the larger question—could militant nationalism, socialist or other, live in peace with rival militant nations?—and he warned that the nature of war in this century was such that it would undermine liberal, socialist, and, by implication, conservative values as well.

There was a qualitative change in the nature of state intervention under total seige. In every belligerent nation the government organized production, allocated raw materials and finished goods, and censored public opinion until few dared to speak of the hardships of civilian sacrifice for the war effort. These government controls were akin to communism and at the same time devoid of any radical theory or messianic hope of liberation or emancipation of mankind. Was there anything in a program of state ownership or controls of basic industries that could contradict caesarism or fascism or authoritarianism of any sort? Halévy thought not and liberal socialists must accept that fact for the threat to their liberal principles that it was. It seemed clear to him that conservatives and liberals alike must admit that the state that was prepared for vigorous and militant foreign policy was, by his definition, "socialist" in a new and fearsome way. As he pointed out, the wartime measures that even conservatives resorted to in the Great War would have fulfilled the program of nationalization demanded by Guesdists at the turn of the century.[18]

As we have seen in "The World Crisis" and in his correspondence even before, this was not the first time that Halévy had connected war and socialism. In the midst of World War I he had written that a new era had opened on the day that

Jaurès was assassinated and the conflagration of the war broke out,[19] a new era in class and national conflict. These were connections that he had put aside in the 1920s, with other cassandra-like premonitions. During the war he had seen that its impact on a mass, industrialized society would be so great as to change the very nature of European civilization—to democratize it further in the sense of mass democracy, to alter the power relationship between the states and between social groups within the state, to weaken the hold of parliamentary government on the loyalties of citizens, to intensify nationalism, and to "organize enthusiasm." He had stressed the dynamic relationship of the forces for war with the forces for social revolution, speculating that there were those among the leaders in the great powers who had risked war rather than face the impending social changes. He thought that national fanaticism had triumphed over class hatreds in the origins of the war and that when the hostilities ceased national self-determination had triumphed, having held back social revolution at the gates of Warsaw.[20] He had seen and hoped for the liberal prospects of the peace settlement.

By 1934, however, the revolutionary movements for liberation, whether national or social, were secondary in his thinking. His expressions of faith in liberal or tolerant behavior among peoples were relatively few or faint, such as his thought that England might yet remain faithful to liberalism and to peace, and might continue to fulfill Gregory the Great's prophetic description of them "Angles? Angels!" By the 1930s his whole sense of his epoch and of socialism was one of the statism, organized and hierarchical and oppressive. The historian's subtle differentiations were pushed aside in the "Era of Tyrannies," where one might say by way of criticism and example that it is difficult to distinguish nineteenth-century authoritarianism or caesarism from twentieth-century totalitarianism. His constant assumption of the strong bond of socialism and the powerful nation-state blurs many distinctions between Bismarck's social monarchy and

Napoleon's caesarism and bolshevism and fascism. The
power of the state is the only common feature and is that really socialism? Finally, it is statism rather than revolution or
violence that forced comparisons to his mind, the place of
Hegel or Bismarck, not of Bakunin.

The war was a concrete reality that had made structural
changes in the economy, society, and government, changes
that had strengthened the illiberal states and reinforced illiberal forms of socialism. To him it was axiomatic that fascism
and communism had their origins in the war. Both movements seized power in the midst of anarchy or impending
disorder and forced the concentration of power in industry,
in the state, and in the state over industry, thus continuing
wartime policies and tendencies toward hierarchy and control. Fascism and nazism mixed proletarian ideology with
military ideology; under the control of these movements the
nation entered a permanent state of seige. Halévy's audience
agreed that bolshevism rose from the First World War, but
there were those who resisted tying nazism and fascism directly to the war. The depression and economic instability
figured very little in Halévy's analysis of the era of tyrannies.
He argued that Germany's wartime mobilization had influenced Lenin's vision of war communism and that Mussolini's
and all other fascist movements imitated Lenin's putschism
and experimentation. He refused to discuss the degree to
which the autocratic regime of Russia or the Leninist conception of the party influenced communism when the point was
raised. He did not discuss the possibility that Lenin's war
communism might have owed as much to the Bolsheviks' fear
of decentralizing power with the risk of losing control as it
did to wartime mobilization. He skipped over problems of
chronology, such as the fact that Mussolini rose to power
more than a year after the uprisings in northern Italy were re-
pressed; to his mind, the memory of the uprisings furnished
the support for Mussolini's dictatorship.

If socialism required state ownership of the instruments
of production or a planned economy, then only Russia came

to socialism from the World War. But Halévy's equivocal definition of socialism meant that he thought the rationalization of the economy that took place at the end of the war was socialist too, as were experiments with labor representation in management. That rationalization and those experiments, which he felt both the Bolsheviks and the fascists continued though the western democracies dropped them, led him to see the war as the decisive event in the history of twentieth-century socialism. In his introduction to his edition of Sismondi's writings he accounted for the depression as a phenomena of underconsumption and overproduction, but explained it as having originated in the accelerated industrialization that was forced by the war. In Halévy's mind war and the structural changes arising from the war determined the nature of the era of tyrannies, just as it determined the shift of socialism toward its bureaucratic, hierarchical organization and illiberal forms.

Were the inherent contradictions Halévy found in socialism rooted in the diverse origins of socialist theory, in the structure of contemporary political and economic life or in human nature? It is clear that in the short space of the "Era of Tyrannies" that he would have answered yes to all three views of the contradictions of socialism. In the discussion he concentrated upon the diverse origins of statist socialism, not referring much to the libertarian and even liberal origins that had impressed him in the earliest period of his studies—the cross fertilization between the utilitarians and the working-class radicals, the liberal origins of Saint-Simon's thought, and the critique of the classical economics made by Sismondi and Hodgskin. Here he chose to emphasize conservative, authoritarian, monarchical, and Christian features of nineteenth-century European socialism, the influence of Lassalle on Bismarck,[21] the Saint-Simonian influence through the Duc de Morny on Napoleon III or the ambiguous role of Louis Blanc, whose socialism glorified the Terror and Robespierre the Incorruptible over the French Voltairean liberal tradition. Halévy believed and reminded his listeners that the young

Marx in Paris in 1848 was swayed by Blanqui, the intellectual heir to Babeuf.[22]

Halévy's response to two of his correspondents indicated that he thought some of the difficulties facing socialism originated in human nature. Both questioned whether there were internal contradictions in socialist thought. Weren't the difficulties actually those which arose from external conditions, from the resistance of the bourgeoisie to socialist measures or from the complexities of economic institutions that required a strong state or the specific problems of attempting socialist measures in a period of restricted economy, of scarcity rather than prosperity, of stagnation rather than growth? They argued that abstract theory could not be expected to be applied perfectly and immediately. Halévy thought that the contradictions in socialism arose from something he called human nature, from the fact that both the proprietor and the worker needed freedom, the one to pursue profits and the other to pursue higher wages and better conditions, and that these freedoms were mutually exclusive if pushed to an extreme. It was the nature (i.e. the economic role) of the entrepreneur or the manager, whether it was the state or an individual or a corporation in a corporativist system, to insist upon the freedom to innovate, to accelerate production, to change conditions, and in the nature of the worker to desire freedom from the pressures of innovation, accelerated production, and changing conditions. He did not consider this difficulty resolved by placing one's faith in a future in which the nature of workers and work supposedly would change.[23]

There was a sense, of course, in which Halévy's posing of contradictions, his contrast between liberating and regimenting socialism in the twentieth century, unnecessarily limited his conception of alternatives. Bouglé accused him of suffering from "an abuse of contradictions," making it impossible for him to see a third way of political and intellectual liberalism coupled with economic controls.[24] Yes, economic liberalism was dying, but political and intellectual liberty might yet be saved. The possibility did not elude Halévy, but he was skeptical. He recalled that he had been hopeful of a reconciliation of liberalism and social reform on the eve of the World War but that his hope was stillborn as a result of the war. In fairness, it must be said that we have seen from his essays in the 1920s that he still hoped for Bouglé's third alternative then as he did when reviewing the American New Deal.[25] In a world where he thought the liberals were no more than an intermediate or center party between "a caesarist *étatisme* and a democratic *étatisme*, between a corporatism with capitalistic and Christian tendencies and a syndicalism with emancipationist tendencies."[26] there was no doubt that he hoped as much as Bouglé did for the democratic, syndicalist form of *étatisme*. The crucial question was could the democratic way survive another war?

Halévy had experienced some hopes in the postwar period that Britain might once again reconcile the class conflict; the Labour Party was, after all, the most democratic and pacific of Europe's socialist parties. In his expectations and judgments of the Labour Party we can see a fundamental conflict in Halévy's approach to socialism, perhaps to Britain. British socialism and working-class movements were the ones he knew best. He had always admired them for their commitment to democratic and parliamentary government. He had found in British socialism's tendency to eschew doctrinal politics a source of strength. As much nonconformist as socialist, certainly not Marxist, heirs to the tradition of utilitarianism, liberalism, and evangelicalism, the Labour Party offered hope for democratic and liberal socialism. Certainly as a scholar Halévy had done as much as any man to draw attention to these diverse currents in the British Left, but his postwar judgments were critical of the lack of doctrinal power, the merely trade-unionist mentality, the dearth of political skill and the ineffectual leadership the party and the class had to offer. Under the pressure of impending war that he felt so strongly in the 1930s he despaired of Britain, and of the British Left in particular.

Early in the 1920s he was critical of Labour's capacity for

politics. He had written that the party included the intellect of the country and yet, in spite of so much vitality, intelligence, organization, and public support, the party did not have a single representative in the capitol or a daily paper, did not control a municipal council, and had abandoned all administration to the benevolent control of bourgeois notables.[27] The prerequisites of a political party seemed to matter little to them. They were secure in trade-union activity and cautious parliamentary politics; they were curiously hidebound in their attempts to face economic hardship, which they were forced to face from the very end of the war.

The lack of rigid ideology had been the source of English political flexibility and of working-class strength. Labourites had concentrated on realizable economic and political demands and had contributed to the well-being of their constituents through reforms that Halévy had urged for France. Before the war he had berated his countrymen for their incapacity in enacting exactly these reforms. In the postwar era he doubted Labour would have been able to realize these reforms had they held power rather than the Liberals. He thought a merely trade-unionist mentality would not solve the problems of the postwar era, not the economic ones and surely not foreign affairs. The very qualities he admired in the English working classes and their leadership were the characteristics with which he found fault between the wars. He criticized them for indecisiveness. He suspected that the Labour Party was "afraid of the responsibilities of power."[28] For economic policy Labour had fallen back on classical economics—he accused them of having connived in the liquidation of the wartime emergency laws. Measures of relief for unemployment came not from Labour leadership but from Liberals like Lloyd George or John Maynard Keynes. He said they had no collectivist solution, that they had six million supporters but had failed to nationalize railways or mines or turn any of their opportunities of the twenties to their advantage. The Labour Party had seemed pleased merely to demonstrate that it could govern in 1924 with Ramsay MacDonald, not to do anything toward socialism or toward the alleviation of the distress of its members and following.

Halévy's theoretical conclusions from Labour Party behavior in the 1920s—as opposed to specific explanations for each action—was that socialist doctrines were easily assimilated to the militant nation state and that this presented a problem for liberal socialists. The Labour Party's Gladstonian pacifism, internationalism, and economic cosmopolitanism conflicted with its demand for a state capable of protecting the well-being of its citizenry. He said: "In the west liberal socialists would like to speak the language of Gladstone and the language of Lenin at the same time."[29] Labour's ambivalent position in the Parliament illustrated his point. Parliament embodied the nineteenth-century principle, one might say the Whig principle, of preserving liberty against the natural absolutist tendencies of the state by constantly challenging its authority, by criticizing and supervising it, and by virtually refusing obedience to it.[30] Labour politicians found such a delicate balancing act difficult, oriented as they were toward opposition to the actual state while trying to move toward a stronger government in order to realize their program. What would be the outcome of Labour's failure to satisfy legitimate and realizable desires? Who would realize the ambitions of working men? Or if they remained unfulfilled what action might be expected from the mass of men armed only with revolutionary rhetoric against critical economic need?

By 1934, bitterly disappointed, Halévy raised a general criticism, asking the reason for the paralysis and inefficiency of socialist parties in the west.[31] Privately, he confided to Bouglé: "In England as in every other country [the Labour Party] has left everything, by the force of inertia and imbecility combined with revolutionary phraseology which moves fools, to some 'national socialism' more or less mussolinian."[32] He thought the very structure of the economic organization of modern industrialized society, which demanded greater organization and control of production and distribution, rendered the idea of workers controlling their destiny more and more illusory. The conditions of industrialization required an ever stricter work discipline from the very men who had turned to socialism for emancipation from the rigors of the factory system. These conditions did not change with the socialists' taking of power. Thus, socialism had whetted the workers' appetites for freedom and for an increased share of the national life, but economic conditions of the 1930s offered a less abundant life, regardless of the form of government. And who would furnish the statesmanship to guide labor and everyone else through such times as faced them? Not the men who, when the Tories took England off the gold standard, complained: "But you didn't tell us we could do that."

Halévy's view of socialism was always too attracted to theory and too much impressed by the lack of British socialist theorists. He was too much impressed by the Webbs' own view of their impact on the labor movement and on collectivism. He emphasized Cole's guild socialism rather than the shop stewards' movement. Perhaps he underestimated working-class solidarity in Britain, dismissing it as merely trade unionist with mere economic concerns. His analysis of Labour's support—more pacifist than labor—underplayed the emotional and spiritual commitment to justice, to building the new Jerusalem.

But why was he so hard on Britain and on Labour? Because the Labour Party had become the spokesman for democracy, for the League of Nations, for peace, and for a number of other liberal causes. Halévy asserted there was no other heir to the liberal heritage and the incompetence and irresponsibility of the heir apparent threatened the system itself. British socialism, like continental democratic socialism, had "risen as a paralytic and inert party awakening expectations which it is unable to satisfy." His final judgment was that Labour's record since the war led him to shudder "at the thought of the Labour Party ever having a real majority, not for the sake of capitalism, but for the sake of socialism." [33] Further, unless Labour, and for that matter democratic socialism everywhere, proved itself capable of handling domestic and foreign policy, Halévy was afraid that the democratic left would not resist authoritarianism for long. In the 1930s even the Marxists in the west seemed humane, internationalist, and pacifist in stark relief to bolshevist or fascist forms of "socialism." And he accused Labour of campaigning on a platform of "peace everywhere, forever and at any price." [34]

The fascist and communist alternatives were too omnipresent and too threatening to allow for the kind of incompetence and impotence that Halévy thought he saw in the Labour Party. If socialism in the hands of tried and true parliamentarians was in danger, then how much greater was the danger in other states? He did not believe that democratic government would fall from internal pressures, but in the face of the external threat his thoughts were not very sanguine in those days of the Popular Front. He shared the commitments of the men of the Popular Front, but he had little faith that European federation or collective security could establish conditions that would make the world safe for democracy and not the habitat of tyrannies. He had been Wilsonian and an ardent supporter of the League, but that meant for him the acceptance of responsibility by England and France, not deferring it to the League in the hope of not having to take it at all. Whatever hope others had that the Soviet Union would preserve peace, he reminded them that the tyrannies of Berlin and Rome were nearer at hand, were narrowly nationalist, and offered no prospect other than war, a war from which he did not think the democracies would emerge as parliamentary and liberal states. His cousin René Berthelot thought the tyrannies faced greater internal contradictions than the democracies and that war would endanger those regimes more than it would the democratic ones—a prediction that in the long run, the very long run of World War II, seems to have been true. [35] But Halévy was not reassured. War had forced the Jacobin regime into caesarism, and the First World War had taught "men of revolution and men of action that the modern structure of the state put almost unlimited powers at their command."[36] Another war and the very nature of democratic regimes would be irrevocably changed. Historical precedent reinforced his pessimism in 1936.

The most provocative of Halévy's propositions was his comparison of communism and fascism. The discussion returned again and again to this thesis. Bouglé found his equation of the two movements shocking. He argued that although their methods might be comparable, the goals of the tyrannies differed, and they worked for the benefit of different classes.[37] An ardent defender of Soviet Marxism argued against Halévy that the German and Italian regimes were different from the communist dictatorship; the latter would soften, suppress itself, wither away when it was no longer necessary and was at that moment in the process of evolving greater democracy. The dictatorship of the proletariat existed in order to raise the economic, intellectual, and cultural level of mankind, which fascism, for all of its extraordinary capacity to impose discipline, had not shown itself capable of lifting. Hitler and Mussolini aggressively threatened Europe with national wars, but the Soviets were fundamentally peace-loving.[38]

Raymond Aron observed that the common features of the totalitarian regimes might be important to a "liberal who reacts sentimentally against the loss of formal and democratic liberties,"[39] but to his mind the class struggle and the will of the proletarian classes was the central social fact of the times. The decisive problem for democratic countries arose not from liberalism but from the fact that class antagonisms were as strong as national passions. It was obvious, he said, that both communist and fascist regimes directed their economies, but while Italy defended capitalism and moved toward war, the U.S.S.R. directed its economic life toward the common good. Nazism made the fundamental differences even clearer. Another participant struck this same note saying that Halévy's analysis was merely a superficial parallel built on the fact that socialism and fascism were led to use the same means, although they looked toward opposite goals. National socialism was "a movement directly opposed to socialism, resembling it only because, like socialism, it has been adapted to the modern world." [40] It was the nature of that modern world that Halévy thought he was discussing.

Halévy responded somewhat impatiently to the discussion of Soviet totalitarianism. He shook off the arguments of several of his listeners, who differentiated the regimes on the basis of their ultimate ends, and cited the communist promise of emancipation of man and the withering away of the state. He was not a hostile critic of socialism but discussions that accepted rationalizations of the dictatorship of the proletariat were unacceptable to him. "Alas! There lies the tragedy. I am sure that nothing could be truer than my statement. Every socialist government coming to power is forced to use complicated scholastics to explain how it must act when, professing a doctrine of complete socialism, it takes over in a non-socialist society. Here the Marxist formulas come in." [41] He too was capable of being moved by the heroic struggle of the Russian people to modernize, and he had seen it first hand,[42] but he believed an intellectual owed a special duty to the truth. The Soviets promised a temporary dictatorship but practiced a morality in which the individual sacrificed his desires for the good of the state. The greatest good for the greatest number did not ensure liberty (at least not in the thinking of all men). Even the discussion of liberty and its reconciliation with the needs of the revolution had been relegated to the distant future in the Leninist revolution. Meanwhile, a heroic and fundamentally warlike morality was the actual state of mind.

He could not suspend judgment and submit his intellect to formulas. Was the dictatorship merely the suspension of legality such as Marx might have foreseen, resembling the grant for six months of plenipotentiary powers to Poincaré to save the franc? Was it to last for several decades or for a cen-

THE ERA OF TYRANNIES

tury or two? "I cease being interested in the state of anarchy that they tell us will succeed it. What interests me is the present and the near future; beyond that lies what Jules Romains calls the ultra-future." As for the promise of some future state of the human race, when a perfect socialism would be united with perfect freedom, he asked, "What freedom? The freedom to do nothing as in the abbey of Thélème, or the absence of obedience to a master, along with incessant labor like an ant or a bee?" He claimed such freedom was beyond the limits of his imagination. Such dreams were certainly against the grain of his temperament. "When I see men giving themselves up to these dreams, I cannot help but think of Kant's dove trying to fly in the void, or of Hegel's swimmer without water."[43]

Was it really necessary to convert to one of the twentieth century's secular religions to better the lives of one's fellow men? He had never thought it was and even the experience of the 1930s had not convinced him otherwise. He wrote to young Etienne Mantoux to stop awhile among the Scandinavians or the Dutch and "see what can be done for the well-being and the culture of the popular classes by the development of certain secondary virtues, which are lacking in the French."[44] They had a secret there which one could find without a journey to Moscow, he thought. For oneself, one must ask what would be the effect on one's conduct of converting to communism. Would Mantoux be able to produce happy results by his social action? Then he ought to convert. But if conversion would merely enable him to disengage from all responsibility for society by taking an intransigent attitude, to protest without cease, and to do nothing while awaiting the final overthrow, then he advised Mantoux that he ought not to become a communist. It was the same response that he had made as a young man when his fellow Dreyfusards had converted to socialism or when Victor Basch urged non-negotiable demands and refusal to cooperate as a "socialist" policy.

Several times in the "Era of Tyrannies" discussion Halévy tried to explain his insights autobiographically. With the same unassuming quality of his letter to Mantoux he thought he could teach a lesson of tolerance from the "accidental nature" of beliefs: "If we have learned it well, we have to ask if it is worthwhile to massacre each other for beliefs whose origins are so flimsy."[45] He credited, one might almost say reduced, his liberal and republican opinions to a function of his age or environment, saying that in the years that he had attended the Ecole Normale Supérieure there were no socialists there and the political milieu of the nation was not Dreyfusard but the calm corruption that followed the Boulanger Affair and the Panama Scandals. He was a "liberal," an anticlerical, a democrat, and a republican, all that the word Dreyfusard would come to characterize in French political life, but he was not a socialist.

Charles Gillispie has observed that the historian could well learn humility from Halévy's modest approach to his own political commitments.[46] One could well learn that lesson of tolerance and of humility from Halévy, but not from the accidental nature of his allegiance to liberalism rather than to socialism. One could learn that lesson from his life, his work, and from the "Era of Tyrannies," which was something in the nature of an *apologia pro vita sua*.

There are serious reasons for doubting that Elie Halévy would have followed his brother's path or joined the socialist generation of Péguy, Mathiez, or Albert Thomas had he been born five years later. A careful study of his political behavior at several periods of crisis—the Dreyfus agitation, the First World War, in the deepening class conflict in France—indicates that he was a Dreyfusard with or without Dreyfus. His commitment was to justice and to toleration, not to factionalism and sectarianism; he rejected opportunism from any political quarter. Julien Benda observed that Halévy thought it was easy to be impartial because the ideologues all justified their politics with such good arguments. But he was a man who could choose between the arguments and could discern differences between the facts and the arguments as well. That was his role in the "Era of Tyrannies."

As we have seen, his fight for justice in l'Affaire for an

innocent individual did not become a struggle against the state, as did that of many of his contemporaries. In the First World War he did not succumb to chauvinist passions or to pacifism. He opposed war but acted to affirm as much of the life of reason and of universal humanitarianism as he could. At the end of his life he remained committed to the liberal, rational republicanism of his youth, to the perfect independence of his thought. The events of his life reveal his remarkable capacity for holding to his principles in spite of shifts in the political winds. Instead of arguing that the intellectual environment of his university years had made him "liberal," he might as well have argued that his temperament made him unfit for duty as a "doctrinaire."

He offered evidence of his abiding liberalism in his autobiographical comments. He said that as a young man he had seen in the Webbs, who were older than he and already important figures in the socialist movement in England when he met them, an "essentially anti-liberal," and "ostentatiously imperialistic" socialism. He thought it might well have been their fault that he was impressed by all that was illiberal in the socialist idea. "The independence of small nations could well mean something to believers in liberal individualism, but not to them, precisely because they were collectivists," for them "the future lay with great administrative nations, where governing was done by the bureaucrats and order maintained by the policemen." The Webbs and Shaw betrayed no principles with their enthusiasm for fascist or communist experiments. Neither had Halévy betrayed his liberalism. He had identified with the Liberals and Labourites who became pro-Boers out of "generosity and a love of liberty and humanity" and over the years his affirmation of liberal humanism had not diminished, had in fact been strengthened because the course of events seemed to leave fewer and fewer who were willing to affirm it.[47] His truer friends in England, truer than the Webbs, were Bertrand Russell and Graham Wallas. His friends in France were Bouglé, Léon, Brunschvicg, and of course Chartier, none of them socialists. It was not chance that led Halévy to liberalism rather than socialism; it was choice.

It is certainly true that Halévy's liberal individualism remained particularly wary of the imperialistic, anti-democratic, and illiberal aspects of socialism. He had found a conflict between the internationalism professed by socialists and the exigencies of legislating and organizing within national frontiers.[48] He had observed the anti-Semitism that demagogues had tapped in the "socialist" working classes during the Dreyfus Affair. He thought it was obvious that socialism was a political force within a nation-state and that nationalist and separatist passions were more powerful than internationalist, brotherly sentiments. It was useless to argue that national hatreds were the illegitimate offspring of "false" socialism. He noted that even the democratic idea could take on less liberal, less parliamentary forms when joined with socialism.[49] The irrationalist and anti-liberal protests of the syndicalist movement were married without much difficulty to nationalist and racist hatreds; he had observed such unions forged by the demagogues in France during the Affair and again in the South African labor movement. Long before Henri de Man and Marcel Déat became Hitler's supporters, Halévy sensed their motivations and the exact nature of their anti-democratic, corporatist doctrine.[50]

Much of the lecture was formulated in Halévy's most challenging manner. He may very well have intended, as Alain commented, to astonish and scandalize the naive beliefs of his audience, many of whom were socialists by sentiment. Halévy was perfectly aware of the fact that democratic socialists had come more and more in the postwar world to express the hopes for peace and for change that would preserve liberty and critical thought. Anti-fascist, anti-bolshevist, a liberal, who, as Alain said, never refused combat, Halévy raised his shocking hypotheses in a laconic manner. It is impossible to know if he feared that his observations might have the unintended effect of debilitating the resistance to fascism when he hoped to encourage the love of liberty; one can only note that he was dissatisfied with the results of his session.

His remarks were not very well received either on the level of a "political and social treatment" or as the merest outline, albeit a lucid and provocative one, of the issues that were the major interest of his last decade of work. Bouglé's comment that this lecture was his testament is certainly apt in the sense that Halévy bore witness to the values of his entire life that day. And it is also true in the sense that this lecture was his legacy by the chance that he died the following year. He added no further comment on the significant generalizations that he had made that day about the nature of socialism, revolution and war, nationalism and totalitarianism in this century. The theses that he had advanced were not widely accepted—in point of fact were hardly acceptable—when he made them.

In a sense that November discussion was for the end of Halévy's life what the Dreyfus Affair had been for his youth—his positive moral commitment to human freedom and political liberty, a commitment that he made although he was acutely ware of the conflicts of political ends and means. He appeared to be a hostile critic of socialism. He was certainly hostile to the tyrannical traits and tendencies that he perceived in it. But he shared the values of most of the participants in the discussion who hoped for the peace, democracy, and justice that democratic socialists defended. He admitted that if he were forced to choose he could live with a communist regime but that he must unalterably oppose fascism. But part of the commitment of his youth was to speak the truth as he saw it, and he saw tyrannical tendencies in socialism, especially when coupled with war. One might make distasteful political choices from necessity, but one need not leap into faith, blind oneself to the truth, or abdicate one's intellectual duty to speak it.

Notes

INTRODUCTION

1. Review of *Era of Tyrannies* by Elie Halévy, *Times Literary Supplement*. November 23, 1967, p. 1102.

2. Bourgin, *De Jaurès à Léon Blum; L'Ecole Normale et la politique*, pp. 147ff.

3. Thomson, *Democracy in France since 1870*, ch. 1.

4. Thibaudet, *Les Idées politiques de la France*.

1. THE MAKING OF A HISTORIAN

1. Pierre Guiral, *Prévost-Paradol: 1829–1870*, pp. 17–18. See also Daniel Halévy's introduction to Ludovic Halévy, *Les Carnets: 1862–1869*, vol. 1. All translation from French unless otherwise indicated is the author's.

2. *La Grande Encyclopedie*, 19:756–57.

3. Halévy, *Les Carnets*, 1:168–78.

4. *Ibid.*, p. 170.

5. Daniel Halévy's introduction to *Les Carnets*, 1:64.

6 Alain (Chartier), *Correspondance avec Elie et Florence Halévy*, pp. 21–23 (hereafter referred to as *Correspondance*).

7. George Painter, *Proust*, 1:74

8. A number of young men who attended the Lycée Condorcet testified to Darlu's personal and intellectual power. See Dominique Parodi, *La Philosophie contemporaine en France*, p. 15. As to Darlu's place in the Halévy family, Elie Halévy to Mme. Ludovic Halévy, February 22, 1898, Halévy papers, Guy-Loé collection.

9. Halévy, "Era of Tyrannies," *Era of Tyrannies*, R. K. Webb trans., (Garden City, N.Y.: Anchor, 1965), p. 269.

10. *Revue de Métaphysique et Morale* (1893), 1:376 (hereafter referred to as the *Revue de Métaphysique*).

11. H. Stuart Hughes, *Consciousness and Society*, pp. 13–14.

12. Halévy to Xavier Léon, August 30, 1891, *Correspondance*, p. 380.

13. Dominique Parodi, *La Philosophie contemporaine en France*, p. 15.

14. Halévy to Léon, rapport sur une visite à M. Boutroux, 1892, Halévy papers, Guy-Loé Collection.

15. Halévy to Léon, August 30, 1891. *Correspondance*, p. 380. Halévy expressed his antipathy to Bergsonianism frequently over the years. (Halévy to Bouglé, March 30, 1901, and Halévy to Léon, December 7, 1908, Halévy papers, Guy-Loé collection.)

16. Halévy to Bouglé, October 1, 1913, *Correspondance*, p. 337.

17. Xavier Léon's introduction to the *Revue de Métaphysique* (1893), 1:3.

18. *Ibid.*, p. 1. See also Halévy's letter to Léon, August 30, 1891, *Correspondance*, p. 380, n. 4. For a discussion of the influence of the neo-Kantianism of Renouvier see John A. Scott, *Republican Ideas and the Liberal Tradition in France 1870–1914*, pp. 52–85, and Elisabeth Waelti, "La Morale Kantienne de Charles Renouvier et son influence de XIXᵉ siècle en France" (Ph.D. dissertation, University of Berne, Switzerland, 1947).

19. Halévy to Bouglé, March 30, 1901, Halévy papers, Guy-Loé collection.

20. [Elie Halévy and Léon Brunschvicg], "La Philosophie au Collège de France," (1893), pp. 369–81.

21. *Ibid.*, p. 370. See Charles Digeon, *La Crise allemande de la pensée française, 1870–1914*.

22. Halévy, "Les 'Seminaires' philosophiques et l'état actuel des études de philosophie aux universités de Berlin et de Leipzig," (July–December 1896), pp. 504–21 (hereafter referred to as "Les 'Seminaires' ").

23. *Ibid.*, p. 521.

24. *Ibid.*, p. 510.

25. Halévy to Bouglé, December 13, 1896, Halévy papers, Guy-Loé collection.

26. Halévy to Bouglé, lundi, July 16 (1900), Halévy papers, Guy-Loé collection.

27. Halévy to Bouglé, February 4, 1903, *Correspondance*, p. 329.

28. Steven Lukes, *Emile Durkheim: His Life and World*, pp. 534–35. See also Halévy to Bouglé, March 15, 1903, *Correspondance*, p. 329.

29. Halévy to Bouglé, Oct. 5, 1892, Nov. 13, 1895, Sept. 1900, Halévy papers, Guy-Loé collection.

30. Halévy to Bouglé, January 22, 1896, Halévy papers, Guy-Loé collection.

31. Halévy to Bouglé, September 14, 1905, *Correspondance* (dated Sept. 12, 1905), pp. 332–33.

32. [Halévy and Brunschvicg], "La Philosophie au Collège de France," (1893), p. 376.

33. *Ibid.*, p. 377.

1. THE MAKING OF A HISTORIAN

34. John Passmore makes a point of the revival of philosophical interest in Plato, particularly of the later Dialogues. *A Hundred Years of Philosophy*. 2nd. ed., p. 11. Passmore says Lutoslawski's *The Origin and Growth of Plato's Logic* (1897) drew attention to the later Dialogues. Rodier's review of Halévy's *La Theorie platonicienne des sciences* (*Revue de Métaphysique*, (1897), 5:725–63), indicated that Halévy's theme of unity in the Dialogues was an unusual interpretation.

35. Halévy, *La Theorie platonicienne des sciences*, p. 378 (hereafter referred to as *La Théorie*).

36. Gillispie, "The Work of Elie Halévy: A Critical Appreciation," *Journal of Modern History* (1950), 22:237 (hereafter Gillispie, "Elie Halévy").

37. Halévy to Bouglé, March 22, (1901), Halévy papers, Guy-Loé collection.

38. Emile Boutmy, *The English Peoples: A Study of Their Political Psychology*, E. English, trans.

39. David Thomson, *Democracy in France since 1870*, 5th ed., p. 59, citing Pierre Tissler, *I Worked for Laval* (1942), pp. 7–17. For a more balanced estimation of the Ecole Libre des Sciences Politiques and its influence on French administrative and diplomatic circles see Theodore Zeldin, "Higher Education in France 1848–1940," *Journal of Contemporary History* (1967), 2:78. Also, Richard Challener, "The French Foreign Office in the Era of Philippe Berthelot," in Gilbert and Craig, eds., *The Diplomats*, vol. 1, *The Twenties*, 62–63.

40. Halévy to Bouglé, January 15 and March 8, 1905, Halévy papers, Guy-Loé collection.

41. Halévy to Xavier Léon, October 7, 1911, Halévy papers Guy-Loé collection.

42. George Painter, *Proust*, 1:226.

43. Halévy to Bouglé, November 16 and 18, 1897, Halévy papers, Guy-Loé collection.

44. Silvera, *Daniel Halévy and His Time: A Gentleman Commoner in the Third Republic*, p. 91, citing an anti-Semitic reference in Daniel's diary for December 2, 1898.

45. Halévy to Bougle, November 16, 1897. There is only one other reference to Semitic identifications in all Elie Halévy's letters that have survived. In World War I he teased his dear friend Xavier Léon, who was Jewish, that Léon would be chosen as the liaison to the Americans because he had such a good Catholic name. His own name sounded much too Jewish, he quipped.

46. Halévy to Bouglé, February 22, 1899, Halévy papers, Guy-Loé collection.

47. Halévy to Bouglé, March 31, 1898, Halévy papers, Guy-Loé collection.

1. THE MAKING OF A HISTORIAN

48. *Ibid.*

49. Halévy to Bouglé, January 1, 1899, Halévy papers, Guy-Loé collection.

50. Halévy to Bouglé, mardi, 1898, Halévy papers, Guy-Loé collection.

51. Halévy to Bouglé, February 1, 1898, Halévy papers, Guy-Loé collection.

52. Halévy to Bouglé, Sunday, October 1899, Halévy papers, Guy-Loé collection.

53. Halévy to Bouglé, February 1, 1898, Halévy papers, Guy-Loé collection.

54. Daniel Halévy, "Apologie pour notre passé," *Luttes et problèmes* (Paris: Rivière, 1911). See also Charles Péguy, *Notre Jeunesse* first published in 1910 in the *Cahiers de la quinzaine* in answer to Halévy's *Apologie.*

55. Halévy to Bouglé, mardi, February 7, 1899, Halévy papers, Guy-Loé collection.

56. *Ibid.*

57. Halévy to Bouglé, December 2, 1897, Halévy papers, Guy-Loé collection.

58. *Ibid.*

59. *Ibid.*

60. Halévy to Léon, mercredi (November 24, 1897), Halévy papers, Guy-Loé collection.

61. Halévy to Bouglé, lundi, January 10, 1898, and Halévy to Bouglé, mardi, 1898, Halévy papers, Guy-Loé collection.

62. Halévy to Bouglé (February 16, 1900), Halévy papers, Guy-Loé collection.

63. Halévy to Bouglé, January 1 (1899), and January 27, 1900, Halévy papers, Guy-Loé collection.

64. Halévy to Bouglé, January 27, 1900, Halévy papers, Guy-Loé collection.

65. Halévy to Bouglé, August 15, 1902, August 10, 1902, Halévy papers, Guy-Loé collection.

66. Halévy to Bouglé, November 1902, "lundi 24," Halévy papers, Guy-Loé collection.

2. The Growth of Philosophic Radicalism

1. Halévy to Celestin Bouglé, June 26, 1896, *Correspondance*, p. 325.

2. Halévy, "Quelques Remarques sur l'irreversibilité des phénomènes psychologiques," (1896), pp. 756–77; Halévy "L'Explication du sentiment," (1897), pp. 703–24; "De l'association des idées," Communication au Premier Congrès international de philosophie, (1900), pp. 219–35; *De Concatenatione quae inter affectiones mentis propter similitudinem fieri dicitur* (1901).

3. See Melvin Richter's listing of the topics to which Halévy contributed. "A Bibliography of Signed Works by Elie Halévy," pp. 66–70.

1. THE MAKING OF A HISTORIAN

4. Halélvy to Bouglé, October 19, 1896, Halévy papers, Guy-Loé collection.

5. Halévy to Bouglé, June 26, 1896, *Correspondance*, p. 325.

6. *The Growth of Philosophic Radicalism*, Mary Morris, trans. (Boston: Beacon Press, 1955), p. xix (hereafter referred to as *Philosophic Radicalism*).

7. Halévy to Bouglé, October 14, 1897, Halévy papers, Guy-Loé collection.

8. Halévy, *Supplément, Revue de Métaphysique* (1901), 9:11.

9. *Ibid*.

10. *Philosophic Radicalism*, p. 154.

11. *Ibid*., pp. 238–48.

12. Halévy was convinced that Bentham had not been a democrat before 1810 and that it was James Mill who converted him (*Philosophic Radicalism*, pp. 257–64). Halévy's stress on the role of James Mill was not Stephen's view—Leslie Stephen, *The English Utilitarians*, vol. 2 *James Mill* (London: Duckworth, 1900), pp. 7–30. In terms of the conversion to democracy and universal suffrage A. V. Dicey remarked that the school was very divided (*Lectures on the Relation between Law and Public Opinion in England in the Nineteenth Century*, pp. 162–68, citing Halévy, *Philosophic Radicalism*, pp. 168–69). Mill was the first utilitarian to try to base a theory of representative government on utility (*Philosophic Radicalism*, p. 257). (Stephen will hereafter be referred to as *The English Utilitarians* and Dicey as *Law and Public Opinion*.)

13. *Philosophic Radicalism*, p. 314.

14. Dicey's ninth lecture in *Law and Public Opinion* qualified the complete identification of Individualism and Benthamism, recounting the debt which the "Collectivists," by which he meant liberals of the Lloyd George and Churchill vintage, owed to Benthamism. That debt included a legislative dogma, an instrument, and a tendency; i.e., the utilitarian dogma, the omnipotent parliament, and improved governmental machinery (pp 303–10). The notes to this text indicate the areas in which Halévy's book had led Dicey to make any qualifications of his original edition. J. Bartlet Brebner was the first to analyze Dicey's shifts in "Laissez-faire and State Intervention in Nineteenth Century Britain," 59–73, especially p. 71, n. 15. See also Henry Parris, "The Nineteenth Century Revolution in Government: A Reappraisal Reappraised," for a more systematic analysis of Dicey.

15. Halévy to Léon, December 1916, Halévy papers, Guy-Loé collection.

16. Halévy, *Philosophic Radicalism*, p. 84; see also Stephen, *The English Utilitarians*, vol. 1; *Jeremy Bentham*, pp. 201–06.

17. *Philosophic Radicalism*, p. 235.

18. *Ibid*., p. 390. See pp. 380–94 for general discussion of questions of evidence and liberal safeguards.

19. *Ibid*., p. 390.

2. THE GROWTH OF PHILOSOPHIC RADICALISM

20. *Ibid.*, p. 403.

21. *Ibid.*, p. 432.

22. *Ibid.*, p. 431.

23. This was the basis of Sismondi's criticism of Ricardo. Halévy published a small volume of Sismondi's writings in 1933 with a long introduction that has been translated for the *Era of Tyrannies*. Discussion of this essay and Sismondi's place in Halévy's thinking about socialism is in chapter four.

24. Halévy, *The Era of Tyrannies*, Appendix 2, pp. 315–16.

25. *Philosphic Radicalism*, pp. 337, 514.

26. Halévy, *Thomas Hodgskin*, A. J. Taylor, trans. (London: Ernest Benn, 1956). Trygve Tholfsen argues that Halévy's concentration on the Methodists as the source of stability ignored the Enlightenment radical tradition of self-reliance, independence, self-government, and prudence as a stabilizing force in British society. Trygve Tholfsen, "The Intellectual Origins of Mid-Victorian Stability," p. 58. Halévy's explanation, by reason of its deliberate contrast to the experience of France with the political results of philosophe ideas, has a sub-theme the stabilizing and reforming effect of a doctrine that logically ought to have upset England as well as France. It is true that Halévy did not dig deeply into the ideas of working class radicals other than those of such theorists as Hodgskin, but *Philosophic Radicalism* and *Thomas Hodgskin* both touched on the role, the special nature of the role of working-class theorists in the non-revolutionary activity of the aristocracy of labor. See as well Halévy's review article of several books on the Chartists in *Quarterly Review* (1927), 236:62–75, in which his description of the nature of working-class radical leaders dwells upon just these characteristics as an antidote to the studies that would dwell on their socialist and revolutionary characteristics.

27. *Philosophic Radicalism*, p. 370.

28. *Ibid.*

29. Stephen made much more of this criticism of the Philosophic Radicals' lack of historical foundation than Halévy did, perhaps because Halévy's thesis was that they were rationalists and not empiricists. Therefore Stephen's criticism that their ahistorical science was paradoxical in empiricists was not pertinent to Halévy's argument.

30. *Philosophic Radicalism*, pp. 492–96.

31. Halévy to Bouglé, October 19, 1896, Halévy papers, Guy-Loé collection.

32. Halévy to Mme. Léon Halévy, February 6, 1893, Halévy papers, Guy-Loé collection.

33. Halévy to Bouglé, "vendredi" (1902–3), Halévy papers, Guy-Loé collection.

34. *Philosophic Radicalism*, pp. 497–98, 501.

35. *Ibid.*, p. 501. See Halévy and Brunschvicg "Notes critiques: L'An-

2. THE GROWTH OF PHILOSOPHIC RADICALISM

née philosophique 1893," *Revue de Métaphysique* (1894), 2:557–78. On the other hand Halévy's critique of Vilfredo Pareto's paper "L'Individuel et le social," given at the fourth general meeting of the Congrès du Genève and printed in *Revue de Métaphysique* (1904), 12:1103–13 said, in part, that he did not address himself to the assumptions regarding the *collective.*

36. Halévy to Bouglé, January 22, 1896, Halévy papers, Guy-Loé collection.

37. The most characteristic example of this rephrasing of problems in sociological language was his response to Max Lazard's comment at the "Ère de tyrannies" meeting in 1936 that Halévy tended to approach concrete social facts indirectly as they were reflected in doctrines about them. Halévy then expressed his thesis about socialism in terms of classes and social groups rather than ideas, without altering his meaning, pp. 274–75.

38. Halévy, "Lévy-Bruhl, 'La Mythologie primitive,' " (1936), pp. 155 56.

39. *Philosophic Radicalism*, p. 485.

40. *Ibid.*, p. 486.

41. Bernard Semmel's introduction to Halévy's *Birth of Methodism in England* (Chicago: University of Chicago Press, 1973), pp. 13–16.

42. Halévy, *Philosophic Radicalism*, p. xviii.

43. *Ibid.*

44. Brebner, "Elie Halévy," in *Some Modern Historians of Britain: Essays in Honor of R. L. Schuyler*, p. 242.

45. *Ibid.*

46. See Halévy's essay "Les Principes da la distribution des richesses," (1906), pp. 545–95, as well as the concluding pages of "La Doctrine économique de Saint-Simon," written at the same time and reprinted in the *Era of Tyrannies*. See the conclusion of *Philosophic Radicalism* (p. 499).

47. Halévy, *Philosophic Radicalism*, p. 514.

48. *Ibid.*

49. *History of the English People in the Nineteenth Century*, vol. 3: *Triumph of Reform*, p. 101.

50. *Ibid.*, p. 100.

51. *Ibid.*, pp. 99—100.

52. *Ibid.*, p. 100.

53. *Ibid.*, p. 115. For Halévy's interpretation of the new powers granted to the New Poor Law Commissioners, see also p. 124.

54. Jennifer Hart, "Nineteenth Century Social Reform: A Tory Interpretation of History." S. E. Finer, *The Life and Times of Sir Edwin Chadwick.* Gertrude Himmelfarb, "Bentham Scholarship and the Bentham 'Problem,' " and "Bentham's Utopia: The National Charity Company" and "The Haunted House of Jeremy Bentham." E. C. Midwinter, "State Intervention at the Local Level: The New Poor Law in Lancashire." Oliver MacDonagh, "The Nineteenth Century Revolution in Government: A Reappraisal," and

2. THE GROWTH OF PHILOSOPHIC RADICALISM

Early Victorian Government 1832–70. Henry Parris, "The Nineteenth Century Revolution in Government: A Reappraisal Reappraised." David Roberts, *Victorian Origins of the British Welfare State*. Lionel Robbins, *The Theory of Economic Policy in English Political Economy*. Nancy Rosenblum, *Bentham's Theory of the Modern State*.

55. "Before 1835," H. J. Laski, ed., *A Century of Municipal Progress*, pp. 34–35.

3. THE "HALÉVY THESIS"

1. Halévy to Bouglé, May 10, 1906, Halévy papers, Guy-Loé collection.
2. Halévy, *England in 1815*, p. 591.
3. *Ibid.*, p. xiii.
4. Halévy, *History of the English People in the Nineteenth Century*, vol. 4: *Victorian Years 1841–1895*, p. 337. This particular chapter, "Religious Beliefs," is the only finished one of the mid-century tableau which he intended to parallel the survey of social forces of *England in 1815*. Trygve Tholfsen's point that Halévy explicitly excluded the Victorian period from the reach of his argument on the stabilizing effect of intellectual forces ignores this fact and the significant generalizations that Halévy made on precisely this effect ("The Intellectual Origins of Mid-Victorian Stability," p. 58).
5. Halévy, *History of the English People*, vol. 5: *Epilogue: Imperialism and the Rise of Labour (1895–1905)*, p. x.
6. Halévy, *England in 1815*, p. 585.
7. Halévy, *The Growth of Philosophic Radicalism*, pp. 492–95. See also *England in 1815*, pp. 586–87.
8. *England in 1815*, p. 586.
9. Ibid., p. 586 n.
10. Halévy, *England in 1815*, p. 587.
11. Hobsbawm, "The British Secret," pp. 548–49.
12. Halévy, *History of the English People*, vol. 5: *Epilogue: Imperialism and the Rise of Labour (1895–1905)*, p. x. This same theme is treated in Halévy "L'Angleterre: Grandeur, decadence et persistance du liberalisme en Angleterre," *Inventaires, La Crise sociale et les nationales* (1936), pp. 5–23. See also his treatment of Cardinal Newman in vol. 4: *The Victorian Years*, 352–64, 374–75, which he wrote in his last months.
13. K. W. Swart, *The Sense of Decadence in Nineteenth Century France*, pp. 172–78. Steven Lukes has an excellent summary of this tradition in *Emile Durkheim*, pp. 195–99.
14. Halévy to Bouglé, July 30, 1905, Halévy papers, Guy-Loé collection.
15. Halévy to Léon, July 31, 1905, *Correspondance*, p. 332.
16. Halévy, *The Birth of Methodism in England*, Bernard Semmel, trans. (Chicago: University of Chicago Press, 1971), pp. 33–34. This was originally two articles: "La Naissance du Methodisme en Angleterre," published in

La Revue de Paris, (juillet-août 1906) 13:519–39, 841–67. (Hereafter referred to as *The Birth of Methodism.*)

17. *Ibid.,* p. 33.

18. Halévy to Bouglé, December 19, 1900, Halévy papers, Guy-Loé collection.

19. Daniel to Elie Halévy, April 2, 1902, Halévy papers, Guy-Loé collection.

20. Halévy to Bouglé, May 20, 1904, Halévy papers, Guy-Loé collection.

21. Halévy to Bouglé, March 8, 1905, Halévy papers, Guy-Loé collection. The contemporary history which intrigued him was the general subject of England in the nineteenth century, specifically the preparation of a small book on the rise of imperialism in England, *L'Angleterre et son empire* (1905).

22. Halévy to Bouglé, July 30, 1905, Halévy papers, Guy-Loé collection.

23. Halévy to Bouglé, May 10, 1906, Halévy papers, Guy-Loé collection.

24. Bernard Semmel's introduction to Halévy's *The Birth of Methodism,* p. 16.

25. Taine, *History of English Literature,* 3:73–74.

26. *Ibid.,* p. 75.

27. Halévy, *The Birth of Methodism,* pp. 35, 38–40, 43–45, 49.

28. *Ibid.,* pp. 41 and 46.

29. See Halévy's refutation of this view, *The Birth of Methodism,* p. 75.

30. *Ibid.,* p. 74.

31. *Ibid.,* p. 75.

32. Halévy, *England in 1815,* p. 586. Halévy's comment notes the subtle, often excessively subtle, argument of "Die Protestantische Ethik und der Geist der Kapitalismus," which appeared in *Archiv für Sozialwissenschaft und Sozialpolitik,* vols. 20 and 21 in 1904–5. Weber's essays were not reviewed or summarized in *Revue de Métaphysique,* which did summarize foreign journals including sociological ones, or *l'Année Sociologique* or *Revue Philosophique.*

33. W. G. Pogson Smith, "Reviews of Books: *La Formation du Radicalisme philosophique,*" and Paul Mantoux, "*La Formation du Radicalisme philosophique,*" *Revue de Synthèse Historique* (1901), pp. 121–25.

34. Halévy to Bouglé, May 10, 1903, Halévy papers, Guy-Loé collection.

35. Halévy to Lucien Herr, December 30, 1910, Halévy papers, Guy-Loé collection.

36. Graham Wallas' introduction to Halévy's *History of the English People in the Nineteenth Century,* vol. 1: *England in 1815,* E. I. Watkin and D. A. Barker, trans. (London: Ernest Benn, 1923).

37. Halévy, *The Birth of Methodism,* pp. 39–40.

3. THE "HALÉVY THESIS"

38. Gustave Lanson review of Halévy, *L'Angleterre en 1815*, *Le Matin*, 1913. Halévy papers, Guy-Loé collection.

39. See Esther de Waal's review of John Kent, *Age of Disunity* "Revolution in the Church," *Victorian Studies* (June 1967), 10:435–39, or Eric Hobsbawm, "The British Secret," or his "Methodism and the Threat of Revolution," *Labouring Men*, pp. 27–39 (hereafter referred to as "Methodism and the Threat of Revolution").

40. Halévy, *England in 1815*, pp. 5–9.

41. *Ibid.*, p. 44.

42. *Ibid.*, p. 200.

43. *Ibid.*, pp. 337 and 383.

44. Gillispie, "Elie Halévy," p. 243. This is also the burden of Hobsbawm's argument in "Methodism and the Threat of Revolution."

45. Halévy, *The Birth of Methodism*, pp. 62–72.

46. Halévy, *England in 1815*, p. 383.

47. *Ibid.*, p. 387.

48. Gillispie is one of the few commentators on Halévy who noted his attitude, perhaps overdoing it, p. 244. "Halévy's indulgence, not altogether unmixed with contempt."

49. Halévy, *History of the English People*, vol. 2: *The Liberal Awakening*, p. vi.

50. Halévy, *England in 1815*, p. 424.

51. *Ibid.*, pp. 331–35.

52. Himmelfarb, "The Victorian Ethos: Before and After Victoria," *Victorian Minds*, pp. 292–99.

53. Eric Hobsbawm and George Rudé, *Captain Swing*, p. 13.

54. *Ibid.* See also E. P. Thompson, *The Making of the English Working Class*, pp. 195–97.

55. J. L. and Barbara Hammond, *The Town Labourer 1760–1832*, *The Village Labourer 1760–1832*, *The Skilled Labourer 1760–1832*.

56. E. P. Thompson, *The Making of the English Working Class*, p. 375.

57. J. L. and Barbara Hammond, *The Age of the Chartists; 1832–54; A Study of Discontent*, p. 287.

58. Hobsbawm, "Methodism and the Threat of Revolution," p. 37; *Primitive Rebels* (New York: Norton, 1965), pp. 128–32, 145.

59. Himmelfarb, *Victorian Minds*, pp. 296–97, quoting Halévy, 4:337.

60. Halévy, 4:337.

61. John D. Walsh, "Elie Halévy and the Birth of Methodism," p. 6. See also Owen Chadwick, *The Victorian Church*, 1:370–448; K. S. Inglis, *Churches and the Working Classes in Victorian England*, pp. 325–36; W. R. Ward, *Religion and Society 1790–1850*, pp. 1–105, 135–76; Thomas W. Laquer, *Religion and Respectability: Schools and Working Class Culture 1780–1850*; and James Obelkevich: *Religion and Rural Society*.

3. THE "HALÉVY THESIS"

62. Halévy, *History of the English People*, vol. 5: *Epilogue: Imperialism and the Rise of Labour, 1895–1905*, p. x.

63. Halévy, "The Policy of Social Peace in England," *Era of Tyrannies*, pp. 183—208.

64. Halévy, "The World Crisis of 1914–1918," *Era of Tyrannies*, pp. 246–47.

4. STUDIES IN SOCIALISM

1. The publication of his course lectures as the *Histoire du socialisme européen* (1948) drew together pieces from several sources: some finished lectures which date from the period of the first course at Ecole Libre des Sciences Politiques (1901–3); his students' notes from the period of the 1930s; and his own notes, which were usually brief topical outlines. In 1932–33 there was a photocopy of his lectures on the course "L'Evolution du socialisme anglais de 1815 à nos jours," published by the Librairie des Facultés, and the following year a portion of the course "Le Socialisme en Europe au XXᵉ siècle" was issued. "Les Amis de Elie Halévy" (under Celestin Bouglé's direction until his death in 1940 and then led by Raymond Aron) edited the pieces that they drew together from these diverse sources. The friends were Halévy's former pupils, including Robert Marjolin, Michel Debré, Jean-Marcel Jeanneney, Pierre Laroque, and Etienne Mantoux, the author of *The Carthaginian Peace or the Economic Consequences of Mr. Keynes*. Mantoux was killed in the last months of World War II, before the edition was finished and before his own manuscript was published.

2. *L'Ère des tyrannies* (Paris: Gallimard, 1938) has been translated as the *Era of Tyrannies* by R. K. Webb and published by Anchor in 1965. The work includes: "La Doctrine economique de Saint-Simon," (1907), and (1908); "La Politique de paix sociale en Angleterre. Les 'Whitley Councils' " (1919); "Le Problème du contrôle ouvrier," Conference au Comité National d'Etudes Politiques et Sociales (1921); "L'Etat présent de la question sociale en Angleterre," (1923), pp. 5–29; *Sismondi* Collection Reformateurs Sociaux (1933); "Socialism and the Problem of Democratic Parliamentarianism," (1934); *The World Crisis of 1914–1918: An Interpretation* (1929); "L'Ère des tyrannies," (1936).

3. Melvin Richter, "A Bibliography of Signed Works by Elie Halévy," p. 46. For the effect on English speaking critics of the delayed and random nature of the publication of Halévy's work on socialism, see particularly the review in the *Times Literary Supplement*, November 23, 1967, p. 1102, of *Era of Tyrannies* and the review of the same work by Geoffrey Barraclough, "Historian at the End of His Tether," *New York Review of Books* (January 6, 1966), 3:20–22.

4. Raymond Aron, *Main Currents in Sociological Thought: The Sociologist and the Revolution of 1848*, 1:332. Aron's analysis of Marx follows Halévy's

interpretation rather closely and in Aron's summation of the three sociological approaches he groups himself with Halévy and Montesquieu among the "political sociologists" who are liberal and non-dogmatic and who stress the autonomy of the political order.

5. Halévy to Bouglé, October 1, 1913, *Correspondance*, p. 337.

6. "Extraits du journal d'Elie Halévy," May 1888, *Correspondance*, p. 22.

7. Charles Andler, *La Civilisation socialiste*; Charles Andler, *Le Socialisme d'état en Allemagne*; Celestin Bouglé, *Socialisme français. Du "socialisme utopique" à la "democratie industrielle;"* Celestin Bouglé, *Proudhon* (Paris: Alcan, 1933); Celestin Bouglé, *La Sociologie de Proudhon* (Paris: Colin, 1911); Hubert Bourgin, *Les Systemes socialistes*; Hubert Bourgin, *Proudhon;* Sebastien Charléty, *Essai su l'histoire du Saint-Simonisme*; E. Dolleans, *Histoire du mouvement ouvrier*; Emile Durkheim, *Le Socialisme. Sa Definition. Ses Debuts. La Doctrine Saint-Simonienne*; Charles Gide, *Fourier, Précurseur de la coopération;* Charles Gide and Charles Rist, *Histoire des doctrines économiques depuis les physiocrats jusqu'à nos jours*; Georges Guy-Grand, *Proudhon et l'enseignement du peuple;* Daniel Halévy, *Essais sur le mouvement ouvrier en France;* Maxime Leroy, *Le Socialisme des producteurs: Henri de Saint-Simon;* Georges Sorel, "Essai sur la philosophie de Proudhon," *Revue Philosophique,* 33 (1892); Georges Weill, *L'École Saint-Simonienne* (Paris: Alcan, 1896).

8. Halévy review of "Emile Durkheim, Le Socialisme. Sa Définition: Ses Debuts. La Doctrine Saint-Simonienne." (1929).

9. "Vocabulaire technique et critique de la philosophie," *Bulletin de la Société Française de Philosophie*, 3, 5, 8, 10, 16, 23. See Richter, "Bibliography" for a listing of the topics.

10. *La Doctrine de Saint-Simon. Exposition. Premiere Année, 1829,* Bouglé and Halévy, eds. (1924). Georg Iggers' translation and introduction to *The Doctrine of Saint-Simon: An Exposition. First Year, 1829* (Boston: Beacon Hill, 1958) includes the footnotes and substantial critical notes from the Halévy and Bouglé edition.

11. Aaron Noland, *The Founding of the French Socialist Party, 1893–1905, pp.* 82–85, 137–164. Harvey Mitchell, *Labor and the Origins of Social Democracy in Britain, France, and Germany 1890–1914*, pp. 60–64.

12. Halévy's friend Charles Andler was one of the first translators and commentators on Marx in France. His translation and his "adventurous commentary" (as Halévy described it) on the *Communist Manifesto* was the major French source until the Molitor translation of 1934. See Halévy's review of Molitor's translation of Marx's works, *Revue des Sciences Politiques* (1935), 58:150.

13. Both of the Halévy brothers continued their devotion to these institutions long after the more rigid political positions of the pre-war period had allowed the *université populaire* to atrophy. See Halévy's comments in

4 . STUDIES IN SOCIALISM

"Comment l'Angleterre organise ses universités populaires" *Manuel general de l'instruction primaire* (February–March, 1920), 87:303–05.

14. Daniel to Elie Halévy, January, 1901, Halévy papers, Guy-Loé collection; Daniel Halévy, *Essais sur le mouvement ouvrier en France.*

15. Halévy to Bouglé, Oct. 29, 1901. Halévy papers, Guy-Loé collection.

16. Halévy to Bouglé, October, 1898, Halévy papers, Guy-Loé collection.

17. J. E. S. Hayward, "Solidarity: The Social History of an Idea in Nineteenth Century France," pp. 261–284. See also Hayward's article "The Official Social Philosophy of the French Third Republic: Léon Bourgeois and 'Solidarisme,' " 19–48. Theodore Zeldin, *France 1848–1945,* vol. 1, *Ambition, Love, Politics,* pp. 640–81.

18. John A. Scott, *Republican Ideas and the Liberal Tradition in France,* p. 179.

19. Halévy to Bouglé, May 10, 1906, Halévy papers, Guy-Loé collection.

20. Halévy to Bouglé, December 25, 1906, Halévy papers, Guy-Loé collection.

21. Halévy to Bouglé, September 6, 1906, Halévy papers, Guy-Loé collection.

22. Halévy to Bouglé, February 7, 1899, Halévy papers, Guy-Loé collection.

23. "Era of Tyrannies," *Era of Tyrannies,* p. 271.

24. "Les Principes de la distribution des richesses," (1906), p. 594. This article was written in September 1905, according to Halévy's correspondence with Bouglé, October 2, 1905, Halévy papers, Guy-Loé collection.

25. "Saint Simonian Economic Doctrine," *Era of Tyrannies,* pp. 98–99.

26. Victor Basch, "De la démocratie," *Bulletin de la Société Française de Philosophie* (1907), 7:107–09, 111–12.

27. Halévy to Bouglé, December 27, 1906, Halévy papers, Guy-Loé collection.

28. "Les Principes de la distribution des richesses," p. 594.

29. Halévy to Bouglé, May 10, 1906, Halévy papers, Guy-Loé collection. In another letter to Bouglé, February 27, 1904, Halévy said: "The French quarrel over doctrines. Theories of socialism are French but the realities are German."

30. Werner Sombart, *Socialism and the Social Movement.* Sombart also distinguished moral criticism such as Christian socialism or "ethical economists" from those who accepted industrialization, which Halévy did not do. By the sixth edition Sombart's commitment to industrialization changed, as did his grouping together of socialism and capitalism as progressive forces.

4. STUDIES IN SOCIALISM

31. Ludwig von Mises, *Socialism*, pp. 239–80.

32. Halévy's lectures appended to the first edition of *Histoire du socialisme européen* include "Friedrich List and National Political Economy," "Marxism and Syndicalism," "Two English Theorists: Ruskin and Carlyle," "German Historism."

33. Halévy, *Histoire du socialisme européen*, p. 18.

34. "Vocabulaire technique et critique," *Bulletin de la Société Française de Philosophie* (January–February, 1917), 17:54.

35. *Ibid.*, p. 55, n.

36. Halévy to Bouglé, October 29, 1901, samedi 9 (November 1901), Halévy papers. November 24, 1901, *Correspondence*, p. 327. Also *Histoire du socialisme européen*, p. 75.

37. Halévy, *Histoire du socialisme européen*, p. 126.

38. Halévy, "The World Crisis of 1914–1918: An Interpretation," *The Era of Tyrannies*, p. 214 (hereafter referred to as "The World Crisis"). See also "Saint-Simonian Economic Doctrine" (1907), *Era of Tyrannies*, p. 21.

39. Georges Sorel, "Le Materialisme historique," *Bulletin de la Société Française de Philosophie* (1902), 2:91–122. Halévy, *Thomas Hodgskin*, A. J. Taylor, trans. (London: Ernest Benn, 1956). The two early lectures—"La Conception materialiste de l'histoire" and "Le Capital. La theorie de la valeur"—date from 1901–03. The article "Les Principes de la distribution des richesses," pp. 545–95. There is no indication in the interpretation of "La Jeunesse de Marx et la formation du Marxisme 1836–48" and "La Lutte des classes et l'evolution du capitalisme" that would date them, although the footnotes cite the Molitor (1924) translation of Marx's work, but neither indicates an altered view of Marx.

40. Halévy reviewing A. Aftalion "Les Fondements du socialisme," *Bulletin de la Société Française de Philosophie* (1924), 13:6.

41. Halévy, *Histoire du socialisme européen*, pp. 94–95.

42. Raymond Aron, "Séance pour le centenaire de Elie Halévy," pp. 27–28.

43. Halévy to Bouglé, November 21, 1907, printed in part in *Histoire du socialisme européen*, p. 76 n.

44. Halévy, *Histoire du socialisme européen*, pp. 76ff. The early lectures include a substantial inquiry into the historicists, the work of Friedrich List and of the *Kathedrasozialisten*. Privately Halévy dismissed the historicist school as intellectual lightweights when he wrote to Bouglé: "Neither Schmoller, nor Wagner, nor all the professors, nor all the electics interests me. I am sticking totally to Karl Marx. (Surely you have read the chapter on the division of labor?) Marxism will be the pivot of my course this winter. The course, if it becomes a regular one, could be entitled: 'Critique or critical appreciation of modern socialism.' Do you approve?" (November 9, 1901, Halévy papers, Guy-Loé collection.) He, nonetheless, included their contributions to economic thought in his lectures. More importantly he ac-

knowledges their importance in the nurture of German *statist* tendencies.

45. Georges Sorel, "Le Materialisme historique," p. 115.

46. Sorel had already published an important little book, *L'Avenir socialiste des Syndicats* (1897), under the influence of Ferdinand Pelloutier, the leader of the syndicalist movement in France, whose book *Histoire des Bourses du Travail* (1902) Sorel and Daniel Halévy had published. Since 1899 Sorel, Daniel Halévy, Edward Berth, and Victor Griffuelhes were regular contributors to Hubert Lagardelle's paper *Le Mouvement Socialiste*, the tribune of the syndicalist movement. Halévy thought Sorel was the disciple of Croce and the Italians and that Sorel's influence on his generation was so considerable that he deserved attention himself. See his obituary, "Georges Sorel 1847–1922," *Revue de Métaphysique* (1922), 29:1–2. Both Halévy and Werner Sombart thought Sorel was Roberto Michel's mentor, but Halévy dismissed Michel's work as lacking the brilliant insights one expects from the Sorellans. See Halévy's review of Michel's *Die Verelendungstheorie,* (1929), pp. 470–71.

47. Sorel, "Le Materialisme historique," p. 110.

48. Halévy's comment to Sorel's statement, *ibid.*, p. 97.

49. Halévy's comment, *ibid.*, p. 119.

50. Halévy, *Histoire du socialisme européen*, p. 126. See also his comment on A. Aftalion's "Les Fondements du socialisme," p. 5.

51. Halévy's comment on Aftalion, p. 5.

52. André Lichtenberger, *Le Socialisme au XVIIIe siècle* (Paris: Alcan, 1895); Celestin Bouglé, *Socialismes français;* Maxime Leroy, *Histoire des idées sociales en France*, vol. 1; George Lichtheim, *The Origins of Socialism* (New York: Praeger, 1969); J. L. Talmon, *The Origins of Totalitarian Democracy* (New York: Norton, 1970).

53. Halévy, *Histoire du socialisme européen*, p. 18.

54. *Ibid.*, pp. 21–23.

55. Halévy to Bouglé, November 1902, "lundi 24," Halévy papers, Guy-Loé collection.

56. Halévy to Bouglé, December 19, 1901, *Correspondance*, p. 327.

57. Halévy, *Thomas Hodgskin*, pp. 167–68.

58. Halévy, *Philosophic Radicalism*, pp. 223–24, for discussion of the Godwinian argument that ego and egoism would cease with the end of ownership. See also *Thomas Hodgskin*, pp. 32–36.

59. Halévy, *Thomas Hodgskin*, pp. 80, 55, 110, and 105, the latter quoting Hodgskin's *Popular Political Economy*, four lectures delivered at London Mechanics Institution in 1827.

60. *Ibid.*, p. 115, quoting Hodgskin, *The Natural and Artificial Right of Property*, pp. 19–21.

61. Halévy, *Histoire du socialisme européen*, p. 35.

62. Halévy, *Thomas Hodgskin*, p. 169.

63. Halévy, *Histoire du socialisme européen*, p. 343. During *la belle*

4 . STUDIES IN SOCIALISM

époque the influence of Ruskin was important on the thought of Proust and others, but also on the socialist impulse that developed from the aesthetic rejection of the bourgeoisie.

64. *Times Literary Supplement* (March 23, 1956) 55:175 makes the second point. See also François Bedarida's excellent article, "Elie Halévy et le socialisme anglais," pp. 377–79.

65. Halévy, *Thomas Hodgskin*, p. 180.

66. Halévy to Bouglé, January 5, 1902, Halévy papers, Guy-Loé collection. Gillispie's observation that from *Philosophic Radicalism* one might gain the impression that Halévy believed that the "chief practical influence of ideas comes after they have hardened into dogmas and . . . that what often converts ideas to dogmas is their applicability to real interests in definite circumstances" is even more apt a comment regarding socialist ideology (Gillispie, "Elie Halévy," p. 236).

67. "La Doctrine économique de Saint-Simon," (1907 and 1908). Also Halévy and Bouglé, "Introduction," *La Doctrine de Saint-Simon. Exposition. Première Année, 1829.* Reprinted as "Saint-Simonian Economic Doctrine," *The Era of Tyrannies.*

68. *Ibid.*, p. 21.

69. *Ibid.*, pp. 40–45. Halévy believed the influence of the theocratic school reinforced Saint-Simon's authoritarian tendencies. This coincided with Comte's secretaryship to Saint-Simon, but Halévy argued that these tendencies were present in the last months of Augustin Thierry's collaboration with Saint-Simon and led to the break (*ibid.*, p. 35). Here Halévy took sides against the positivists, including Comte, who argued that Saint-Simon's system made this break from liberalism under the influence of Comte, de Bonald, and de Maistre.

70. *Ibid.*, pp. 50 and 53.

71. *Ibid.*, p. 54.

72. *Ibid.*, p. 58.

73. *Ibid.*, pp. 81–82.

74. *Ibid.*, p. 90, quoting *Exposition de la doctrine de Saint-Simon,* 1:134.

75. Halévy, *The Era of Tyrannies*, p. 96.

76. *Ibid.*, pp. 98–99.

77. *Ibid.*, pp. 103–04.

78. Maxime Leroy, *Le Socialisme des producteurs: Henri de Saint-Simon; La Vie de Comte de Saint-Simon* (Paris: 1925); M. Bourbannais, *Le Neo-Saint Simonisme et la vue sociale d'aujourd'hui* (Paris: Presses Universitaires Françaises, 1923); G. Brunet, *Le Mysticisme sociale de Saint-Simon* (Paris: PUF, 1925); G. Gignoux, *Revue d'histoire des doctrines économiques et sociales* (Paris: A. Colin, 1923); Gottfried Salomon, *Saint-Simon und der Sozialismus. Wege zum Socialismus* (Berlin, 1919). Vergeot's *Le Credit comme stimulant et régulateur de l'industrie: La Conception de Saint-Simon* was published in 1918.

79. Roy F. Harrod, *John Maynard Keynes* (New York: Harcourt, 1951), pp. 379–86.

4. STUDIES IN SOCIALISM

80. Halévy, "La Politique de paix sociale en Angleterre. Les 'Whitley Councils' " (1919); "Le Problème du contrôle ouvrier" (1921); and "L'Etat present de la question sociale en Angleterre" (1922). All three discussions are reprinted in the *Era of Tyrannies*.

81. Halévy, "The Policy of Social Peace," *Era of Tyrannies*, p. 106.

82. Halévy to Léon, March 19, 1919, Halévy papers, Guy-Loé Collection.

83. Halévy, "The Problem of Worker Control," *Era of Tyrannies*, p. 179.

84. Elie Halévy comments on Bouglé, "La Sociologie de Proudhon," *Bulletin de la Société Française de Philosophie* (1912), 11–12:173–75, 177, 190, 196.

85. Halévy, "Sismondi: A Critique of Industrialist Optimism," *Era of Tyrannies*, p. 20.

86. Halévy, "Saint-Simonian Economic Doctrine," *Era of Tyrannies*, p. 101.

87. Halévy used this same lineage from Bismarckian socialist insurance to Saint-Simon by way of Blanc and Lassalle in a review essay of Gaston Isambert's "Les Idées socialistes en France de 1815 à 1848" (1906). Halévy in this review raised this genealogy to question the general thesis that the French socialist tradition was humanitarian, fraternal, *solidariste*, in contradistinction to the German determinist, materialist, and statist heritage, Although Halévy's work on socialism can be fitted loosely within this thesis. Halévy did not stress his sense of contradictions inherent in socialism strongly before the war, but the idea was there as early as 1906. He pointed to the Blanquist secret revolutionary societies after the Lyons insurrection of 1831 with their fusion of revolutionary and socialist ideals. Although the stress is not so great as after the war, Halévy's sense of the organizing and terrorist potential of socialism itself, regardless of its nationality, is apparent. The Bolshevik Revolution furnished parallels among Babeuf, Blanqui, Gustave Hervé, and Lenin (*Histoire du socialisme européen*, p. 60). See also "Era of Tyrannies," p. 278.

88. Halévy, "Saint-Simonian Economic Doctrine," pp. 102–103.

5. THE ORDEAL OF THE WORLD WAR

1. See Halévy's comments during the session of the Société Française de Philosophie of December 30, 1907. T. Ruyssen, "Pacifisme et patriotisme," *Bulletin de la Société Française de Philosophie* (1908), 8:54, 59, 61. Halévy's letter to Alain of March 8, 1913 passionately rejected an article by Alain that attacked the draft on pacifist grounds. The letter is printed in the *Correspondance*, pp. 130–32.

2. Halévy, "The World Crisis of 1914–18: An Interpretation," *The Era of Tyrannies*, p. 247.

3. Halévy to Léon, November 21, 1917, *Correspondance*, p. 366.

4. Halévy to Léon, December 16, 1916, Halévy papers, Guy-Loé collec-

tion. "If I should have the misfortune to bury you and I want to give the impression of your political wisdom, I would only have to publish a collection of your letters that you have sent to me for the last twenty months. I would not be able to say as much for any other of my correspondents."

5. Halévy to Léon, November 26, 1914, printed in part in *Correspondance*, p. 342.

6. Halévy to Léon, October 11, 1915, *Correspondance pp.* 352–53. See also Halévy to Léon, February 3, 1916, p. 356.

7. Halévy to Léon, November 26, 1914, *Correspondance*, p. 342.

8. Halévy to Léon, February 11, 1915, and June 5, 1915, Halévy papers, Guy-Loé collection.

9. Halévy to Léon, June 5, 1915, *Correspondance*, p. 348.

10. Halévy to Léon, February 11, 1915, printed in part, *Correspondance*, pp. 344–45.

11. Halévy to Léon, September 23, 1914, *Correspondance*, p. 340, and November 26, 1914, *Correspondance*, p. 342.

12. Halévy to Léon, October 21, 1914, printed in part, *Correspondance*, p. 341.

13. Halévy to Léon, September 23, 1914, *Correspondance*, p. 340.

14. Halévy to Léon, December 16, 1916, Halévy papers, Guy-Loé collection.

15. Halévy to Léon, October 21, 1914, *Correspondance*, p. 341.

16. Halévy to Léon, September 12, 1916, Halévy papers, Guy-Loé collection.

17. Halévy to Léon, December 13, 1916, Halévy papers, Guy-Loé collection.

18. Halévy to Léon, December 9, 1916, Halévy papers, Guy-Loé collection.

19. Halévy to Léon, March 28, 1917, and April 24, 1917, Halévy papers, Guy-Loé collection.

20. Halévy to Léon, October 12, 1917, Halévy papers, Guy-Loé collection.

21. Halévy's unpublished and incomplete essay on the French parliamentary system, which was written some time after the condemnation of Malvy. Halévy papers, Guy-Loé collection.

22. Halévy to Léon, December 1916, Halévy papers, Guy-Loé collection.

23. Halévy did write one piece of propaganda during the war which was published anonymously in 1917, *La Part de la France*, a pamphlet in the form of a letter from a French soldier to American soldiers. A remarkably restrained pamphlet, it attempted to explain the sources of French pride to the American allies. The work was identified by Halévy's niece and executor, Docteur Henriette Noufflard Guy-Loé. The work is listed in Melvin Richter's "Bibliography."

5 . THE ORDEAL OF THE WORLD WAR

24. Halévy to Léon, December 15, 1914, *Correspondance*, p. 343.

25. Halévy to Léon, October 9, 1916, *Correspondance*, pp. 360–61.

26. Halévy to Léon, April 12, 1916, Halévy papers, Guy-Loé collection.

27. Halévy to Léon, November 14, 1915, Halévy papers, Guy-Loé collection.

28. Halévy to Léon, March 1, 1915, *Correspondance*, pp. 345–46.

29. Halévy to Léon, October 5, 1916, *Correspondance*, p. 360 and September 12, 1915, *Correspondance*, p. 352.

30. Halévy to Léon, November 22, 1917, Halévy papers, Guy-Loé collection.

31. Halévy to Léon, August 20, 1916, Halévy papers, Guy-Loé collection.

32. Halévy to Léon, January 10, 1917, Halévy papers, Guy-Loé collection.

33. Halévy to Léon, September 18, 1917, Halévy papers, Guy-Loé collection.

34. Halévy to Léon, January 10, 1917, Halévy papers, Guy-Loé collection.

35. Halévy to Léon, September 29, 1917, Halévy papers, Guy-Loé collection.

36. Halévy to Léon, December 30, 1918, Halévy papers, Guy-Loé collection. See also Halévy to Bouglé, March 23, 1918, and June 8, 1918, *Correspondance*, pp. 367–68.

37. Halévy to Léon, December 30, 1918, Halévy papers, Guy-Loé collection. See also March 24, 1916, *Correspondance*, pp. 356–57.

38. Halévy to Léon, January 14, 1919, Halévy papers, Guy-Loé collection.

39. "Introduction," *History of the English People*, vol. 2: *The Liberal Awakening* (New York: Barnes and Noble, 1916), pp. ix–x.

40. Melvin Richter, "Elie Halévy," *International Encyclopedia of Social Sciences*.

41. Angleterre carton, Halévy papers, Ecole Normale Supérieure. There are many letters, memos from labor leaders, employers, administrators from whom Halévy received information or of whom he made inquiries about the workings of the Whitley Councils, the nationalization proposals in the coal industry, inspection schemes, etc. There are as well innumerable clippings and drafts of legislation sent by English friends.

42. Sebastien Charléty, "Elie Halévy, 1870–1937," pp. 422–26.

43. Halévy, "Viscount Morley 'Les Souvenirs de Lord Morley,' " *Revue de Métaphysique* (1918). Actually Halévy wrote three reviews related to "honest John." "Morley, 'Recollections' " (August–December 1918; the long essay in *Revue de Métaphysique*; and "J. H. Morley, *John Viscount Morley, An Appreciation and Some Reminiscences*" (1925).

44. "Viscount Morley 'Les Souvenirs de Lord Morley,' " p. 96.

5 . THE ORDEAL OF THE WORLD WAR

45. Halévy to chief subeditor of *The Spectator*, January 12, 1930, Halévy papers, Guy-Loé collection.

46. Halévy, "Le Problème des nationalities," *Revue de Métaphysique* (1939). This paper was given at Oxford in September 1920 and reprinted in memoriam. It was originally printed in the *Proceedings of the Aristotelian Society*, (1919–20).

47. *Ibid.*, p. 148.

48. Halévy, "L'Opinion anglaise et la France" (1923).

49. *Ibid.*, p. 359.

50. In general Halévy resisted parallels between 1815 and 1918. He did comment that he brought new insights to the problems of England after the Napoleonic Wars because of his personal experience of the Great War, that his own judgment of Canning was negative and his positive estimation of Peel reflected his wartime re-evaluations (2:ix–x).

51. Halévy, "L'Opinion anglaise et la France," p. 365.

52. Halévy, "Les Rapports franco-anglais de 1882 à 1914" (October 15, 1937), p. 1003.

53. Halévy, "Les Origines de la discorde anglo-allemande" (February 1, 1921). The *Daily Telegraph* had published before the war a series of articles by a Silesian Junker, Baron von Eckardstein, in which he revealed, as he repeated in his *Souvenirs*, that he, as secretary to the ambassador to London under Count Hatzfeldt, had participated in discussions with important English figures. These discussions, had they been successful, would have drawn England from isolation into an alliance aimed at France and Russia (*Daily Telegraph*, August 15, 19, 26, 28, September 7, 10, 11, 1912). Halévy's second article was "Les Origines de l'Entente (1902–3)" (1924).

54. Halévy, *L' Angleterre et son Empire* (1905).

55. Halévy, "Franco-German Relations since 1870," *History* (1924), p. 18.

56. *Ibid.*, p. 28. In World War II Halévy's student, Etienne Mantoux, the son of historian Paul Mantoux, wrote *The Carthaginian Peace* to forestall the resurrection of the revisionism inspired by Keynes's *Economic Consequences of the Peace*. He wrote his book in English and left the manuscript with Halévy's widow shortly before he died in the liberation of France.

57. Halévy, "Documents anglais sur les origines de la guerre" (1927), p. 788. This theme, particularly in the *Epilogue*, has influenced the work of George Dangerfield, *The Strange Death of Liberal England*.

58. Halévy, "L'Angleterre sur le seuil de la guerre (aôut 1913–*aôut* 1914)" (1931), pp. 32, 36.

59. Halévy, "The World Crisis: An Appreciation," *The Era of Tyrannies*, p. 215.

60. *Ibid.*, p. 216. This fundamentally liberal argument continues in Carl Schorske, *German Social Democracy* (Cambridge, Mass.: Harvard University Press, 1955), and Rudolf Caper, *Failure of a Revolution* (Cambridge: Cam-

bridge at the University Press, 1955). For a critique of this thesis see James McRandle, "The German Revolution," *The Track of the Wolf* (Evanston, Ill.: Northwestern University Press, 1965). The failure of the German Social Democratic Party to make a revolution, either democratic or socialist, perplexes most historians of modern Germany. Halévy never thought that it was capable of attempting revolution.

61. "The World Crisis," *The Era of Tyrannies*, pp. 221–22.

62. *Ibid.*, p. 223.

63. *Ibid.*, p. 224.

64. *Ibid.*, p. 233.

65. *Ibid.*, p. 234. For this thesis Halévy acknowledged his debt to Albert Sorel whom he had always admired.

66. *Ibid.*, p. 235.

67. *Ibid.*, p. 241.

68. *Ibid.*, pp. 243 and 245.

69. *Ibid.*, p. 244.

70. Halévy, *The History of the English People*, vol. 6: *Epilogue: The Rule of Democracy* (New York: Barnes and Noble, 1961), pp. 621ff.

71. Charles Seignobos review of Halévy, *Epilogue: Vers la democratie sociale et vers la guerre, 1905–1914* in *Revue Critique d'Histoire et de Litterature* (1932), p. 565.

72. Halévy to Bouglé, August 20, 1903, *Correspondance*, p. 329.

73. Barraclough, "Historian at the End of His Tether," pp. 20–22.

74. Stern, "A Note on 'The World Crisis of 1914–1918,' " *The Era of Tyrannies*, p. 323.

75. Halévy, "The World Crisis," p. 245.

76. *Ibid.*, p. 246.

77. *Ibid.*, p. 247.

6. The Era of Tyrannies

1. Halévy, "The Era of Tyrannies," *The Era of Tyrannies*, p. 265.

2. *Ibid.*, p. 266.

3. *Ibid.*, p. 267.

4. *Ibid.*

5. Max Lazard's comment, *Bulletin de la Société Française de Philosophie: Séance du 28 novembre 1936*, p. 186 (hereafter referred to as *Bulletin 1936*).

6. Communication from Marcel Mauss, printed in the *Appendice, Bulletin 1936*, p. 234.

7. Halévy actively supported the Italian antifascists, particularly Salvemini and the Rosselli brothers. The latter, though exiles in France, were assassinated by Mussolini's agents. He frequently requested aid for refugee Jews or political liberals trying to get to England. His letters from Italy were extremely critical of the regime.

8. Halévy, "The Era of Tyrannies," p. 306.

6. THE ERA OF TYRANNIES

6. THE ERA OF TYRANNIES

9. Maublanc's comment, *Bulletin 1936,* 36:219.

10. Halévy, "The Era of Tyrannies," p. 274.

11. *Ibid.,* p. 275.

12. Berthelot comment, *Bulletin 1936,* pp. 207–19.

13. Halévy's response to Robert Marjolin, "The Era of Tyrannies," p. 281.

14. Halévy, "The Era of Tyrannies," p. 272.

15. *Ibid.,* pp. 315–16.

16. *Ibid.,* p. 307.

17. Halévy, "Socialism and the Problem of Democratic Parliamentarianism," *The Era of Tyrannies,* pp. 260–61.

18. Halévy, "The Era of Tyrannies," p. 275.

19. Halévy to Léon, March 24, 1916, *Correspondence,* p. 358.

20. Halévy, "The World Crisis," *The Era of Tyrannies,* pp. 244–45.

21. Halévy, "The Era of Tyrannies," pp. 265–66, 272–73. See also "Saint-Simonian Economic Doctrine," pp. 100–04.

22. "The Era of Tyrannies," pp. 274 and 280.

23. *Ibid.,* pp. 313–14.

24. Bouglé's comment, *Bulletin 1936,* pp. 198–99.

25. Halévy, "The Policy of Social Peace in England," *The Era of Tyrannies,* pp. 105–07. See also "The Problem of Worker Control," pp. 159–81, and "The State of The Social Question in England," pp. 183–207.

26. Halévy, "Saint-Simonian Economic Doctrine," *The Era of Tyrannies,* pp. 103–04.

27. Halévy, "Après les elections anglaises," *Revue de Paris* (1919), p. 215.

28. *Ibid.*

29. Halévy, "The Era of Tyrannies," p. 313.

30. Halévy, "Socialism and the Problem of Democratic Parliamentarianism," pp. 260–64. This is also the theme of Halévy's contribution to "L'Angleterre: Grandeur, decadence et peristance du liberalisme en Angleterre," *Inventaires,* (1936).

31. Halévy, "Socialism and the Problem of Democratic Parliamentarianism," *The Era of Tyrannies,* pp. 258–60.

32. Halévy to Bouglé, April 20, 1934, Halévy papers, Guy-Loé collection.

33. Halévy, "Socialism and the Problem of Democratic Parliamentarianism," *The Era of Tyrannies,* pp. 250 and 255.

34. Halévy, "State of the Social Questions in England," *The Era of Tyrannies,* p. 206.

35. Berthelot's comment, *Bulletin 1936,* p. 219.

36. Halévy "The Era of Tyrannies," p. 316.

37. Bouglé's comment, *Bulletin 1936,* p. 197.

38. Maublanc, *Bulletin 1936,* pp. 221–23.

6. THE ERA OF TYRANNIES

39. Aron, *Bulletin 1936*, p. 227.

40. Roger Lacombe's comment, "The Era of Tyrannies," Appendix ii, p. 297.

41. Halévy, "The Era of Tyrannies," p. 280.

42. Halévy to Mantoux, September 20, 1934, *Correspondance,* pp. 372–73. Halévy and his wife traveled in the Soviet Union in the 1930s and were frequent visitors to Italy.

43. Halévy, "The Era of Tyrannies," pp. 283–84, 313–14.

44. Halévy to Mantoux, September 20, 1934, *Correspondance,* p. 373.

45. Halévy, "The Era of Tyrannies," p. 270.

46. Gillispie, "Elie Halévy," p. 249.

47. Halévy, "The Era of Tyrannies," p. 271.

48. Halévy, "Socialism and the Problem of Democratic Parliamentarianism," *The Era of Tyrannies,* p. 261.

49. Halévy, "The Era of Tyrannies," p. 315.

50. See Ehrmann's comment on this point of Halévy's *Histoire du socialisme européen* in "Recent Writings on the French Labor Movement," *Journal of Modern History* (1950), 22:151–58.

Bibliography

Manuscript Collections

Elie Halévy papers. Collection of Docteur Henriette Noufflard Guy-Loé. Sucy-en-Brie, Seine et Oise, France.
Elie Halévy papers. Collection of the Ecole Normale Supérieure.
Xavier Léon papers. Collection of the Bibliothèque Victor Cousin.

Works by Elie Halévy

[Halévy and Léon Brunschvicg]. "La Philosophie au Collège de France." *Revue de Métaphysique et de Morale* (1893), 1:369–81.
Review of *Platon, sa philosophie,* by Charles Benard. *Revue de Métaphysique et de Morale* (1893), 1:288–301.
Review of *Theon de Smyrne: Exposition des connaissances mathematiques utiles pour la lecture de Platon,* by J. Dupuis. *Revue de Métaphysique et de Morale* (1893), 1:281–88.
Review of *La Causalité efficiente,* by G.-F. Fonsegreve. *Revue de Métaphysique et de Morale* (1893), 1:607 14.
Review of *Salomé,* by Oscar Wilde. *The Cambridge Observer* (1893), 1:3–4.
Review of *L'Année philosophique,* F. Pillon, ed. *Revue de Métaphysique et de Morale* (1894), 2:473–96, 563–90.
La Théorie platonicienne des sciences. Paris: Alcan, 1896.
"Quelques Remarques sur l'irreversibilité des phénomènes psychologiques." *Revue de Métaphysique et de Morale* (1896), 4:756–77.
"Les 'Seminaires' philosophiques et l'état actuel des études de

philosophie aux universités de Berlin et de Leipzig." *Revue International de l'Enseignement* (1896), 32:504–21.

Review of *Die Lehre des Socrates als sociales Reform-system*, by A. Doring. *Revue de Métaphysique et de Morale* (1896), 4:86–117.

Review of Der echte und der Xenophontische Socrates, by K. Joel. *Revue de Métaphysique et de Morale* (1896), 4:86–117.

"L'Explication du sentiment." *Revue de Métaphysique et de Morale* (1897), 5:703–24.

"Quelques Remarques sur la notion d'intensité en psychologie." *Revue de Métaphysique et de Morale* (1898), 6:589–607.

"De l'association des idées." Communication au Premier Congrès International de Philosophie, *Bibliothèque du Congrès de 1900;* Paris: Armand Colin, Pp. 219–35.

De Concatenatione quae inter affectiones mentis propter similitudinem fieri dicitur. Paris: Alcan, 1901.

La Formation du radicalisme philosophique. Vol. 1: *La Jeunesse de Bentham.* Vol. 2: *L'Evolution de la doctrine utilitaire de 1789 à 1815.* Paris: Alcan, 1901.

Review of "De l'organisation et du rôle des sciences politiques," by Gabriel Alix, Léon Abrami, Georges Lecarpentier, Gaston Salaun, and Robert Savary. *Revue des Sciences Politiques* (1902), 17:273–77.

Thomas Hodgskin (1787–1869). Paris: Société Nouvelle de Librairie et d'Édition, 1903.

La Formation du radicalisme philosophique. Vol. 3: *Le Radicalisme philosophique.* Paris: Alcan, 1904.

Review of "L'Individuel et le social," by Vilfredo Pareto. *Revue de Métaphysique et de Morale* (1904), 12:1103–13.

L'Angleterre et son empire. Paris: Pages Libres, 1905.

"La Naissance du Methodisme en Angleterre." *Revue de Paris,* (1906), 13:519–39, 841–67.

"Notre Enquête sur l'évolution pacifique de la vie internationale." *La Paix par le Droit* (1906), 16:49–53.

Les Principes de la distribution des richesses." *Revue de Métaphysique et de Morale* (1906), 14:545–95.

Review of *Les Idées socialistes en France de 1815 à 1848,* by Gaston Isambert. *Revue des Sciences Politiques* (1906), 21:407–09.

"La Doctrine économique de Saint-Simon." *La Revue du Mois* (1907), 4:641–76 and (1908), 6:39–75.

Review of *La Reine Victoria, d'après sa correspondance inédite.* Jacques Bardoux, trans. *Journal des Savants* (1908), 6:530–42.

Histoire du peuple anglais au XIXe siècle. Vol. 1: *l'Angleterre en 1815.* Paris: Hachette, 1912.

"Le Droit de dissolution en Angleterre." *Correspondance de l'Union pour la Vérité* (1912) 20:656–64.

"La Question de la population." *La Revue du Mois* (1913), 16:84–85.

Review of *Londres et les ouvriers de Londres,* by D. Pasquet. *Revue des Sciences Politiques* (1914), 32:232–38.

[anonymously published]. *La Part de la France. Lettre ouverte d'un soldat français aux soldats américains.* Paris: Attinger Frères, 1917.

Review of *Les Souvenirs,* by John Morley. *Revue de Métaphysique et de Morale* (1918), 25:83–97.

Review of *Recollections* by John Morley. *Revue des Sciences Politiques* (1918), 40:316–17.

"La Politique de paix sociale en Angleterre. Les 'Whitley Councils.' " *Revue d'Economie Politique* (1919), 33:385–431.

"Après les élections anglaises." *Revue de Paris* (1919), 26:207–24.

"La Nouvelle Loi scolaire anglaise." *Revue de Paris* (1919), 26:596–621.

"Le Problème des élections anglaises." *Revue Politique et Parliamentaire* (1919), 98:227–46.

"The Problem of Nationalities." *Proceedings of the Aristotelian Society.* London. (1919–20), N.S. 20:237–42.

"Comment l'Angleterre organise ses universités populaires." *Manuel general de l'instruction primaire* (February–March 1920), 87:303–5.

"Comment Lord Palmerston passa grand homme." *Revue des Sciences Politiques* (1921), 44:523–46.

"Chartism." *Quarterly Review,* (1921), 236:62–73.

"Le problème du contrôle ouvrier." Conference au Comité National l'Études Politiques et Sociales. (March 1921) Reprinted in *l'Ère des Tyrannies. Études sur le socialisme et la guerre.* Paris: Gallimard, 1938.

"Les origines de la discorde anglo-allemande," *Revue de Paris* (1921) 28:563–83.

"France and Silesia." *New Statesman* (1921), 17:185.

"Comment fut votée la loi anglaise de fabriques en 1833." *Revue d'Histoire Economique et Sociale* (1922), 10:252–65.

L'État present de la question sociale en Angleterre." *Revue Politique et Parliamentaire* (1922), 112:5–29.

Histoire du peuple anglais au XIXe siècle. Vol. 2: *Du lendemain de Waterloo à la veille du Reform Bill* (1815–1830). Vol. 3: *De la crise du*

Reform Bill a l'avenement de Sir Robert Peel (1830–1841). Paris: Hachette, 1923.

"L'Opinion anglaise et la France." *Revue Politique et Parliamentaire*, (1923), 117:354–71.

Review of *Les Fondements du socialisme*, by Albert Aftalion. *Revue des Sciences Politiques* (1923), 46:309–10.

Review of *Insurance by Industry Examined*, by Joseph L. Cohen. *Revue des Sciences Politiques* (1923), 46:465.

Review of *Workshop Organization*, by G. D. H. Cole. *Revue des Sciences Politiques* (1923), 46:624–25.

Review of *History of Modern Europe 1878–1919*, by G. P. Gooch. *Revue des Sciences Politiques*, (1923), 46:469–70.

Review of *The Life and Work of Sir James Kay Shuttleworth*, by Frank Smith. *Revue des Sciences Politiques* (1923), 46:301–02.

Review of *British History in the Nineteenth Century 1782–1901*, by G. Trevelyan. *History* (1923), 7:308–10.

Review of *The Miners' Unions of Northumberland and Durham*, by E. Welbourne. *Revue des Sciences Politiques* (1923), 46:623.

Review of *The Third Winter of Unemployment*. *Revue des Sciences Politiques* (1923), 46:624.

La Doctrine de Saint-Simon. Exposition. Première Année, 1829. Elie Halévy and Celestin Bouglé eds. Paris: Rivière, 1924.

"Franco-German Relations since 1870." *History* (1924), 9:18–29.

"Les Origines de l'Entente (1902–3)." *Revue de Paris* (1924), 31:293–318.

Review of *La Génèse de la guerre*, by H. H. Asquith. *Revue des Sciences Politiques* (1924), 47:608–10.

Review of *Delivrons-nous du marxisme*, by Lucien Deslinieres. *Revue des Sciences Politiques* (1924), 47:607–08.

Review of *Wilberforce: A Narrative*, by R. Coupland. *History* (1924), 9:255–57.

Review of *Lord Shaftesbury*, by J. L. Hammond and Barbara Hammond. *History* (1924), 9:255–57.

Review of *The Triumph of Lord Palmerston*, by B. Kingsley Martin. *Revue des Sciences Politiques* (1924) 47:607.

Review of *The Cambridge History of British Foreign Policy*, A. W. Ward and G. P. Gooch, eds. *History* (1924), 9:70–71.

Review of *Freedom and Unity*, by R. Coupland. *History* (1925), 10: 187.

BIBLIOGRAPHY

Review of *King Edward VII. A Biography*, by Sidney Lee. *Revue des Sciences Politiques* (1925), 48:275–81.

Review of *John Viscount Morley, An Appreciation and Some Reminiscences*, by J. H. Morgan. *Revue des Sciences Politiques* (1925), 48:603–04.

Review of *La Crise du Ministère Walpole en 1733–1734*, by Paul Vaucher. *Revue des Sciences Politiques* (1925), 48:464–66.

Review of *Robert Walpole et la politique de Fleury (1731–42)*, by Paul Vaucher. *Revue des Sciences Politiques* (1925) 48:464–66.

Histoire du peuple anglais au XIXe siècle. Épilogue (1895–1914). Vol. 5: *Les Imperialistes au pouvoir (1895–1905)*. Paris: Hachette, 1926.

"Une Chapitre de l'histoire des Trade Unions." *Revues des Études Cooperatives: Problèmes d'Economie Nationale et Internationale* (1926), 20:353–82.

Review of *The Evolution of French Canada*, by Jean Charlemagne Bracq. *History* (1926), 11:167.

Review of *Great Britain. The Nations of To-Day: A New History of the World*, John Buchan, ed. *History* (1926), 11:174–75.

Review of *Organized Labour: An Introduction to Trade Unionism*, by G. D. H. Cole. *Revue des Sciences Politiques* (1926), 49:140–41.

Review of *The International Anarchy, 1904–1914*, by G. Lowes Dickinson. *Revue des Sciences Politiques* (1926), 49:293–94.

Review of *The Church of England*, by Arthur C. Headlam. *Revue des Sciences Politiques*, (1926), 49:146–47.

Review of *English Political Institutions*, by J. A. R. Marriott. *History* (1926), 49:184–85.

Review of *L'Angleterre et sa politique étrangère et interieure (1900–1914)*, by François Novion. *Revue des Sciences Politiques* (1926), 49:318.

Review of *Isvolsky and the World War*, by Friedrich Stieve. *Revue des Sciences Politiques* (1926), 49:292–93.

Review of *The Foreign Policy of Canning*, by Harold Temperley. *Revue des Sciences Politiques* (1926), 49:315–16.

Review of *The Selbourne Memorandum: A Review of the British South African Colonies in 1907*, Basil Williams, ed. *History* (1926), 11:271.

"L'Année politique 1925 en Angleterre." *L'Année politique française et étrangère* (1926), 2:156–92.

"Documents anglais sur les origines de la guerre." *Revue de Paris* (1927), 34:776–95.

BIBLIOGRAPHY

"Conditions of Life in Europe. Reaction and Readjustment to Changed Conditions in All the Nations Party to the Napoleonic Wars." *Universal History of the World*. J. A. Hammerton, ed. 7:4279–95.

Review of *Wages and the State*, by E. M. Burns. *Revue des Sciences Politiques* (1927), 50:470–71.

Review of *A Short History of the British Working Class Movement*, by G. D. H. Cole. *History* (1927), 11:351–52.

Review of *The International Anarchy*, by G. Lowes Dickinson. *Revue des Sciences Politiques* (1927), 50:463.

Review of *The Later Correspondence of Lord John Russell (1840–1878)*, G. P. Gooch, ed., *History* (1927) 12:80–81.

Review of *Palmerston*, by Phillip Guedella. *Revue des Sciences Politiques* (1927), 50:291–92.

Review of *The Rise of Modern Industry*, by John and Barbara Hammond. *History* (1927), 12:173–74.

Review of *England and the World*, F. S. Marvin, ed. *History* (1927), 12:353–54.

Review of *Marx-Engels Archive*, F. Rjazanov, ed. *History* (1927), 12:279.

Review of *The Two Party System in English Political History*, by George Trevelyan. *History* (1927), 12:278–79.

Review of *Une Politique française*, by Duc de Doudeauville. *History* (1927), 12:278–79.

The Growth of Philosophic Radicalism. Mary Morris trans. New York: Macmillan, 1928.

"La Politique du roi Edouard." *Revue des Sciences Politiques* (1928), 51:83–93.

Review of *La Théorie du materialisme historique; Manuel populaire de sociologie marxiste*, by N. Boukharine. *Revue des Sciences Politiques* (1928), 51:144–45.

Review of *Joseph Parkes of Birmingham and the Part which He Played in Radical Reform Movements, 1825–1845*, by Jessie K. Buckley. *History* (1928), 12:362–63.

Review of *British Foreign Secretaries, 1807–1916: Studies in Personality and Policy*, by Algernon Cecil. *History* (1928), 13:275–76.

Review of *Recent Revelations of European Diplomacy* by G. P. Gooch. *Revue des Sciences Politiques* (1928), 51:459.

Review of *Mémoires*, Edward Grey. *Revue des Sciences Politiques* (1928), 51:137.

Review of *British War Budgets,* by F. W. Hirst and J. E. Allen. *Revue des Sciences Politiques* (1928), 51:136–37.

Review of *England,* by Dean Inge. *History* (1928), 13:283.

Review of *King Edward VII. A Biography,* by Sidney Lee. *Revue des Sciences Politiques* (1928), 51:83.

Review of *The Mechanism of the Modern State; A Treatise on the Science and Art of Government,* by J. A. R. Marriott. *History* (1928), 13:82–83.

Review of *Les Questions fondamentales du marxisme,* by G. F. Plekanov. *Revue des Sciences Politiques* (1928), 51:144–45.

Review of *Historisch-Kritische Gesamtausgabe,* F. Rjazanov, ed. *History* (1928), 13:283.

Review of *La Politique exterieure de l'Allemagne, 1870–1914.* Documents Officiels publiés par le ministère allemand des affairs étrangères. *Revue des Sciences Politiques* (1928), 51:138.

"Documents diplomatiques françaises." *Revue de Paris* (1929), 36:45–63.

Review of *A Short History of the British Working Class Movement.* Vol. 2 *(1848–1900), Vol. 3 (1900–1927),* by G. D. H. Cole. *History* (1929), 14:85–86.

Review of *Le Socialisme, sa définition—ses debuts. La doctrine Saint-Simonienne,* by Emile Durkheim. *Revue des Sciences Politiques,* (1929), 52:471.

Review of *Parliament and War,* by F. R. Flournoy. *History* (1929), 13:368–69.

Review of *The Political Principles of Some Notable Prime Ministers of the Nineteenth Century; A Series of Lectures,* by F. J. C. Hearnshaw. *History* (1929), 13:367.

Review of *The Social Philosophy of William Morris,* by Anna A. Von Helmholtz-Phelan. *Revue des Sciences Politiques* (1929), 52:317.

Review of *British War Budgets,* by F. W. Hirst and J. E. Allen. *History* (1929), 14:184.

Review of *Au dela du marxisme,* by Henri de Man. *Revue des Sciences Politiques* (1929), 52:316–17.

Review of *August Comte et la science économique,* by Roger Mauduit. *Revue des Sciences Politiques* (1929), 52:624.

Review of *Die Verelendungstheorie,* by Robert Michels. *Revue des Sciences Politiques* (1929), 52:470–71.

Review of *The Pre-War Mind in England: An Historical Review,* by Caroline E. Playne. *History* (1929), 14:170–72.

BIBLIOGRAPHY

Review of *The Cause, A Short History of the Women's Movement in Great Britain*, by Ray Strachey. *Revue des Sciences Politiques* (1929), 52:466–67.

The World Crisis of 1914–1918. An Interpretation. The Rhodes Memorial Lectures, 1929. Oxford: Clarendon Press, 1930.

Review of *Recent Revelations in European Diplomacy and Supplementary Chapter on the Revelations of 1928–1929*, by G. P. Gooch. *Revue des Sciences Politiques* (1930), 53:464.

Review of *Sir Arthur Nicolson, Bart., First Lord Carnock. A Study in the Old Diplomacy*, by Harold Nicolson. *Revue des Sciences Politiques* (1930), 53:619.

Review of *Ma Vie, essai autobiographique*, by Leon Trotsky. *Revue des Sciences Politiques* (1930), 53:464–65.

"L'Angleterre sur le seuil de la guerre (août 1913-août 1914)." *Revue de Paris* (1931), 38:14–44.

Review of *Perspectives socialistes*, by Marcel Deat. *Revue des Sciences Politiques* (1931), 54:307.

Review of *England und Europa (Vorwiegend von 1870. Eine Studie zur Geschichte Bismarck und der Reichsgrundung)*, by Horst Michael. *Revue des Sciences Politiques* (1931), 54:150–51.

Review of *Ma Vie, essai autobiographique*, by Leon Trotsky. Vols. 2 and 3. *Revue des Sciences Politiques* (1931), 54:150.

Histoire du peuple anglais au XIXᵉ siècle. Epilogue (1895–1914). Vol. 6: *Vers la democratie sociale et vers la guerre (1905–1914)*. Paris: Hachette, 1932.

"La Reforme de la marine anglaise et la politique navale britannique (1902–1907)." *Revue des Sciences Politiques* (1932), 55:5–36.

"L'Equilibre anglais et l'Europe." *L'Europe Nouvelle* (1932), 15:238–39.

Review of *King Charles II*, by A. Bryant. *English Historical Review* (1932), 47:708–09.

Sismondi. Collection Reformateurs Sociaux. Paris: Alcan, 1933.

"James Mill." *Encyclopedia of the Social Sciences*, 10:480–81.

Review of *A Philosophical Approach to Communism*, by Theodore Brameld. *Revue des Sciences Politiques* (1933), 56:612.

"Socialism and the Problem of Democratic Parliamentarianism." *International Affairs* (1934), 13:490–507.

Review of *Oui, mais Mouscou*, by Pierre Dominique. *Revue des Sciences Politiques* (1934), 57:149–50.

Review of *Le Plan quinquennal*, by G. Grinko. *Revue des Sciences Politiques* (1934), 57:149–50.

Review of *The Soviet State. A Study of Bolshevik Rule*, by Bertram W. Maxwell. *Revue des Sciences Politiques* (1934), 57:151.

Review of *Discours sur le plan quinquennal*, by Joseph Stalin. *Revue des Sciences Politiques* (1934), 57:149–50.

"Before 1835." *A Century of Municipal Progress*, H. J. Laski, W. I. Jennings, and W. A. Robson, eds. London: Allen and Unwin, 1935.

"English Public Opinion and the French Revolutions of the Nineteenth Century." *Studies in Anglo-French History*, A. Coville and H. Temperley, eds. Cambridge: Cambridge at the University Press, 1935.

Review of *Jaurès et l'Allemagne*, by Maurice Lair. *Revue des Sciences Politiques* (1935), 58:158.

Review of *La Russie sous l'uniforme bolchevique*, by Vladimir Lazarevski. *Revue des Sciences Politiques* (1935), 58:150.

Review of *Oeuvres complètes. Le Manifeste communiste*, by Karl Marx. Molitor trans. *Revue des Sciences Politiques* (1935), 58:150.

"L'Angleterre: Grandeur, decadence et persistance du liberalisme en Angleterre." *Inventaires. La Crise sociale et les ideologies nationales.* Paris: Alcan, 1936.

"Palmerston et Guizot (1846–1848)." *Revue des Sciences Politiques* (1936), 59:321–46.

"L'Ère des tyrannies." *Bulletin de la Société Française de Philosophie* (1936), 36:181–253.

Review of *Bilan de la sociologie française contemporaine* by C. Bouglé. *Revue des Sciences Politiques* (1936), 59:156.

Review of *The England of Charles II*, by A. Bryant. *English Historical Review* (1936), 51:738.

Review of *La Mythologie primitive*, by Lucien Lévy Bruhl. *Revue des Sciences Politiques* (1936), 59:155–56.

Review of *Morals and Politics: Theories of Their Relation from Hobbes and Spinoza to Marx and Bosanquet*, by E. F. Carritt. *Revue des Sciences Politiques* (1936), 59:443.

"Les Rapports franco-anglais de 1882 à 1914." *Les Cahiers de Radio-Paris* (1937), 8:998–1003.

"L'Eloge de l'hypocrisie." Philip Maurice Denecke Lecture at Lady Margaret Hall, Oxford. May 11, 1936. Copy Guy-Loé Collection.

Review of *Government and the Press, 1695–1763*, by L. Hanson. *English Historical Review* (1937), 52:545–46.

L'Ère des tyrannies. Etudes sur le socialisme et la guerre. Paris: Gallimard, 1938.

Histoire du socialisme européen. Redigée d'après des notes de cours par un groupe d'amis et d'éleves de Elie Halévy. Paris: Gallimard, 1948.

The Era of Tyrannies. R. K. Webb, trans. Garden City, N.Y.: Anchor, 1965.

Reference Works

Acomb, Evelyn. *The French Laic Laws (1879–1889).* New York: Octagon, 1966.

Alain [Emile Chartier]. *Correspondance avec Elie et Florence Halévy.* Jeanne Michel-Alexandre, ed. 7th ed. Paris: Gallimard, 1958.

—— *Histoire de mes pensées.* Paris: Gallimard, 1936.

Albee, Ernest. *A History of English Utilitarianism.* London: Allen & Unwin, 1957.

Anderson, Malcolm. "The Right and the Social Question in Parliament, 1905–1919." David Shapiro, ed., *The Right in France 1890–1919.* Carbondale, Southern Illinois University Press, 1962.

Anderson, Perry. *Considerations on Western Marxism.* London, NLB, 1976.

Andler, Charles. *La Civilisation socialiste.* Paris: Rivière, 1912.

—— *Le Socialisme d'état en Allemagne.* Paris: Alcan, 1897.

—— *Vie de Lucien Herr.* Paris: Rieder, 1932.

Annan, Noel. *Leslie Stephen: His Thought and Character in Relation to His Age.* Cambridge, Mass.: Harvard University Press, 1952.

Aron, Raymond. *The Century of Total War.* Boston: Beacon Press, 1955.

—— "L'Ère des tyrannies." *Revue de Métaphysique et de Morale* (1939), 39:283–307.

—— *Main Currents in Sociological Thought.* 2 vols. Richard Howard and Helen Weaver, trans. Garden City, N.Y.: Doubleday, Anchor Books, 1968.

—— *L'Opium des intellectuals.* Paris: Calmann Levy, 1955.

—— "Séance pour le centenaire de Elie Halévy, 28 novembre 1970." *Bulletin de la Société Française de Philosophie* (1971), vol. 65.

Aydelotte, William O. "The Conservative and Radical Interpretations of Early Victorian Social Legislation." *Victorian Studies* (1967), 11:225–36.

Barraclough, Geoffrey. "Historian at the End of His Tether." *New York Review of Books* (1966), 3:20–22.

Barker, Ernest. "Elie Halévy." *English Historical Review* (1938), 53:79–87.

Beales, Hugh Lancelot. *The Making of Social Policy*. London: G. Cumberlege, Oxford University Press, 1946.

Bedarida, François. "Elie Halévy et le socialisme anglais." *Revue Historique* (1975), 254:371–95.

Beer, Samuel. *British Politics in the Collectivist Age*. New York: Knopf, 1965.

Bellah, Robert. "Durkheim and History." Robert Nisbet, ed., *Emile Durkheim*. Engelwood Cliffs, N.J.: Prentice-Hall, 1965.

Benda, Julien. "L'Affaire Dreyfus et le principe d'authorité." *Revue Blanche* (1899), 20:190–206.

—— "Elie Halévy." *Nouvelle Revue Française*, 1937. Printed in *Jeunesse d'un clerc*. Paris: Gallimard, 1936.

—— *The Treason of the Intellectuals*. Richard Aldington, trans. New York: Norton, 1969.

Benn, Alfred William. *The History of English Rationalism in the Nineteenth Century*. 2 vols. New York: Russell & Russell, 1962.

Best, Geoffrey. *Mid-Victorian Britain, 1851–1875*. London: Weidenfeld and Nicholson, 1971.

—— *Temporal Pillars. Queen Anne's Bounty and the Ecclesiastical Commissioners and the Church of England*. Cambridge: Cambridge at the University Press, 1964.

Black, R. D. Collison. *Economic Thought and the Irish Question 1817–70*. Cambridge: Cambridge at the University Press, 1960.

Blaug, Marc. "The Classical Economists and the Factory Acts: A Reexamination." *Quarterly Journal of Economics* (1958), 72:211–26.

—— "The Myth of the Old Poor Law and the Making of the New." *Journal of Economic History* (1963), 23:157–84.

—— *Ricardian Economics: A Historical Study*. New Haven: Yale University Press, 1958.

Bouglé, Celestin. *Chez les prophètes socialistes*. Paris: Alcan, 1918.

—— *The French Conception of "Culture générale" and Its Influence upon Instruction*. New York: Bureau of Publications Teachers' College, Columbia University, 1938.

—— *Les Idées égalitaires: Etude sociologique*. Paris: Alcan, 1899.

—— *Les Sciences sociales en Allemagne*. Paris: Alcan, 1896.

—— *Socialisme français*. Du "socialisme utopique" à la "democratie industrielle." Paris: Colin, 1933.

—— *La Sociologie de Proudhon*. Paris: Colin, 1911.

—— *Le Solidarisme*. 2nd ed. Paris: Giard, 1924.

—— *Solidarisme et liberalisme*. Paris: Riedier, 1901.

Bourgin, Hubert, *De Jaurés à Léon Blum: L'Ecole Normale et la politique*. Paris: A. Fayard, 1938.

—— *Proudhon*. Paris: Bellais, 1901.

Boutmy, Emile. *The English Peoples: A Study of Their Political Psychology*. E. English trans. New York: Putnam, 1904.

Boutroux, Emile. *The Contingency of the Laws of Nature*. Fred Rothwell. trans. Chicago: The Open Court, 1916.

Brebner, J. Bartlet. "Elie Halévy." In H. A. Ausubel, J. B. Brebner, and Erling Hunt, eds., *Some Modern Historians of Britain: Essays in Honor of Robert Schuyler*. New York: Dryden Press, 1951.

—— "Halévy: Diagnostician of Modern Britain." *Thought* (1948), 101–13.

—— "Laissez-faire and State Intervention in Nineteenth Century Britain." *Journal of Economic History*. Supplement (1948), 8:59–73.

Briggs, Asa. *The Age of Improvement 1783–1867*. London: Longmans, 1960.

Brogan, D. W. *The Development of Modern France 1870–1939*. London: H. Hamilton, 1967.

—— *French Personalities and Problems*. London: H. Hamilton, 1946.

Brombert, Victor. *The Intellectual Hero: Studies in the French Novel 1880–1955*. Philadelphia: Lippincott, 1961.

Brown, Ford K. *Fathers of the Victorians: The Age of Wilberforce*. Cambridge: Cambridge at the University Press, 1961.

Brunetière, Ferdinand. *Renaissance de l'idealisme*. Paris: Didot, 1896.

Brunschvicg, Léon. *L'Experience humaine et la causalité physique*. Paris: Alcan, 1922.

—— "History and Philosophy." *Philosophy and History: Essays Presented to Ernst Cassirer*. Oxford: Clarendon Press, 1936.

—— *Le Progrés de la conscience dans la philosophie occidentale*. Paris: Alcan, 1927.

Burn, W. L. *Age of Equipoise: A Study of Mid-Victorian Generation*. London: Allen and Unwin, 1964.

Byrnes, Robert. *Antisemitism in Modern France*. Vol. 1: *Prologue to the Dreyfus Affair*. New Brunswick, N.J.: Rutgers University Press, 1950.

Caute, David. *Communism and French Intellectuals, 1914–1960*. New York: Macmillan, 1964.

Chadwick, Owen. *The Victorian Church*. Vol. 1. London: Adam and Charles Black, 1966.

Challener, Richard. "The French Foreign Office in the Era of Philippe Berthelot." Felix Gilbert and Gordon Craig, eds., *The Diplomats*. Vol 1: *The Twenties*. New York: Athenaeum, 1965.

Chapman, Guy. *The Dreyfus Case*. London: Rupert Hart-Davis, Ltd. 1955.

Charlton, D. G. *Positivist Thought in France during the Second Empire*. Oxford: Oxford University Press, 1959.

—— *Secular Religions in France 1815–70*. Oxford: Oxford University Press for University of Hull, 1963.

Charléty, Sebastien. "Elie Halévy, 1870–1937." *Revue des Sciences Politiques* (1937), 52:422–26.

—— *Essai sur l'histoire du Saint-Simonisme*. Paris: Hachette, 1896.

—— *Histoire du Saint-Simonisme* (1825–64). Paris: Paul Hartman, 1931.

Chastenet, Jacques. *Histoire de la Troisiéme République*. Paris: Hachette, 1952.

Checkland, S. G. "The Prescriptions of the Classical Economists." *Economica* (1953) N.S.20:6 1–72.

—— *The Rise of Industrial Society in England 1815–85*. London: Longmans, 1964.

Churchill, Winston. *The World Crisis*. London: Thornton Butterwork, 1915.

Clapham, J. H. *An Economic History of Modern Britain*. 3 vols. Cambridge: Cambridge University Press, 1926–38.

—— Review of *Histoire du peuple anglais au XIXe siecle: Epilogue*. Vol. 2. *English Historical Review* (1933), 48:674–76.

Clark, G. Kitson. *An Expanding Society: Britain 1830–1900*. Cambridge: Cambridge University Press, 1967.

—— *The Making of Victorian England*. Being the Ford Lectures Delivered before the University of Oxford. Cambridge, Mass.: Harvard University Press, 1962.

Clark, Terry N. "Emile Durkheim and the Institutionalization of Sociology in the French University System." *European Journal of Sociology* (1968), 9:37–71.

—— *Prophets and Patrons: The French University and the Emergence of the Social Sciences.* Cambridge, Mass.: Harvard University Press, 1973.

—— "René Worms." *International Encyclopedia of Social Sciences.*

Coates, W. H. "Benthamism, Laissez-faire and Collectivism," *Journal of the History of Ideas* (1950), 11:357–63.

Comte, Auguste. *The Positive Philosophy of Auguste Comte.* Freely translated by H. Martineau. London, 1854.

Coser, Lewis. *Men of Ideas.* New York: Free Press, 1965.

Crawford, Lucy S. *The Philosophy of Emile Boutroux.* New York: Longmans, Green, 1924.

Cromwell, Valerie. "Interpretations of Nineteenth Century Administrations: An Analysis," *Victorian Studies* (1966), 9:245–55.

Cropsey, Joseph. *Polity and Economy: An Interpretation of the Principles of Adam Smith.* New York: Greenwood reprint, 1977.

Cumming, Robert D. *Human Nature and History: A Study of the Development of Liberal Political Thought.* 2 vols. Chicago: University of Chicago, 1969.

Currie, R. and R. M. Hartwell. "The Making of the English Working Class." *Economic History Review.* 2nd Series. (1965), 18:633–43.

Curtis, Michael. *Three Against the Republic: Sorel, Barrès and Maurras.* Princeton, N.J.: Princeton University Press, 1959.

Curtiss, Mina. *Bizet and His World.* New York: Knopf, 1958.

—— *Other People's Letters: A Memoir.* Boston: Houghton-Mifflin, 1978.

Dangerfield, George. *The Strange Death of Liberal England.* New York: Capricorn, 1935.

Davy, Georges. "Emile Durkheim." *Revue de Métaphysique et de Morale* (1919), 26:72–76.

Deane, Phyllis. *The First Industrial Revolution.* Cambridge: Cambridge University Press, 1965.

Dicey, A. V. *Lectures on the Relation Between Law and Public Opinion in England during the Nineteenth Century.* 2d ed. London: Macmillan, 1914.

Digéon, Charles. *La Crise allemande de la pensée française 1870–1914.* Paris: Presses Universitaires Françaises, 1959.

Dolléans, E. *Histoire du mouvement ouvrier.* Paris: Colin, 1939.

Dreyfus, Robert. *De M. Thiers à M. Proust.* Paris: Plon, 1939.

Duguit, Léon. *Law in the Modern State.* Frida and Harold Laski, trans. London: Allen & Unwin, 1919.

Durkheim, Emile. "L'Individualisme et les intellectuals." *Revue Bleu* (1898), 10:7–13.

—— *Montesquieu and Rousseau*. Ann Arbor, Mich.: 1965.

—— *Le Socialisme. Sa Définition. Ses Débuts. La Doctrine Saint-Simonienne*. Paris: Alcan, 1928.

Duveau, Georges. *Les Instituteurs*. Paris: Editions du Seuil, 1957.

Edwards, Clifford. "Some Notes on Recent Periodical Literature on the History of Methodism." *Wesleyan Quarterly Review* (1966), 3:262–66.

Edwards, Maldwyn. *After Wesley: A Study of the Social and Political Influence of Methodism in the Middle Period*. London: Epworth, 1935.

Ehrmann, Henry. *French Labor from Popular Front to Liberation*. New York: Oxford University Press, 1947.

—— "Recent Writings on the French Labor Movement." *Journal of Modern History* (1950), 22:151–58.

Ensor, R. C. K. *Modern Socialism*. 2nd ed. New York: Harper, 1907.

Elwitt, Sanford. "Two Points of View in French Labor History." *Marxist Perspectives*, 1978, pp. 106–22.

Everett, Charles Warren. *The Education of Jeremy Bentham*. New York: Columbia University, 1931.

Fay, C. R. *Great Britain from Adam Smith to the Present Day*. London: Longmans, Green, 1928.

Finer, S. E. *The Life and Times of Sir Edwin Chadwick*. London: Methuen, 1952.

Fouillée, A. *Mouvement idealiste et la reaction contre la science positive*. Paris: Alcan, 1896.

Friedrich, Carl and Zbigniew Brezezinski. *Totalitarian Dictatorship and Autocracy*. 2d ed. Cambridge, Mass.: Harvard University Press, 1965.

Gide, Charles. *Fourier, Précurseur de la coopération: Oeuvres choisies*. Paris: Association pour l'enseignement de la coopération, 1924.

Gide, Charles and Charles Rist. *Histoire des doctrines économiques depuis les physiocrats jusqu'à nos jours*. 2 vols. Paris: Larose and Tenin, 1909.

Gilpin, Robert, *France in the Age of the Scientific State*. Princeton, N.J.: Princeton University Press, 1969.

Girardet, Raoul. *Le Nationalisme français 1871–1914*. Paris: Colin, 1966.

Goguel, François. *La Politique des partis sous la IIIe République*. Paris: Editions de Seuil, n.d.

Gillispie, Charles. "The Work of Elie Halévy: A Critical Appreciation." *Journal of Modern History* (1950), 22:232–49.

Goldberg, Harvey. *The Life of Jean Jaurès*. Madison, Wis.: University of Wisconsin, 1962.

Guiral, Pierre. *Prévost-Paradol: 1829–70. Pensée et action d'un liberal dans le second empire*. Paris: Presses Universitaires Françaises, 1955.

Guy-Grand, Georges. *Proudhon et l'enseignement du peuple*. Paris: Grasset, 1920.

Halévy, Daniel. *Essais sur le mouvement ouvrier en France*. Paris: Bellais, 1901.

—— *La Fin des notables*. Paris: Grasset, 1930.

—— *Luttes et problèmes*. Paris: Rivière, 1911.

—— *My Friend Degas*. Mina Curtiss, trans. and ed. Middletown, Conn.: Wesleyan University Press, 1964.

—— *La République des comités: Essai d'histoire contemporaine (1895–1934)*. Paris: Grasset, 1934.

—— *La République des ducs*. Paris: Grasset, 1937.

Halévy, Ludovic. *Les Carnets*. 2 Vols. Paris: Calmann Levy, 1935.

Hammond, J. L. and Barbara Hammond. *The Age of the Chartists, 1832–54; A Study of Discontent*. London: Longmans, Green, 1930.

—— *Lord Shaftesbury*. 4th ed. London: Longmans, Green, 1936.

—— *Rise of Modern Industry*. London: Methuen, 1925.

—— *The Skilled Labourer (1760–1832)*. London: Longmans, Green, 1919.

—— *The Town Labourer (1760–1832)*. London: Longmans, Green, 1918.

—— *The Village Labourer (1760–1832)*. London: Longmans, Green, 1911.

Hart, Jennifer. "Nineteenth-Century Social Reform: A Tory Interpretation of History." *Past and Present*, No. 31 (1965), 39–61.

Hayek, F. A. "Individualism True and False." *Individualism and Economic Order*. Chicago: Chicago University Press, 1948.

Hayward, J. E. S. "The Co-operative Origins, Rise and Collapse of the 'Universités populaires.' " *Archives Internationales de Sociologie de la Co-operation* (1961), 11:3–17.

—— "Educational Pressure Groups and the Indoctrination of the

Radical Ideology of Solidarism 1895–1914." *International Review of Social History* (1963), 8:1–17.

—— "The Official Social Philosophy of the French Third Republic: Léon Bourgeois and *Solidarisme*." *International Review of Social History* (1961), 6:19–48.

—— "Solidarity: The Social History of an Idea in Nineteenth Century France." *International Review of Social History* (1959), 4:261–84.

Himmelfarb, Gertrude. "Bentham Scholarship and the Bentham 'Problem.' " *Journal of Modern History* (1969), 41:189–206.

—— "Bentham's Utopia: The National Charity Company." *Journal of British Studies* (1970), 10:80–125.

—— *Victorian Minds*. New York: Knopf, 1968.

Hobsbawm, Eric. "The British Secret." *The New Statesman* (1961), 61:548–49.

—— "Methodism and the Threat of Revolution in Britain." *Labouring Men*. New York: Anchor Books, 1967.

Hobsbawm, E. J. and George Rudé. *Captain Swing: The Agricultural Labourer's Rising of 1830*. New York: Pantheon, 1968.

Hughes, H. Stuart. *Consciousness and Society: The Reorientation of European Social Thought, 1890–1930*. New York: Knopf, 1959.

Hutcheson, T. W. "Bentham as an Economist." *Economic Journal* (1956), 66:288–306.

Inglis, K. S. *Churches and the Working Classes in Victorian England*. Toronto: University of Toronto Press, 1963.

—— "English Nonconformity and Social Reform." *Past and Present* (1958), 10:73–88.

—— "Patterns of Religious Worship in 1851." *Journal of Ecclesiastical History* (1960), 11:74–86.

Jackson, J. Hampden. *Clemenceau and the Third French Republic*. New York: Macmillan, 1948.

—— *Jean Jaurès: His Life and Work*. London: Allen and Unwin, 1943.

Jeanneney, Jean-Marcel. "Elie Halévy et le socialisme." *Revue des Sciences Politiques*, (1938), 53:475–80.

Kayser, J. *Les Grandes Batailles du radicalism 1820–1901*. Paris: Rivière, 1962.

Kent, John. *The Age of Disunity*. London: Epworth, 1966.

Keynes, John Maynard. *The End of Laissez-Faire*. London: L. and V. Woolf, 1926.

King, Jere C. *Foch versus Clemenceau*. Cambridge, Mass.: Harvard University Press, 1960.

—— *Generals and Politicians*. Berkeley: University of California, 1951.

Kiernan, V. "Evangelicalism and the French Revolution." *Past and Present* (1952), 1:44–56.

Laforge, Paul. "Socialism and the Intellectuals." George B. de Huszar, ed., *The Intellectuals; A Controversial Portrait*. Glencoe, Ill.: Free Press, 1960.

Laidler, Harry W. *History of Socialism*. New York: Crowell, 1968.

Lanson, Gustave. *Voltaire*. Paris: Hachette, 1906.

Laquer, Thomas W. *Religion and Respectability: Schools and Working Class Culture 1780–1850*. New Haven: Yale University Press, 1976.

Lemaître, Jules. *Jean-Jacques Rousseau*. Paris: Calmann Levy, 1907.

Lévi-Strauss, Claude. "French Sociology." Georges Gurvitch and Wilbert Moore, eds., *Twentieth Century Sociology*. New York: Philosophy Library, 1945.

Lecky, W. E. H. *A History of England in the Eighteenth Century*. London: Longmans, Green, 1878–90.

Lefranc, Georges. *Les Mouvements socialistes sous la Troisième République 1875–1940*. Paris: Payot, 1963.

Léon Xavier. *Fichte et son temps*. Paris: Colin, 1922–27.

Leroy, Maxime. *Histoire des idées sociales en France*. 5th ed. 3 vols. Paris: Gallimard, 1947.

—— *Le Socialisme des producteurs: Henri de Saint-Simon*. Paris: Revière, 1924.

Letwin, Shirley. *The Pursuit of Certainty*. Cambridge: Cambridge University Press, 1965.

Liard, Louis. *L'Enseignement superieur en France, 1789–1889*. Paris: Colin, 1889–94.

Lichtheim, George. *Marxism in Modern France*. New York: Columbia University Press, 1966.

Lorwin, Val. *The French Labor Movement*. Cambridge, Mass.: Harvard University Press, 1954.

Lukács, Gyorgy. *History and Class Consciousness*. Rodney Livingstone, trans. London: Merlin Press, 1971.

Lukes, Steven. *Emile Durkheim: His Life and Work*. London: Allen Lane, Penquin Press, 1973.

—— *Individualism*. Oxford: Blackwell, 1973.

MacDonagh, Oliver. *Early Victorian Government 1830–70*. New York: Holmes-Meier, 1976.

—— "Emigration and the State: An Essay in Administrative History." *Transactions of the Royal Historical Society*, 5th ser. (1955), 5:133–59.

—— "The Nineteenth Century Revolution in Government: A Reappraisal." *Historical Journal* (1958), 1:52–67.

Mack, Mary Peter. "The Fabians and Utilitarianism." *Journal of the History of Ideas* (1955), 16:76–88.

—— *Jeremy Bentham 1748–1792: An Odyssey of Ideas*. New York: Columbia University Press, 1963.

Macpherson, C. B. *The Political Theory of Possessive Individualism*. Oxford: Oxford University Press, 1962.

Mantoux, Etienne. *The Carthaginian Peace or the Economic Consequences of Mr. Keynes*. Oxford: Oxford University Press, 1946.

Mantoux, Paul. "La Formation du Radicalisme philosophique." *Révue de Synthèse Historique* (1901), 121–25.

Manuel, Frank E. *The New World of Henri Saint-Simon*. Notre Dame, Ind.: University of Notre Dame Press, 1963.

—— *The Prophets of Paris*. New York: Harper and Row, 1965.

Marrus, Michael. *The Politics of Assimilation: A Study of the French Jewish Community at the Time of Dreyfus*. Oxford: Oxford University Press, 1971.

Mayer, J. P. *Political Thought in France from the Revolution to the Fifth Republic*. London: Routledge and Kegan Paul, 1961.

Meacham, Standish. "The Evangelical Inheritance." *Journal of British Studies* (1963), 88–104.

Meinecke, Friedrich. *The German Catastrophe. Reflections and Recollections*. Sidney Fay, trans. Cambridge, Mass.: Harvard University Press, 1950.

Michel, Henri. *L'Idée d'état*. Paris: Hachette, 1896.

Midwinter, E. C. "State Intervention at the Local Level: The New Poor Law in Lancashire," *Historical Journal* (1967), 10:106–12.

Mises, Ludwig von. *Socialism: An Economic and Sociological Analysis*. J. Kahane, trans. 2d ed. New York: Macmillan, 1938.

Mitchell, Harvey. *Labour and the Origins of Social Democracy in Britain, France, and Germany 1890–1914*. Itasca, Ill.: Peacock Publishers, 1971.

Moore, D. C. "Political Morality in Mid-Nineteenth Century England." *Victorian Studies* (1969), 13:5–36.

Mornet, Daniel. *Les Origines intellectuelles de la Revolution française.* Paris: Colin, 1933.

Newsome, David. *The Wilberforces and Henry Manning.* Cambridge, Mass.: Belknap Press of Harvard University Press, 1966.

Noland, Aaron. *The Founding of the French Socialist Party, 1893–1905.* Cambridge, Mass.: Harvard University Press, 1956.

—— "Individualism in Jean Jaurès' Socialist Thought." *Journal of the History of Ideas* (1961), 22:63–80.

Nisbet, Robert, *The Sociological Tradition.* New York: Basic Books, 1966.

Nolte, Ernest. *Three Faces of Fascism: Action Française, Italian Fascism, National Socialism.* New York: Holt, Rinehart and Winston, 1963.

Obelkevich, James. *Religion and Rural Society: South Lindsey 1825–1875.* Oxford: Clarendon Press, 1976.

Painter, George. *Proust.* 2 vols. Boston: Little, Brown, 1959.

Parodi, Dominique. *La Philosophie contemporaine en France.* Paris: Alcan, 1919.

Parris, Henry. *Constitutional Bureaucracy.* Clifton, N.J.: Kelley Publishers, 1969.

—— "The Nineteenth Century Revolution in Government: A Reappraisal Reappraised." *Historical Journal* (1960), 3:17–37.

Passmore, John. *A Hundred Years of Philosophy.* 2d ed. New York: Basic Books, 1966.

Peel, J. D. Y. *Herbert Spencer: The Evolution of a Sociologist.* New York: Basic Books, 1971.

Péguy, Charles. *Notre Jeunesse.* 3d. ed. Paris: Gallimard, 1933.

Pelling, Henry. *The Origins of the Labour Party.* Oxford: Oxford University Press, 1965.

—— *Popular Politics and Society in Late Victorian Britain.* New York: St. Martin's Press, 1968.

—— "Religion and the Nineteenth Century British Working Class." *Past and Present* (1964), 27:128–33.

Perkin, Harold. *The Origins of Modern English Society, 1780–1880.* London: Routledge and Kegan Paul, 1969.

Picard, R. *La Philosophie sociale de Renouvier.* Paris: Rivière, 1908.

Pierce, Roy. *Contemporary French Political Thought.* New York: Oxford University Press, 1966.

Plamenatz, John. *The English Utilitarians.* 2d ed. Oxford: Blackwell, 1958.

Radzinowicz, Leon. *A History of English Criminal Law and Its Administration from 1750*. Vol. 1: *The Movement for Reform 1750–1833*. New York: Macmillan, 1948.

Rauschning, Hermann. *The Conservative Revolution*. New York: Putnam, 1941.

—— *The Revolution of Nihilism: Warning to the West*. E. W. Dickes, trans. New York: Longmans, Green, 1939.

Redlich, J. and Hirst, F. W. *The History of Local Government in England*. Bryan Keith Lucas, ed. London: Macmillan, 1958.

Richter, Melvin. "A Bibliography of Signed Works by Elie Halévy." *History and Theory, Supplement* (1968), 7:46–71.

—— *The Politics of Conscience: T. H. Green and His Age*. Cambridge, Mass.: Harvard University Press, 1964.

Ritter, Alan. *Political Thought of Proudhon*. Princeton, N.J., Princeton University Press, 1969.

Roach, John. "Liberalism and the Victorian Intelligentsia." *Cambridge Historical Journal* (1957), 13:58–81.

Robbins, Lionel C. *The Theory of Economic Policy in English Political Economy*. London: Macmillan, 1952.

Roberts, David. *Victorian Origins of the Beitish Welfare State*. New Haven: Yale University Press, 1960.

—— "Jeremy Bentham and the Victorian Administrative State." *Victorian Studies* (1959), 11:193–210.

Rosenblum, Nancy. *Bentham's Theory of the Modern State*. Cambridge, Mass.: Harvard University Press, 1978.

Schapiro, J. Salwyn. "Proudhon: Harbinger of Fascism." *American Historical Review* (1945), 50:714–37.

Scott, John A. *Republican Ideas and the Liberal Tradition in France 1870–1914*. New York: Octagon, 1966.

Sedgwick, A. *Third French Republic, 1870–1914*. New York: Crowell, 1968.

Seignobos, Charles. "Compte rendu de *l'Histoire du peuple anglais au XIXᵉ siecle*." *Revue Critique d'Histoire et de Litterature* (1932), 66:561–75.

—— *L'Évolution de la Troisième République*. Paris: Hachette, 1921.

Semmel, Bernard. *Imperialism and Social Reform: English Social-imperial Thought 1895–1914*. Garden City, New York: Doubleday, 1968.

—— *The Methodist Revolution*. New York: Basic Books, 1973.

—— *The Rise of Free Trade Imperialism: Classical Political Economy, the Empire of Free Trade and Imperialism 1750–1850*. Cambridge: Cambridge University Press, 1970.

Sidgwick, Henry. *Miscellaneous Essays and Addresses*. New York: Macmillan, 1904.

Siegel, Martin. "Science and the Historical Imagination: Patterns in French Historical Thought, 1866–1914." Ph.D. Diss., Columbia University, 1965.

Siegfried, André. *Tableau des partis en France*. Paris: Grasset, 1930.

Silvera, Alain. *Daniel Halévy and His Times: A Gentleman Commoner in the Third Republic*. Ithaca, N.Y.: Cornell University Press, 1966.

Sklar, Judith. "Bergson and the Politics of Intuition." *Review of Politics* (1958), 20:634–56.

Smith, Catherine Haugh. "Elie Halévy 1870–1937." Bernadotte Schmitt, ed., *Some Historians of Modern Europe*. Chicago: University of Chicago Press, 1942.

Smith, W. G. Pogson. "Review of Books: *La Formation du Radicalisme philosophique*." *English Historical Review* (1902), 17:385–91.

Soloway, Richard. "Reform or Ruin: English Moral Thought during the First French Republic." *Review of Politics* (1963), 25:110–28.

Soltau, Roger. *French Political Thought in the Nineteenth Century*. New Haven: Yale University Press, 1931.

Sombart, Werner. *Socialism and the Social Movement*. M. Epstein, trans. 6th ed. New York: Dutton, 1909.

Spring, David. "Clapham Sect: Some Social and Political Aspects." *Victorian Studies* (1961–62), 6:35–48.

Stephen, Leslie. *The English Utilitarians*. 3 vols. London: Duckworth, 1900.

Stoetzel, Jean. "Sociology in France: An Empirical View." Howard Becker and Alvin Boskoff, eds., *Modern Sociological Theory. New York: Dryden Press*, 1957.

Stretton, Hugh. *The Political Sciences*. New York: Basic Books, 1968.

Strong, Tracy. "History and Choices: The Foundations of the Political Thought of Raymond Aron." *History and Theory* (1972), 11:179–92.

Sumler, David. "Domestic Influences on the Nationalist Revival in France, 1909–14." *French Historical Studies* (1970), 6:517–37.

Swart, K. W. "Individualism in Mid-Nineteenth Century (1826–1860)." *Journal of the History of Ideas* (1962), 23:77–90.

—— *The Sense of Decadence in Nineteenth-Century France*. The Hague: Nijhoff, 1964.

Taine, Hippolyte. *Histoire de la litterature anglaise.* 5 vols. Paris: Hachette, 1866–1873.

—— *History of English Literature.* 4 vols. H. Van Laun, trans. Edinburgh: Edmonston & Douglas, 1874.

—— *Notes on England.* W. F. Rae, trans. New York: Henry Holt, 1885.

Taylor, E. R. *Methodism and Politics, 1791–1850.* Cambridge: Cambridge University Press, 1935.

Thibaudet, Albert. *Les Idées politiques de la France.* Paris: Stock, 1932.

—— *La République des professeurs.* Paris: Grasset, 1927.

Tholfsen, Trygve. "The Intellectual Origins of Mid-Victorian Stability." *Political Quarterly Review* (1971), 86:57–90.

—— *Working Class Radicalism in Mid-Victorian England.* New York: Columbia University Press, 1977.

Thompson, David. "The 1851 Religious Census: Problems and Possibilities." *Victorian Studies* (1967), 11:87–97.

Thompson, E. P. *The Making of the English Working Class.* New York: Vintage, 1966.

Thomson, David. *Democracy in France Since 1870.* 5th ed. New York: Oxford University Press, 1969.

Viner, Jacob. *The Long View and the Short.* Glencoe, Ill.: Free Press, 1958.

Waelti, Elisabeth. "La Morale Kantienne de Charles Renouvier et son influence sur la constitution de la morale laïque dans la deuxième moitié de XIXe siècle en France" (Ph.D. Diss., University of Berne, 1947).

Wallas, Graham. "Bentham as Political Inventor." *Contemporary Review* (1926), 129:308–19.

—— "Jeremy Bentham." *Political Science Quarterly* (1923), 38:45–56.

—— *The Life of Francis Place.* London: Longmans, Green, 1898.

Wallwork, Ernest. *Durkheim: Morality and Milieu.* Cambridge, Mass.: Harvard University Press, 1972.

Walsh, John. "Elie Halévy and the Birth of Methodism." *Transactions of the Royal Historical Society.* Fifth series (1975), 25:2–20.

—— "Origins of the Evangelical Revival." G. V. Bennett and J. D. Walsh, eds., *Essays in Modern Church History.* London: A. and C. Black, 1966.

Ward, W. R. *Religion and Society 1790–1850.* London: B. T. Batsford, 1972.

Webb, R. K. *The British Working Class Reader 1790–1848*. London: Allen, 1955.

—— *Harriet Martineau*. New York: Columbia University Press, 1960.

West, E. G. *Education and the State*. London: Institute of Economic Affairs, 1965.

Wolin, Sheldon. *Politics and Vision: Continuity and Innovation in Western Political Thought*. Boston: Little, Brown, 1960.

Zeldin, Theodore. *France, 1848–1945*. 2 vols. Oxford: Clarendon Press, 1973, 1977.

Biographical Notes

Alain, pseud. **Emile Chartier,** (1868–1951), leading French philosopher; author of *Spinoza* (1901); *Les propos* (1906–1914); *Le citoyen contre les pouvoirs* (1926).

Andler, Charles (1866–1933), socialist scholar-philosopher-historian; author of *Les origines du socialisme d'état en Allemagne* (1897) and *La philosophie allemand au XIXe siècle* (1912); translator and commentator on Marxism.

Aron, Raymond (1905   ), French political and social philosopher; author of *Main Currents in Sociological Thought* (1965), *The Opium of the Intellectuals* (1962), and *Democracy and Totalitarianism* (1969).

Babeuf, François Emile (1760–1797), French revolutionary communist.

Bakunin, Mikhail (1814–1876), Russian revolutionary anarchist.

Barbusse, Henri (1873–1935), French author and editor.

Barker, Ernest Sir (1874–1960), British philosopher.

Barrès, Maurice Auguste (1862–1932), French novelist and rightist political figure; author of *Les Deracinés* (1897).

Basch, Victor (1863–1944), French Democratic Socialist delegate; author of *Essais d'esthetique de philosophie et de littérature* (1934), *Les doctrines politiques des philosophes classiques de l'Allemagne* (1927), and *L'individualisme anarchiste: Max Stirner* (1904).

Bazard, Saint-Armand (1791–1832), leading disciple of Saint-Simon, whose joint lectures with Enfantin are drawn together as the *Doctrine de Saint-Simon, Exposition: Première Année 1829* (edited by Bouglé and Halévy in 1924); translator (1828) of J. Bentham's *Defense of Usury*.

Beccaria, Cesare Bonesana, marchese di (1738–1794), Italian philosophe; author of *Dei delitti e delle pene* (1764).

Benda, Julien (1867–1956), French man of letters, friend of Elie Halévy; author of *La traison des clercs* (1927) and many works of literary criticism and philosophy.

Bergson, Henri (1859–1941), French philosopher, professor at the Collège de France; author of *L'évolution creatrice* (1907) and *Les deux sources de la morale et de la religion* (1932).

Bernhardi, Friedrich Adam Julius von (1849–1930), Pan-Germanist, propagandist, military general; author of *British as Germany's Vassal* (1914), *On the War of Today* (1914); and *Germany and the Next War* (1912).

Berr, Henri (1863–1954), historian and philosopher of history; godfather to the *Annales*.

Berthelot, Marcellin (1827–1907) [Halévy's uncle], chemist; minister of education (1886–87); minister of foreign affairs (1895–96); author of many scientific works and articles.

Berthelot, Philippe (1866–1937) [Halévy's cousin], secretary general of the Foreign Ministry (1920–33); son of Marcellin and brother of André (1862–1938), the industrialist; deputy (1898–1902) and senator (1920–27).

Berthelot, René (1872–1960) [Halévy's cousin], professor of philosophy, University of Brussels; author of *Evolutionnisme et platonisme* and *Un romanticisme utilitaire* (1911–22).

Bizet, Georges (1838–1875), French composer, created *Carmen* in collaboration with Ludovic Halévy; married Elie's aunt, Geneviève.

Bizet, Jacques [Halévy's cousin, son of Georges and Geneviève Bizet], poet.

Blackstone, Sir William (1723–1780), British legal theorist; author of *Commentaries on the Laws of England* (4 vols., 1765–69).

Blanc, Louis (1811–1882), socialist; minister of labor (1848); deputy (1848, 1871–72); author of *Histoire de la Révolution française* (12 vols.; 1847–62), *The History of Ten Years, 1830–1840; or France under Louis Philippe* (2 vols.; 1848), and *Organization of Work* (1840).

Blanqui, Louis August (1805–1881), French revolutionary.

Blum, Léon (1872–1950), French socialist; prime minister of France (1936–37, 1938) during the Popular Front; president of Provisional Government (1946–47); author of works of literary criticism before First World War, political speeches and tracts after First World War, and *A l'échelle humaine* during his imprisonment under Vichy.

Bopp, Franz (1791–1867), Prussian philologist and philosopher; author of a comparative grammar of Aryan languages (i.e., German and Slavonic), Sanskrit, Zend, Greek, Latin, Lithuanian, Gothic.

Bouglé, Célestin (1870–1940), professor of social philosophy (sociology) at the Sorbonne (1901–35); director Centre du Documentation Sociale and of the Ecole Normale Supérieure; author of *Les idées égalitaires: étude sociologique* (1899), *Socialismes français: du "socialisme utopique" à la "democratie industrielle"* (1932), and *La sociologie de Proudhon* (1911).

Boulanger, Georges Ernest (1837–1891), French general; minister of war, (1886–87); deputy (1888–89).

Bourgeois, Léon V.A. (1851–1925), French publicist and politician; champion of *Solidarisme*, radicalism, and the League of Nations.

Bourget, Paul (1852–1935), noted French author.

Bourgin, Hubert (1874– ?), author of *Les systèmes socialistes* (1923); *Proudhon* (1901), and *De Juarès á Léon Blum: l'Ecole normale et la politique* (1938).

Boutmy, Emile (1835–1906), founder of the Ecole Libres des Sciences Politiques; author of *The English Constitution* (1891) and *The English People: A Study of their Political Psychology* (1904).

Boutroux, Emile (1845–1921), author of *The Contingency of the Laws of Nature* (1916), *Natural Law in Science and Philosophy* (1914), and *Science and Religion in Contemporary Philosophy* (1909).

Bright, John (1811–1889), Canadian-born publicist of free trade economics; Liberal Party Member of Parliament (1843–89).

BIOGRAPHICAL NOTES

Brunetière, Ferdinand (1849–1906), author of *Art and Morality* (1899), *Manual of the History of French Literature* (1898), and *Bossuet* (1913).

Brunschvicg, Léon (1869–1944), professor of history of philosophy at the Sorbonne 1909– ?; author of *Spinoza et ses contemporaines* (1894), *L'Idealisme contemporaine* (1905), and *Nature et liberté, la génie de Pascal* (1925).

Buisson, Ferdinand (1841–1932), pacifist, educationist, radical founder of Les Etats Unis d'Europe; director of primary education (1878–96); president of the League of the Rights of Man; Nobel Peace Prize (1926); deputy for Paris (1902–14, 1919–24).

Buonnaroti, Filippo Michele (1761–1837), revolutionist; author of *Conspiration pour l'égalité dite de Babeuf* (1828).

Carlyle, Thomas (1795–1881), British author and moralist.

Chadwick, Sir Edwin (1800–1890), Benthamite reformer.

Charléty, Sebastian Camille Gustave (1867–1945), French historian; author of *Essai sur l'histoire du Saint-Simonisme* (1896) and *Histoire de la Restauration 1814–1830* (1921).

Chartier, Emile, *see* Alain.

Chateaubriand, François Auguste Rene, vicomte de (1768–1848), French poet, philosopher, and political figure.

Cobden, Richard (1804–1865), Liberal Member of Parliament 1841–57, 1859–65 publicist for free trade.

Cole, G.D.H. (1889–1959), British socialist; author of *British Working Class Politics, 1832–1914* (1941), *A History of Socialist Thought* (4 vols., 1953–56), and *What Marx Really Meant* (1934).

Combès, Emile (1835–1921), senator (1885–1921); prime minister (1902–05); responsible for laic laws.

Comte, Auguste (1798–1857), founder of positivism; author of *The Cathechism of Positive Religion* (1858).

Constant de Rebecque, Henri Benjamin (1767–1830), French political thinker and novelist; author of *Adolphe* (1816) and *De l'esprit de conquête et de l'usurpation dans leurs rapports avec la civilisation européene* (1814).

Cousin, Victor (1792–1867), leading French eclectic philosopher during the Restoration and July monarchy.

Couturat, Louis (1868–1914), French philosopher; author of the *Algebra of Logic* (1905); active in attempts to establish Esperanto as an international language.

Croce, Benedetto (1866–1952), Italian philosopher; literary and art critic and historian; author of *Materialismo storico ed economia marxistica* (1900), *History as the Story of Liberty* (1938), and *Aesthetics as Science of Expression and General Linguistics* (1930).

Darlu, Alphonse Julien (1849–1921), French idealist philosopher; Halévy's teacher.

Déat, Marcel (1894–1955), French political figure, socialist, and nationalist.

DeLolme, Jean Louis (1740–1806), Swiss jurist and writer on the English constitution.

Dicey, A.V. (1835–1922), English political theorist; author of *Introduction to the Study of the Law of the Constitution* (1889).

Dilke, Sir Charles Wentworth (1843–1911), British political figure and advocate of empire and social reform.

Dolléans, Edouard (1877–1954), author of *Histoire du mouvement ouvrier* (1931) and *Proudhon* (1948).

BIOGRAPHICAL NOTES

Dreyfus, Robert (1873–1939), French literary critic, historian, and memorialist; author of *de Monsieur Thiers à Marcel Proust* and *Souvenirs sur Marcel Proust*.

Durkheim, Emile (1858–1917), noted French sociologist-philosopher; author of *The Division of Labor in Society* (1893), *Suicide* (1897), and *Socialism: Its Definition, Its Origins, and Saint Simonian Doctrine* (1928).

Eckardstein, Hermann, baron von (1864– ?), diplomat; author of memoirs, *Ten Years at the Court of St. James, 1895–1905* (1922).

Edward VII (1841–1910), eldest son of Queen Victoria; king of England (1901–10).

Eichthal, Eugene d' (1854–1936), director, Ecole Libre des Sciences Politiques; vice-president of Midi Railroad.

Enfantin, Barthélemy Prosper (1796–1864), disciple of Saint-Simon; father of the saint-simonienne religion.

Faguet, Emile (1847–1916), French philosopher and literary critic; author of *Politiques et moralistes du dix-neuvième siècle* (1891–1903) and numerous studies of seventeenth-century drama.

Farigoule, Louis, *see* Romains, Jules.

Ferry, Jules (1832–1893), French statesman; minister of public instruction (1879) who expelled Jesuits; formed cabinet (1880–81); prime minister (1883–85).

Fichte, Johann (1762–1814), German philosopher; author of *Addresses to the German Nation* (1807–08).

Filmer, Sir Robert (1590–1653), English political writer who was advocate of divine right of kings in *Patriarchia* (1680).

Fisher, H.A.L. (1865–1940), English historian; teacher at Oxford and vice-chancellor Sheffield University; author of *History of Europe* (1936).

Fourier, Charles (1772–1836), French pre-Marxist Socialist.

Gambetta, Léon Michel (1838–1882), French politician; one of the founders of Third Republic; leader of Opportunists; prime minister (1880–82).

Gide, Charles (1847–1932), French social thinker and reformer.

Godwin, William (1756–1836), English political theorist; author of *Enquiry concerning Political Justice* (1793).

Gooch, G.P. (1873–1968), English historian and editor; Liberal Member of Parliament; author of several histories including *English Democratic Ideas in the Seventeenth Century* (1898) and *Studies in Diplomacy and Statecraft* (1942).

Gregh, Fernand (1873–1960), French author and poet (elected to the Académie, 1953).

Griffuelhes, Victor, French socialist and syndicalist; author of *Le syndicalisme révolutionnaire* (1909).

Guesde, Jules (1845–1922), leader of Socialist Party; author of *Le collectivisme par la révolution, suive du problème et la solution* (1935).

Guizot, Francois P.G. (1787–1874), French historian and statesman of Protestant descent; author of *Histoire de la civilisation en France depuis la chute de l'empire romain* (5 vols. 1828–30), *Histoire de la revolution d'Angleterre* (6 vols. 1858–59), *Histoire des origines du gouvernement representatif en Europe* (2 vols. 1851).

Gumplovicz, Ludwig (1838–1909), Austrian economist and sociologist.

Guy-Grand, Georges (1879– ?), French social thinker.

Halévy, Daniel (1872–1962) [Halévy's brother], French author and publicist; author of *La fin des notables*, (1930), *Essais sur le mouvement ouvrier en France* (1901), and *Péguy et les cahiers de la quinzaine* (1941).

Halévy, Florence Noufflard (?–1957), Halévy's wife.

Halévy, Genevieve (Bizet Strauss), Halévy's aunt.

Halévy, Jacques François Fromental Elias (1799–1862) [Halévy's great-uncle], composer, *La Juive* (1835); admitted to the *Académie des Beaux Arts* (1846); teacher of Bizet and Gounod.

Halévy, Léon (1802–1883) [Halévy's grandfather], French writer and professor at Polytechnique; wrote introduction to Saint-Simon's *Opinions* (1825) and *Resumé de l'histoire des juifs* (1827–28).

Halévy, Ludovic (1834–1908) [Halévy's father], librettist for *Carmen*.

Hanotaux, Gabriel (1853–1944), French historian and statesman; twice foreign minister (1894–1895, 1896–1898); Member of *Académie* (1897); author of *History of Contemporary France 1871–1892* (1903–08).

Hartley, David (1705–1757), English philosopher; author of *Observations on Man* (1749).

Havet, Louis (1849–1925), professor of Latin and Greek philology; ardent Dreyfusard.

Helvétius, Claude Adrien (1715–1771), author (1758) of *De l'esprit; or Essays on the Mind and Its Several Faculties.*

Herder, Johann Gottfried (1744–1803), German critic, poet, historian; collector of folk myths and propagator of historical method of dealing with myths and languages; author of *Ideen zur Geschichte der Menschheit* (4 vols.; 1784–91).

Herr, Lucien, chief librarian, Ecole normale supérieure.

Hervé, Gustave (1871–1944), French anarcho-syndicalist.

Hilbert, David (1862–1943), German mathematician; professor at Göttingen from 1895.

Hobbes, Thomas (1558–1679), English philosopher; author of *De Cive* (1649) and *Leviathan* (1651).

Hobson, John Atkinson (1858–1940), English economist; author of *Problems of Poverty* (1891), *Evolution of Modern Capitalism* (1894), *Imperialism* (1902), *Work and Wealth* (1914), and *Democracy* (1934).

Hodgskin, Thomas (1787–1869), author of *Popular Political Economy* (1827) and *Labour Defended Against the Claims of Capital* (1825).

Hofmannsthal, Hugo von (1874–1929), Austrian poet, dramatist; librettist for *Der Rosenkavalier* (1911) and *Ariadne and Naxos* (1912); founded Salzburg festival.

Holcroft, William (1773–1789), ardent democrat tried with Hardy, Horne Tooke, and others and acquitted.

Huysmans, J.K. (1848–1907), French novelist-poet.

Jaurès, Jean (1859–1914), leader of French Socialist party.

Jevons, William Stanley (1835–1882), English economist and logician; author of *Theory of Political Economy* (1871) and *The State in Relation to Labour* (1882).

Joffre, Marechal, commander of French armies in First World War.

Klein, Felix, (1849–1925), German mathematician known for work on geometry and theory of functions.

Lagneau, Jules (1851–1894), French philosopher; author of *De l'existence de Dieu* (1925).

Lanson, Gustave (1857–1934), French critic; author of *Histoire de la Littérature Française* (1894).

Lassalle, Ferdinand (1825–1864), German sociologist; disciple of Marx; Socialist propagandist regarded as founder of German Social Democratic Party.

Lavisse, Ernest (1842–1922), French historian, specialized in Prussian history; author of *Histoire de France depuis les origines jusqu'à la Revolution*. (1900–11), *The Youth of Frederick the Great* (1893).

Lazard, Max (1875–1953), economist; president, Association pour la lutte contre le chomage et l'organisation du marché du travail.

Leclerc, Max (1864– ?), French publisher and editor.

Leger, Augustin, author of *L'Angleterre religieuse et les origines du Methodisme au XVIII*ᵉ *siècle: la jeunesse de Wesley* (1910).

Lemaitre, Jules (1853–1914), French writer and literary critic.

Léon, Xavier (1868–1935), co-founder with Halévy of *Révue de Métaphysique et Morale* and the *Société Française de Philosophie; author of Fichte et son temps* (1922–27).

LePlay, Pierre Guillaume Frédéric (1806–1882), French engineer and economist, regarded as founder of modern study of social economy in France.

Lévy, Eli Halphen [Halévy's great-grandfather].

Lévy-Bruhl, Lucien (1857–1939), French sociologist-anthropologist; author of *The Philosophy of Auguste Comte* (1900) and *Primitives and the Supernatural* (1931).

Liard, Louis (1846–1917), French philosopher and educator.

List, Georg Friedrich (1789–1846), German political economist and publicist.

Littré, Maximilien Paul Emile (1801–1881), French scholar and lexicographer; regarded as head of the positivist school after death of Comte (1857); author of *Dictionnaire de la Langue Française* (1863–72).

Lloyd George, David, 1st earl of Dwyfor (1863–1945).

Louis Philippe (1773–1850), the citizen king.

Lyon, Georges (1853–1929), French philosopher; author of *Idealisme en Angleterre au XVIII*ᵉ *siècle* (1888).

Mably, Gabriel Bonnot de (1709–1785), French historian; author of *Observations sur l'histoire de la Grèce* (1766), *De la manière de' écrire l'histoire* (1783), and critic of Hume, Robertson, Gibbon, and Voltaire.

MacCulloch, John R. (1789–1864), Scottish economist of wages' fund theory; author of *Principles of Political Economy* (1825).

Mallarmé, Stephane (1842–1898), French symbolist poet, one of the "decadents"; author of *L'Après-Midi d'une Faune* (1876) and *Vers et Prose* (1893).

Man, Hendrik de (1885–1953), Belgium Socialist turned nationalist; author of *Psychology of Socialism* (1927).

Mantoux, Etienne (1913–1945), author of *The Carthaginian Peace; or, The Economic Consequences of Mr. Keynes* (1946).

Mantoux, Paul (1877–1956), historian; director of political secretariat, League of Nations (1920–27); author of *The Industrial Revolution in the Eighteenth Century* (1905).

Marshall, Alfred (1842–1924), English economist, author of *Principles of Economics* (1890).

Mathiez, Albert (1874–1932), historian of the French Revolution; author of *After Robespierre* (1927), *The Thermidorian Reaction* (1929) and *The French Revolution* (1922–27).

Maublanc, René, student and friend of Elie Halévy; author of *Le Marxisme et La Liberté* (1945) and *La philosophie du marxisme et l'enseignement officiel: Dixième mille* (1938).

BIOGRAPHICAL NOTES

Maurras, Charles (1868–1952), French writer, Royalist, and co-editor of *L'Action Française*.

Meilhac, Henri (1831–1897), French librettist.

Menger, Karl (1840–1921), Austrian economist.

Miall, Edward (1809–1881), English political journalist and Independent divine.

Michel, Henry (1857–1904), French political philosopher; author of *L'Idée de l'état* (1896).

Michelet, Jules (1798–1874), French romantic historian; author of *The History of France* (17 vols.; 1833–67).

Miller, Benigne Emanuel Clément (1810–1886), philologist, Byzantinist; member Institut de France and Académie des inscriptions et belles-lettres.

Mises, Ludwig von (1881–   ), Austrian economist, author of *Liberalism* (1927), *Theory of Money and Credit* (1912), and *Planning for Freedom* (1974).

Morley, John Viscount (1838–1923), British Liberal, journalist, administrator, and political figure.

Mornet, Daniel (1878–1954), French literary critic and historian of the Enlightenment.

Morny, Charles Auguste Louis Joseph duc de (1811–1865), half-brother of Napoleon III; chief agent in successful coup d'état (1851).

Morris, William (1834–1896), English poet, artist, and socialist.

Nernst, Walther Hermann (1864–1941), German physicist and chemist.

Noufflard, Florence, *see* Halévy, Florence.

Offenbach, Jacques (1819–1880), French composer of operettas.

Ollé-Laprune, Léon (1839–1898), French philosopher, author of *De la certitude morale* (1880).

Owen, Robert (1771–1858), British industrialist, philanthropist, early socialist.

Paine, Thomas (1737–1809), English-American political revolutionist; author of *The Rights of Man* (1791–92) and the *Age of Reason* (1794, 1796).

Pareto, Vilfredo (1848–1923), Italian economist.

Parodi, Dominique (1870–   ?) French philosopher; author of *Du positivisme à l'idéalisme* (1930), *La philosophie contemporaine en France* (1919), and *Le problème politique et la democratie* (1945).

Pecqueur, Constantin (1801–1887), French socialist thinker; author of *De la république de Dieu* (1844) and *Economie sociale* (1839).

Péguy, Charles (1873–1914), poet, writer, Catholic, and Socialist.

Place, Francis (1771–1854), English Radical politician.

Podmore, Frank (1856–1910), author of *Apparitions and Thought Transference* (1894) and *Robert Owen: A Biography* (1906).

Poincaré, Raymond (1860–1934), deputy (1887–1903), senator (1903–12, 1920), president (1913–20), prime minister (1912–13, 1922–24, 1926–29).

Prévost-Paradol, Lucien Anatole (1829–1870), author of *Essai sur l'histoire universelle* (1865), and *Essai de politique et de littérature* (1859).

Proudhon, P.J. (1809–1865), French moralist, early socialist.

Quinet, Edgar (1803–1875), French politician and philosopher; author of *La République: conditions de la régénération de la France* (1872).

Ravenstone, Percy, author of *A Few Doubts as to the Correctness of Some Opinions Generally Entertained on the Subjects of Population and Political Economy* (1821) and *Thoughts on the Funding System* (1824).

Reinach, Joseph (1856–1921), French journalist, associate of Gambetta; deputy (1889–98, 1906–14) for Basses-Alpes; author of *L'Affaire Dreyfus* (4 vols.; 1898).

Remusat, Charles François Marie count de (1797–1875), French politician and man of letters.

Renan, Ernest (1823–1890), French philosopher, philologist, and essayist; author of *The Future of Science.*

Renouvier, Charles (1815–1903), author of *Les dilemmes de la métaphysique pure* (1901).

Renouvin, Pierre (1893–   ), French diplomatic and political historian.

Ricardo, David (1772–1823), English political economist.

Rist, Charles (1874–1955), French co-operatist, economist; author of *History of Monetary and Credit Theory from John Law to the Present Day* (1940).

Robbins, Lionel Charles, baron (1898–   ), British economist.

Rodbertus, Carl (1805–1875), German socialist and economist.

Romains, Jules, pseud. **Louis Farigoule** (1885–1972), French writer.

Rosebery, Archibald Philip Primrose, 5th earl of (1847–1929), British statesman, leading imperialist, foreign secretary (1886, 1892–94); prime minister (1894–95).

Ruskin, John (1819–1900), English author, art critic, and social reformer.

Salisbury, Robert Arthur T.G. Cecil, 3d marquis of (1830–1903), British statesman; prime minister (1885–92, 1895–1902).

Say, Jean Baptiste, (1767–1832) French economist.

Schlegel, August Wilhelm von (1767–1845), German man of letters and poet.

Schmoller, Gustave von (1838–1917), German economist.

Seignobos, Charles (1854–1942), professor at the Sorbonne (1890–   ?); author of *Histoire de la civilisation contemporaine* (1890) and *Histoire de la civilisation au moyen age at dans les temps modernes* (1890).

Shaftesbury, Anthony Ashley, 7th earl of (1801–1885), philanthropist.

Shaw, George Bernard (1856–1950), British playwright, novelist, critic.

Simiand, François (1873–1935), professor of history of labor, Collège de France (1932–35; author of *Les fluctuations économiques à longue période et la crise mondiale* (1932) and *Le salaire des ouvriers des mines de charbon en France* (1907).

Simmel, Georg (1858–1918), German sociologist.

Sismondi, Jean Charles Simonde de (1773–1842), economist, essayist, critic of classical economics.

Sombart, Werner (1863–1941), German economist.

Sorel, Georges (1847–1922), major philosopher of revolutionary syndicalism; author of *Reflections on Violence* (1908) and *The Illusions of Progress* (1908).

Spencer, Herbert (1820–1903), English philosopher and sociologist.

Staël, Anne Louis de (1766–1817), Swiss-French novelist and writer.

Stephen, Sir Leslie (1832–1904), English man of letters, philosopher, and biographer.

Strauss, David (1808–1874), German theological thinker; author of *The Life of Christ; or, A Critical Examination of His History* (2 vols.; 1835–36).

Strauss, Geneviève Halévy Bizet, *see* Halévy, Genevieve.

Strauss, Richard (1864–1949), German conductor and romantic composer, collaborated with Hugo von Hofmannsthal.

Taine, Hippolyte (1828–1893), French philosopher and critic; author of *The Origins of Contemporary France* (6 vols.; 1871–94).
Tarde, Gabriel (1843–1904), French sociologist; author of *The Laws of Imitation* (1890).
Thibaudet, Albert (1874–1936), French historian and critic.
Thomas, Albert (1878–1932), Socialist party leader; minister of munitions in First World War; director of the International Labor Organization Bureau of the League of Nations.
Thompson, William (1785–1833), Irish landowner and political economist, student of Bentham, supporter of Owen's cooperatives; author of *An Inquiry into the Principles of the Distribution of Wealth* (1824).

Viner, Jacob (1892–1970), political economist.
Von Mises, Ludwig, *see* Mises, Ludwig von. *Theory of Money and Credit* (1912), and *Planning for Freedom* (1974).

Wagner, Adolf (1835–1917), economist; supporter of socialism and social reform.
Wallas, Graham (1858–1932), British political thinker and essayist.
Walras, Marie Esprit Léon (1834–1910), French economist.
Webb, Beatrice Potter (1858–1943) and **Sidney Webb** (1859–1947), authors of *English Poor Law Policy* (1910), *The History of Trade Unionism* (1894), and *Industrial Democracy* (1920).
Weill, Georges (1865– ?), French historian and social thinker; author of *L'Ecole Saint-Simonienne* (1896) and *Histoire du mouvement social au France, 1852–1910* (1904).
Whitefield, George (1714–1770), English-American Methodist leader.
Wilberforce, William (1759–1833), English philosopher and politician.
William II (1859–1941), emperor of Germany (1888–1918).
Worms, René (1869–1926), French sociologist, author of *Philosophie des sciences sociales* (1904–13) and *La science et l'art en économie politique* (1896).

Index